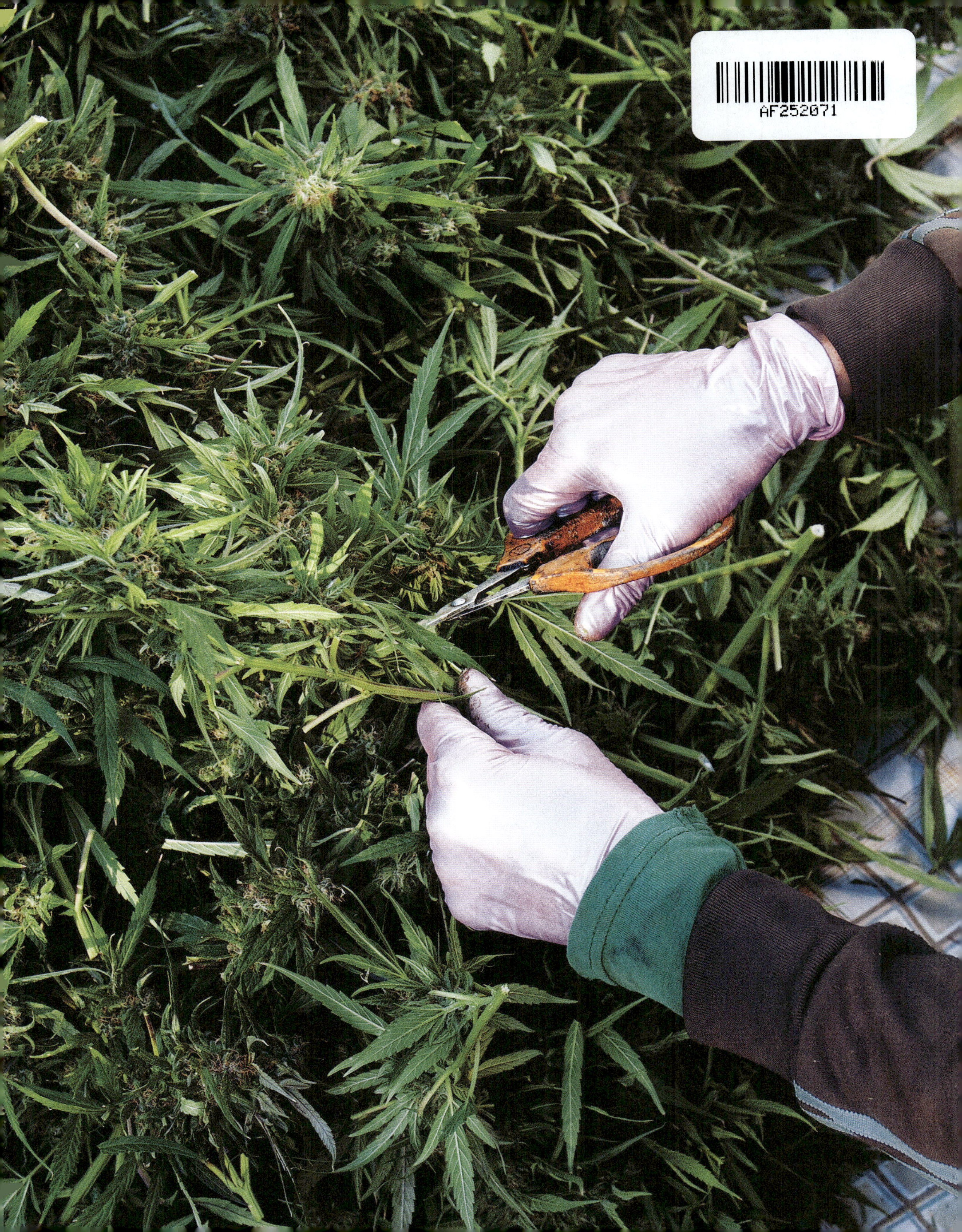
AF252071

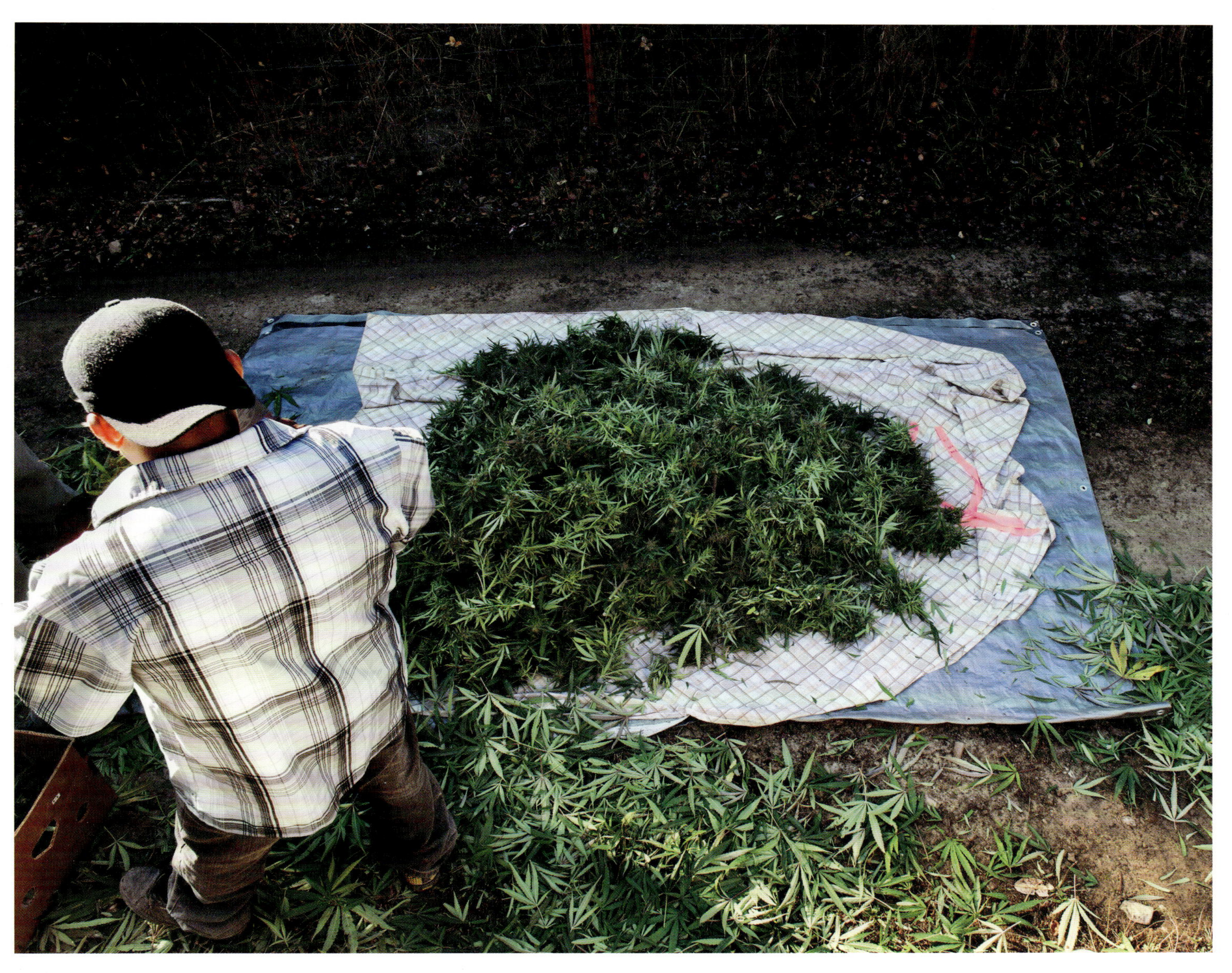

GRASSLAND

H. Lee

KEHRER

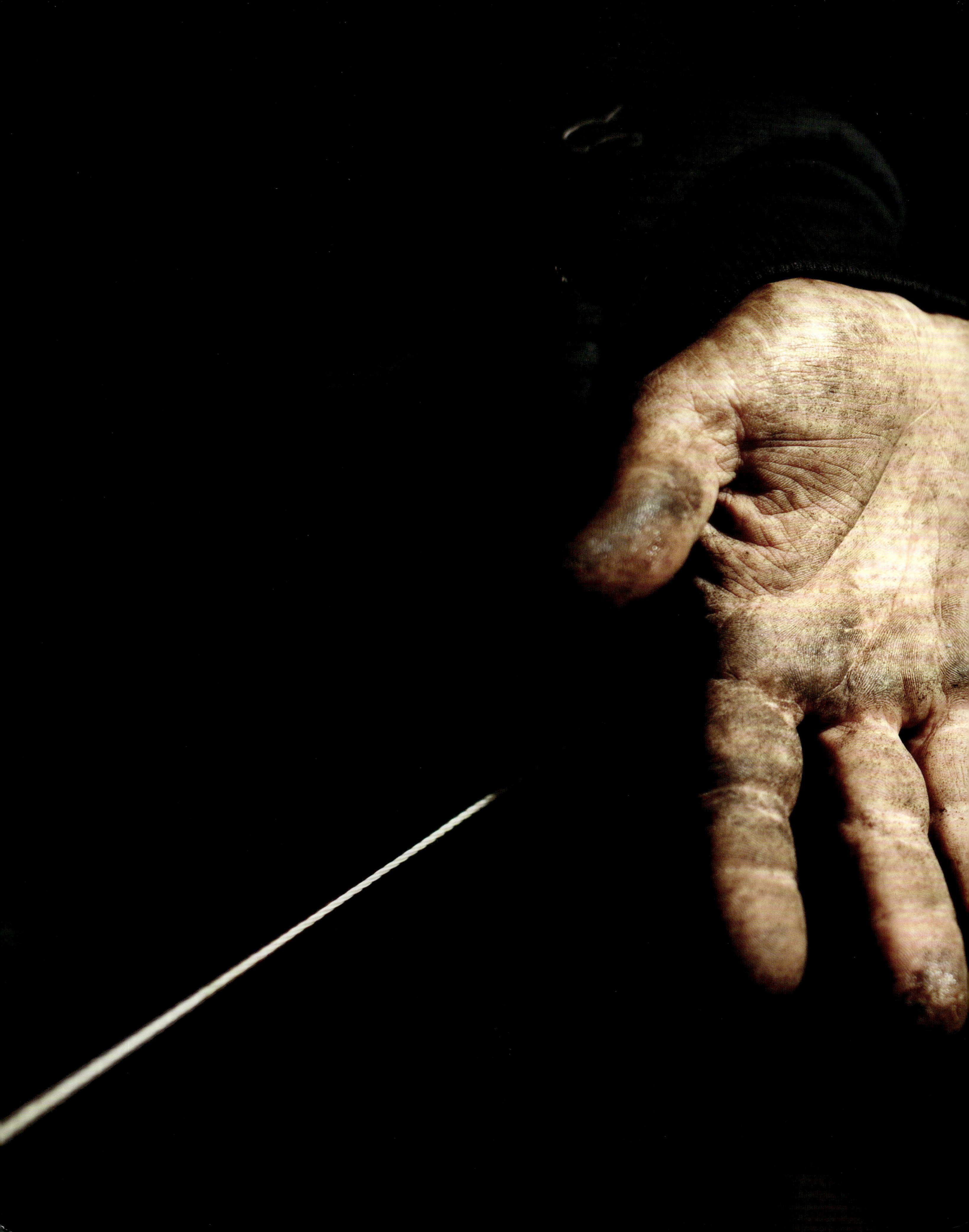

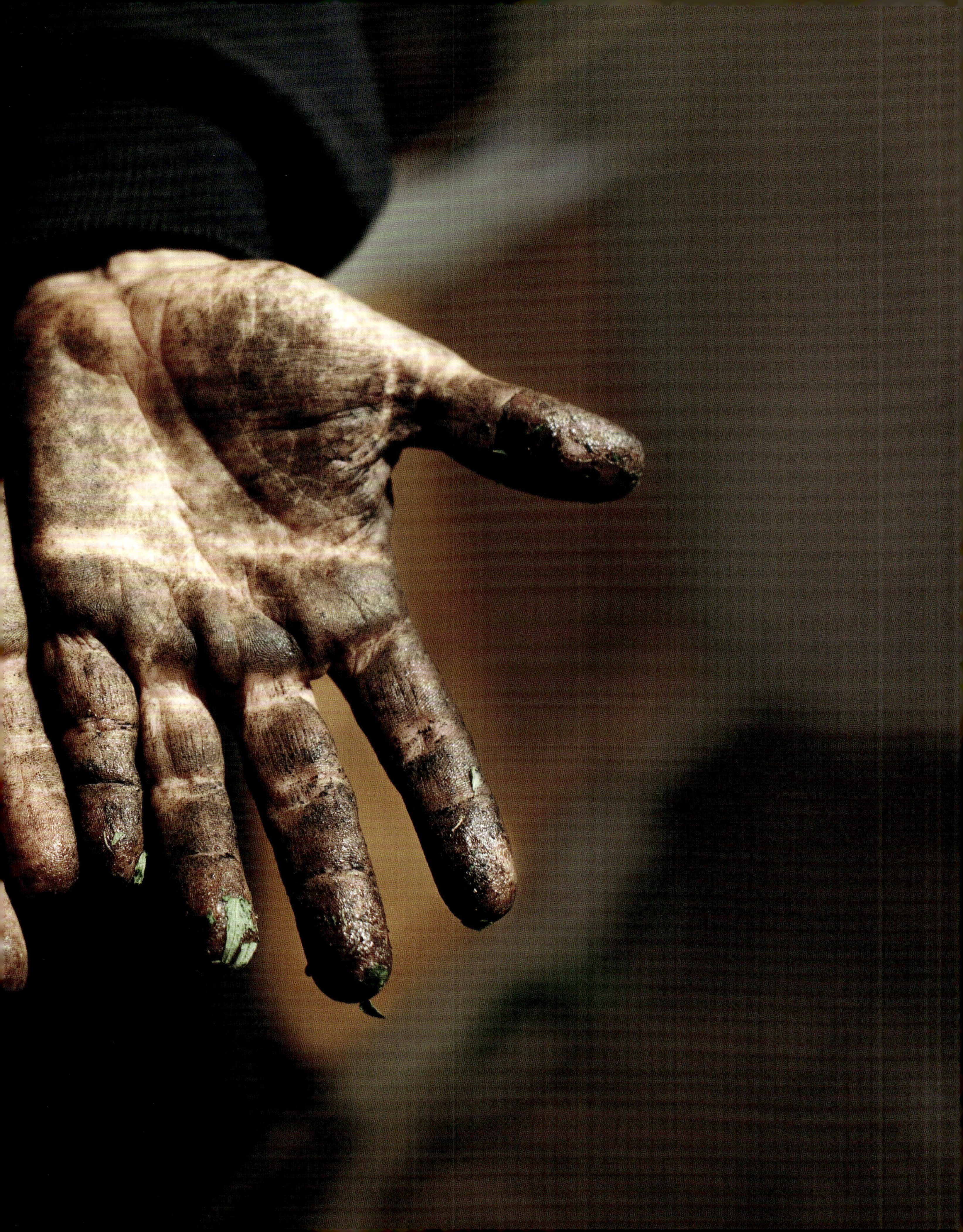

"It would be wryly interesting if in human history the cultivation of marijuana led generally to the invention of agriculture, and thereby to civilization."

—Carl Sagan, *The Dragons of Eden*

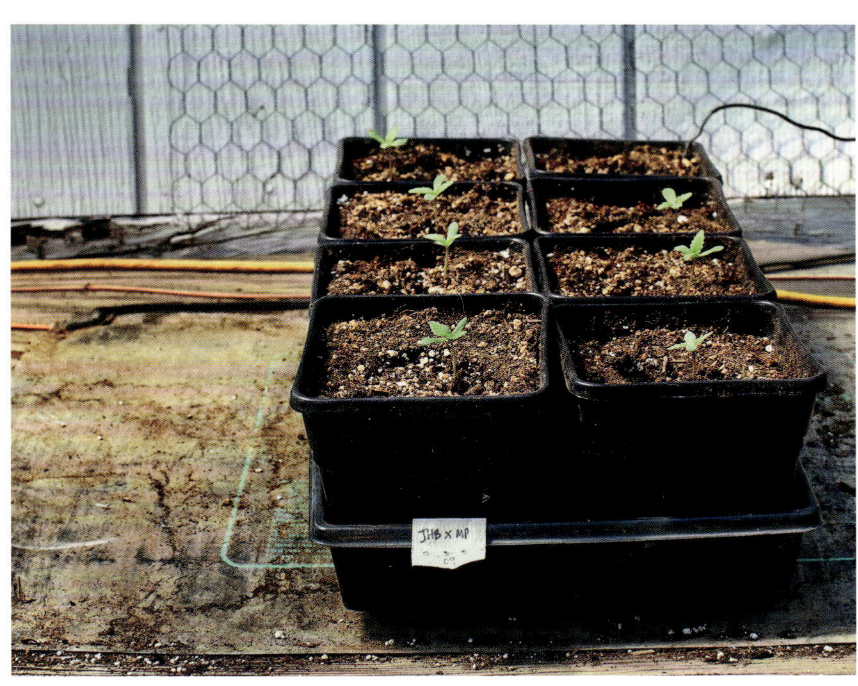
JHB X MP

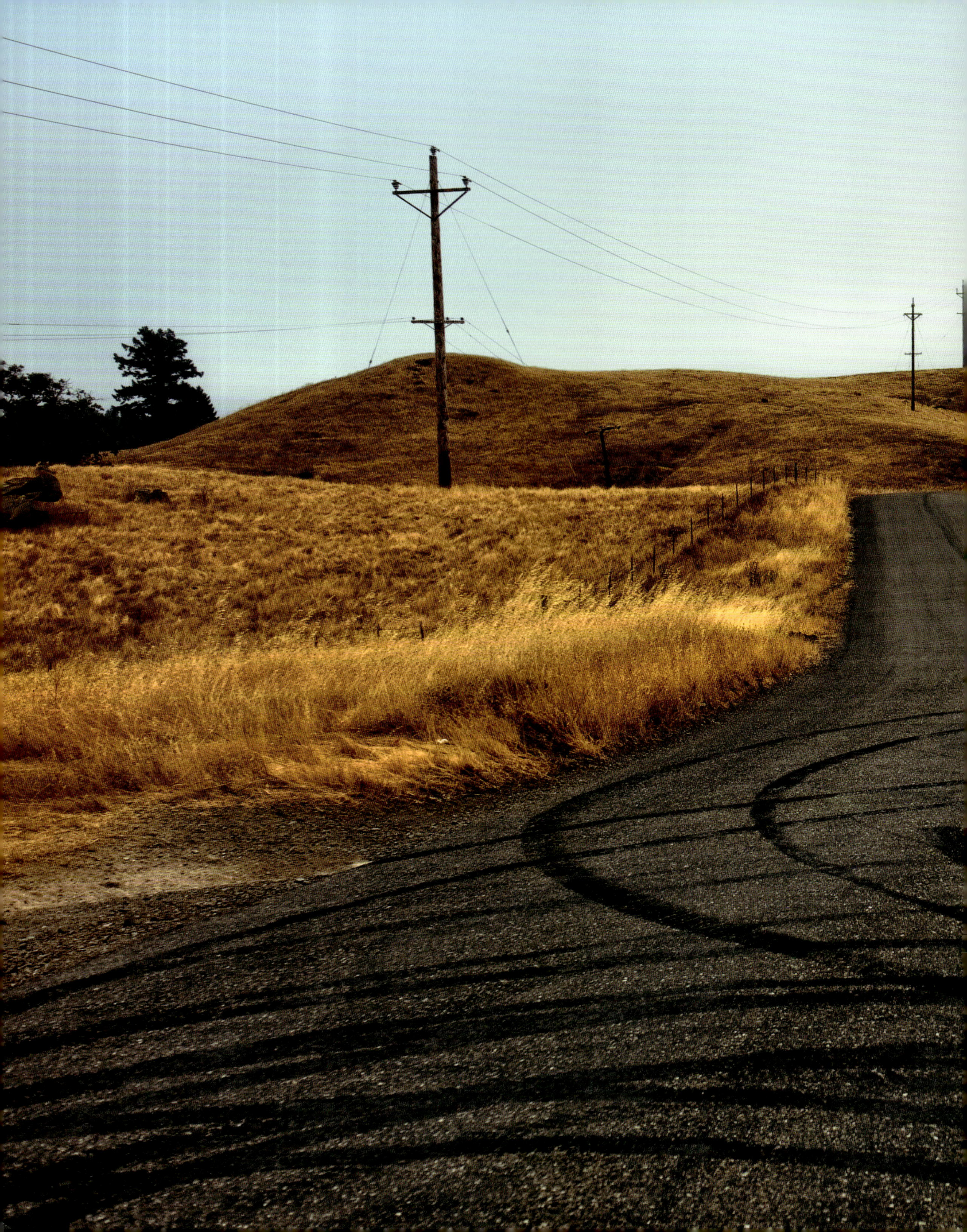

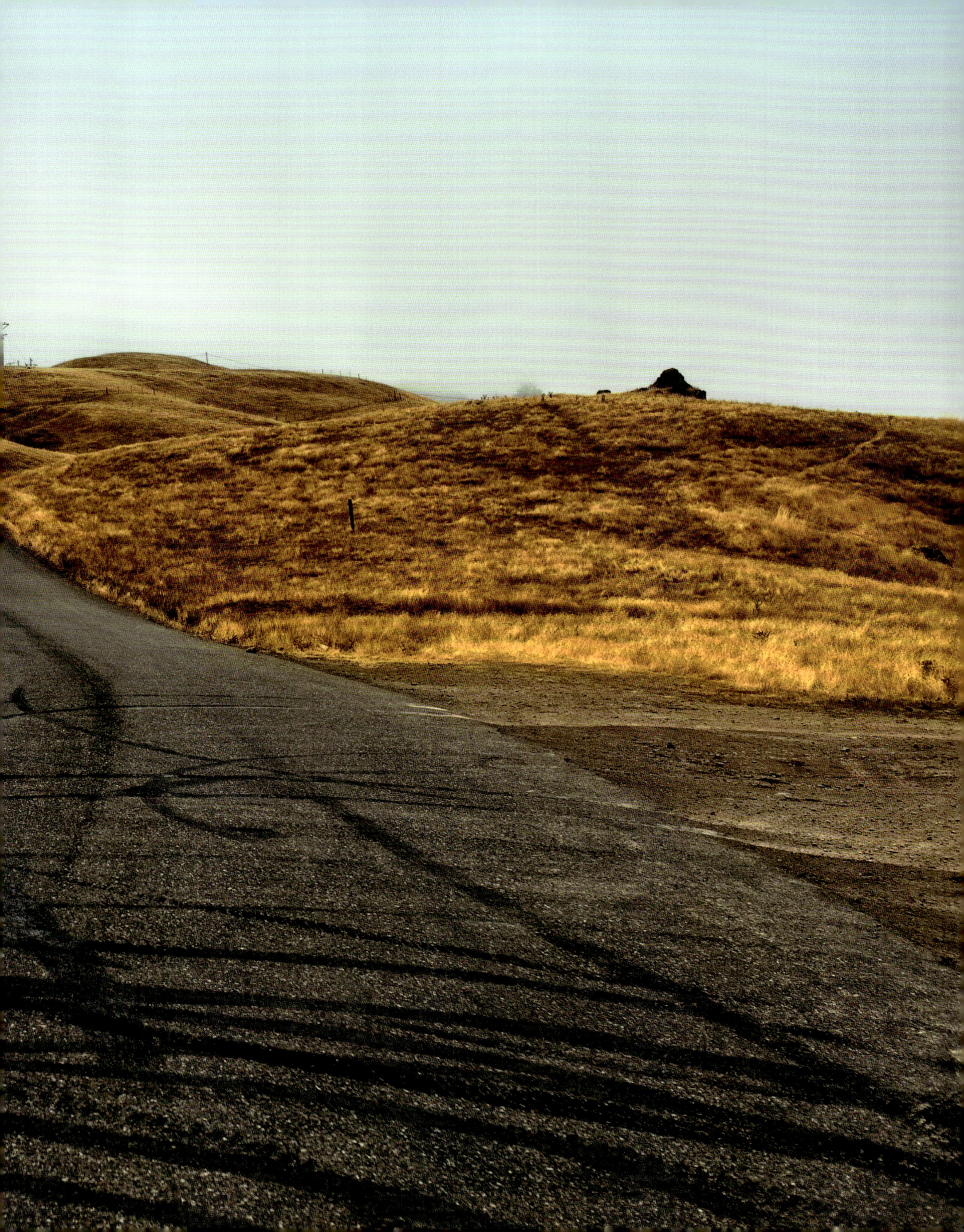

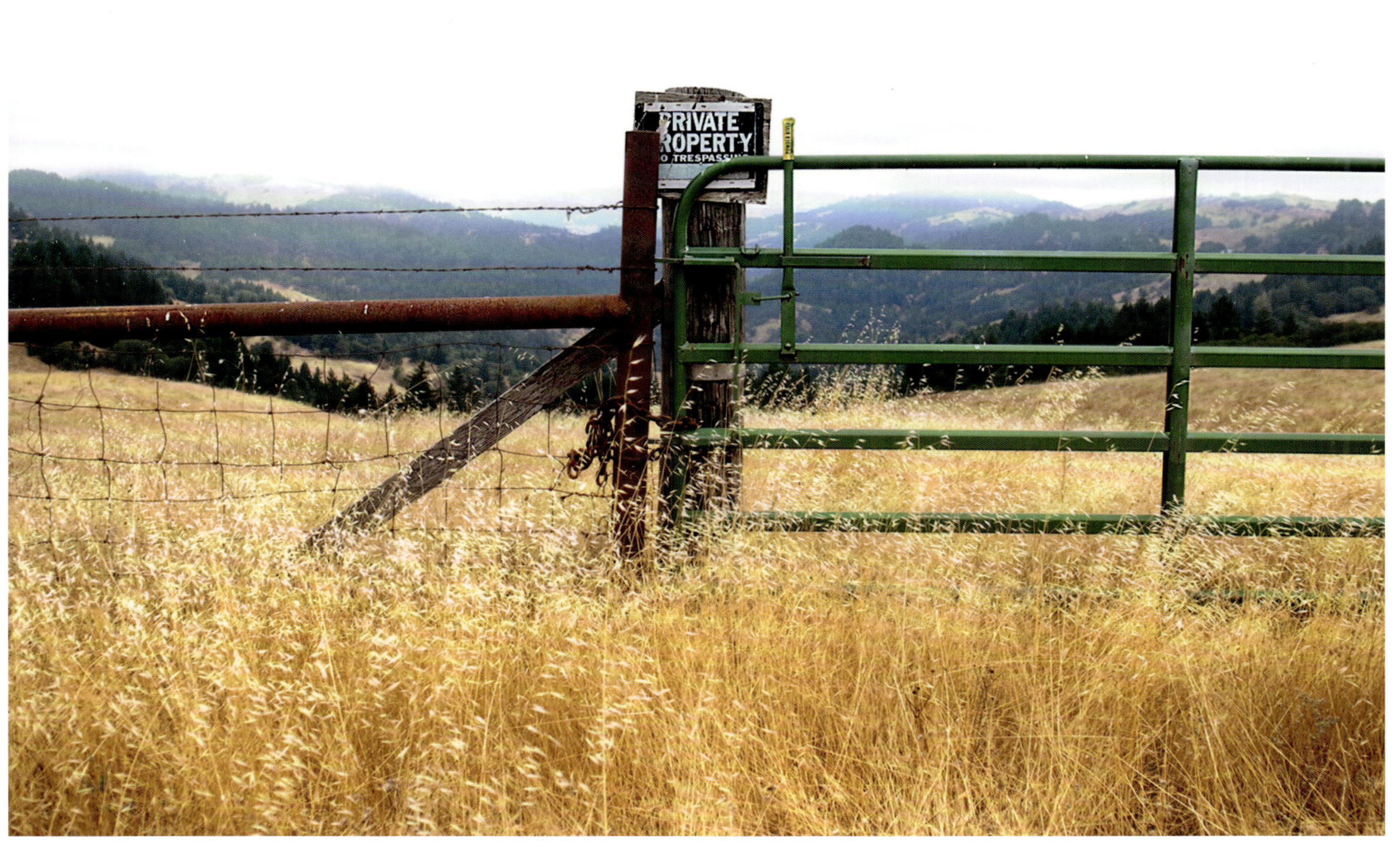

PRIVATE
PROPERTY
NO TRESPASSING

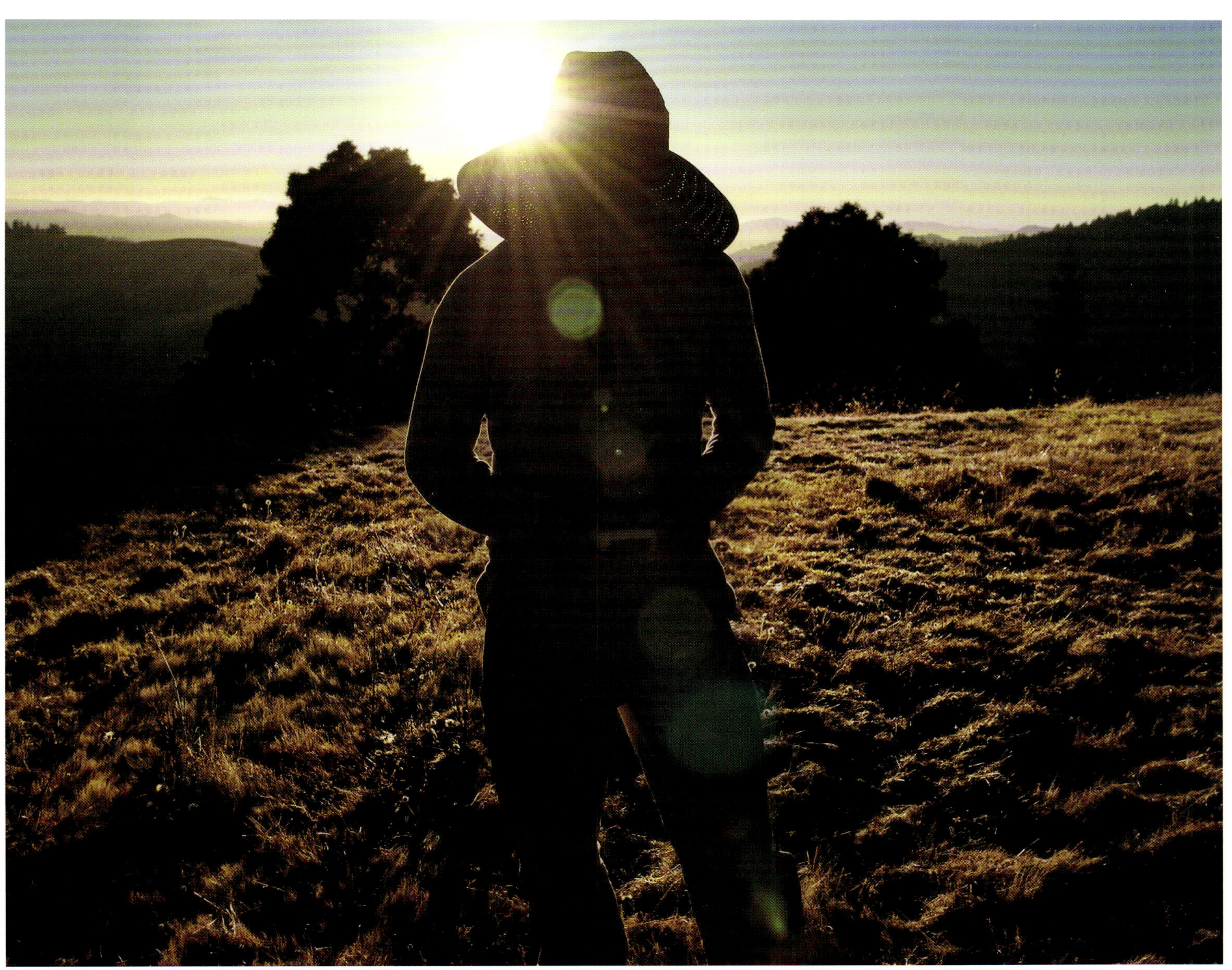

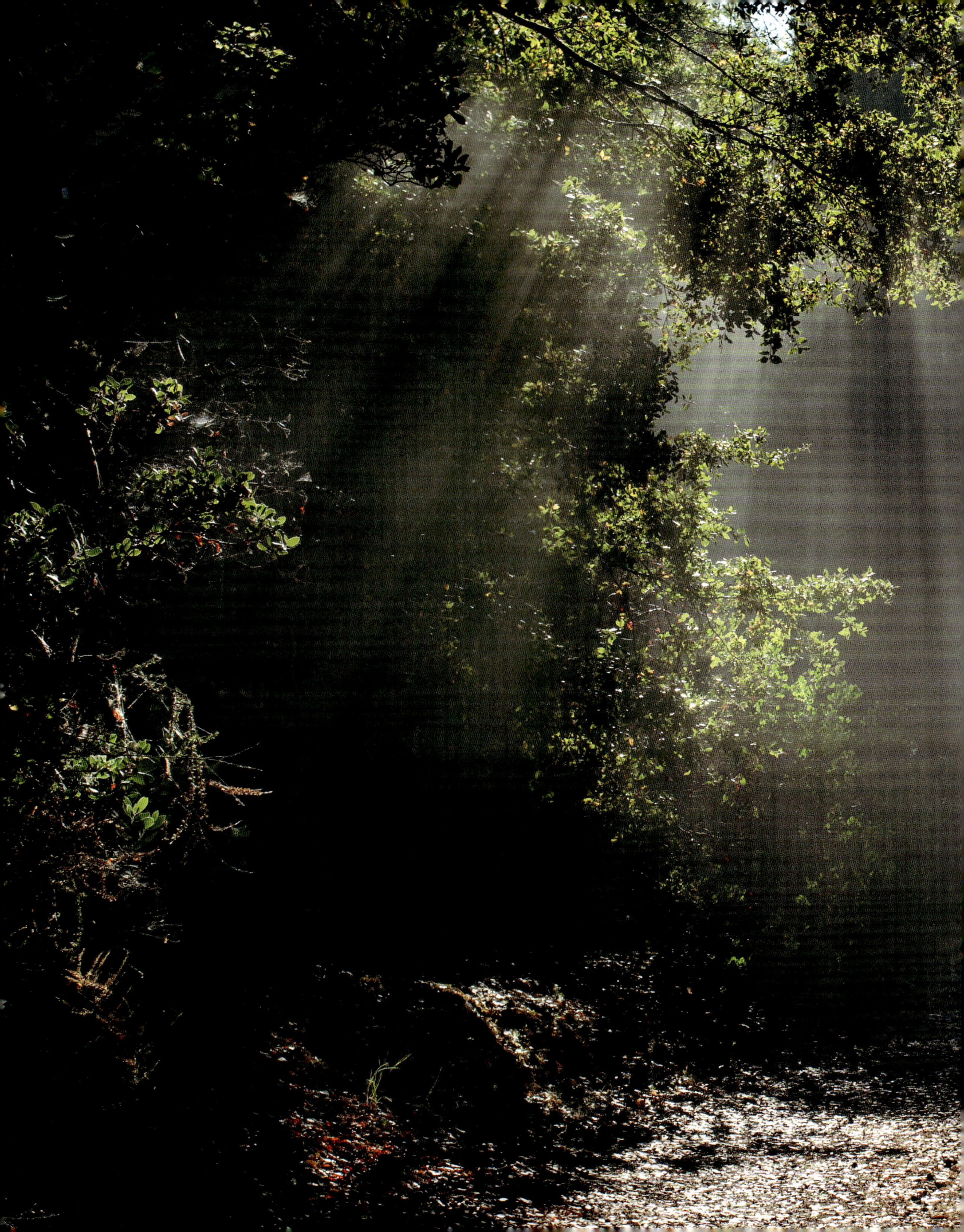

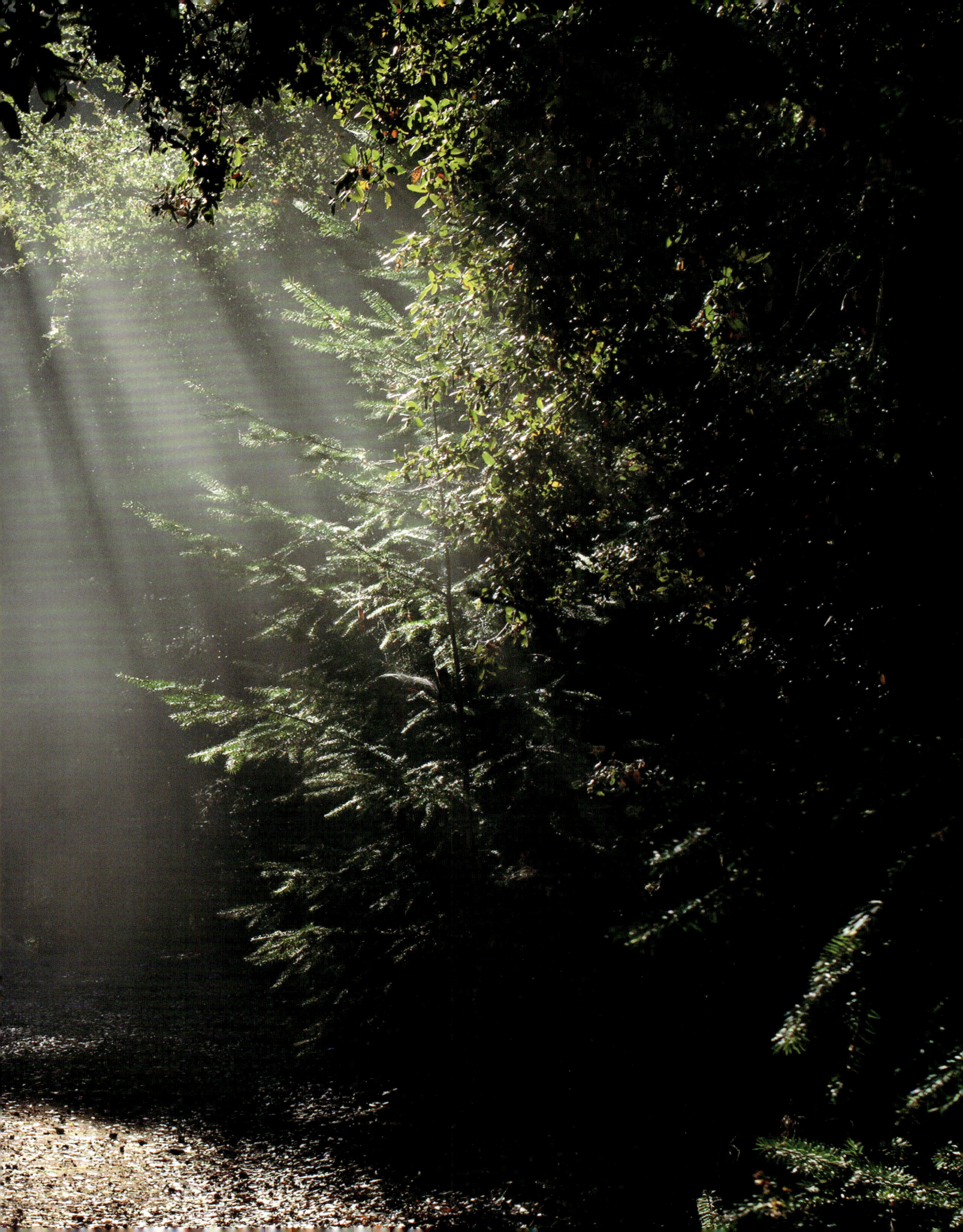

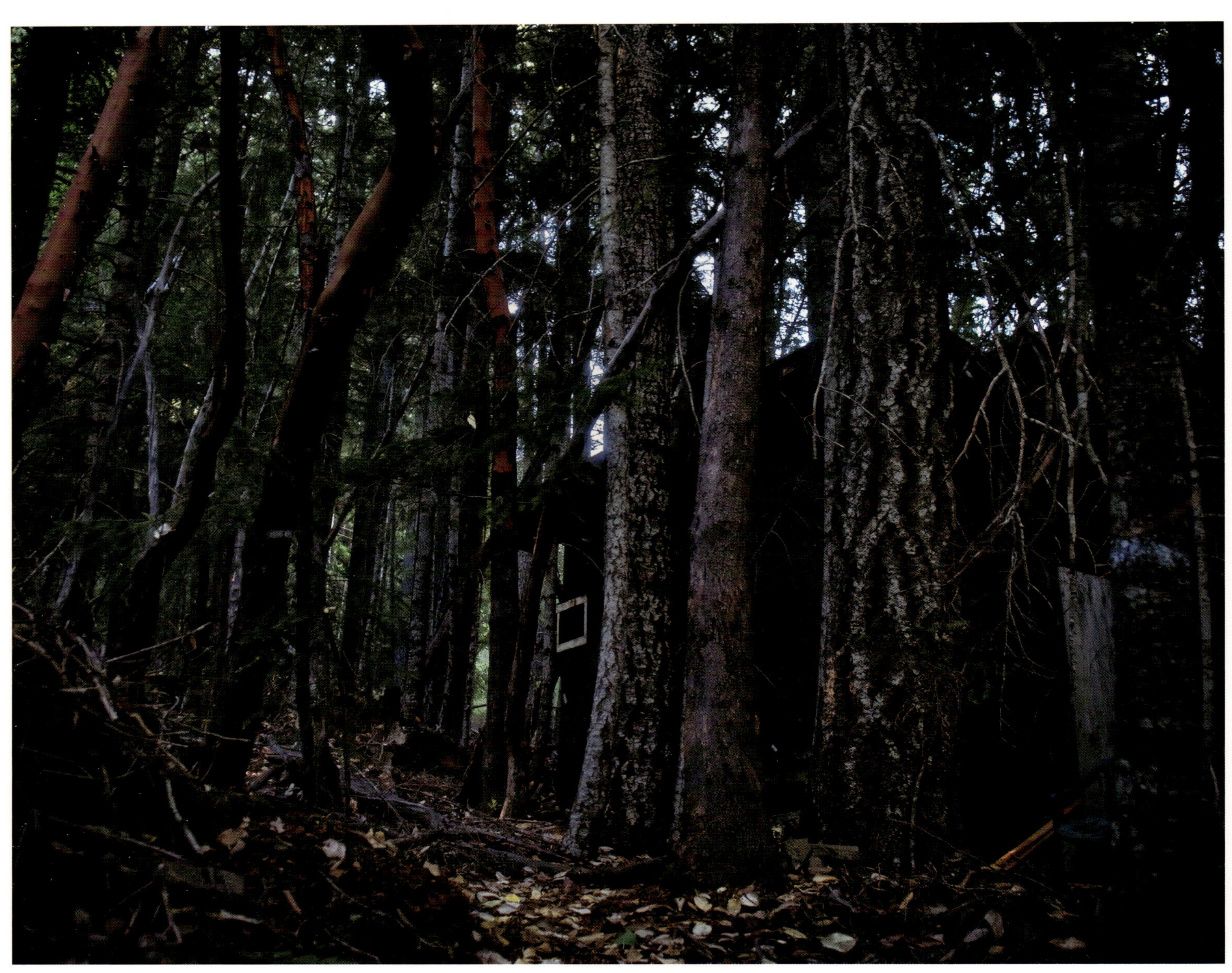

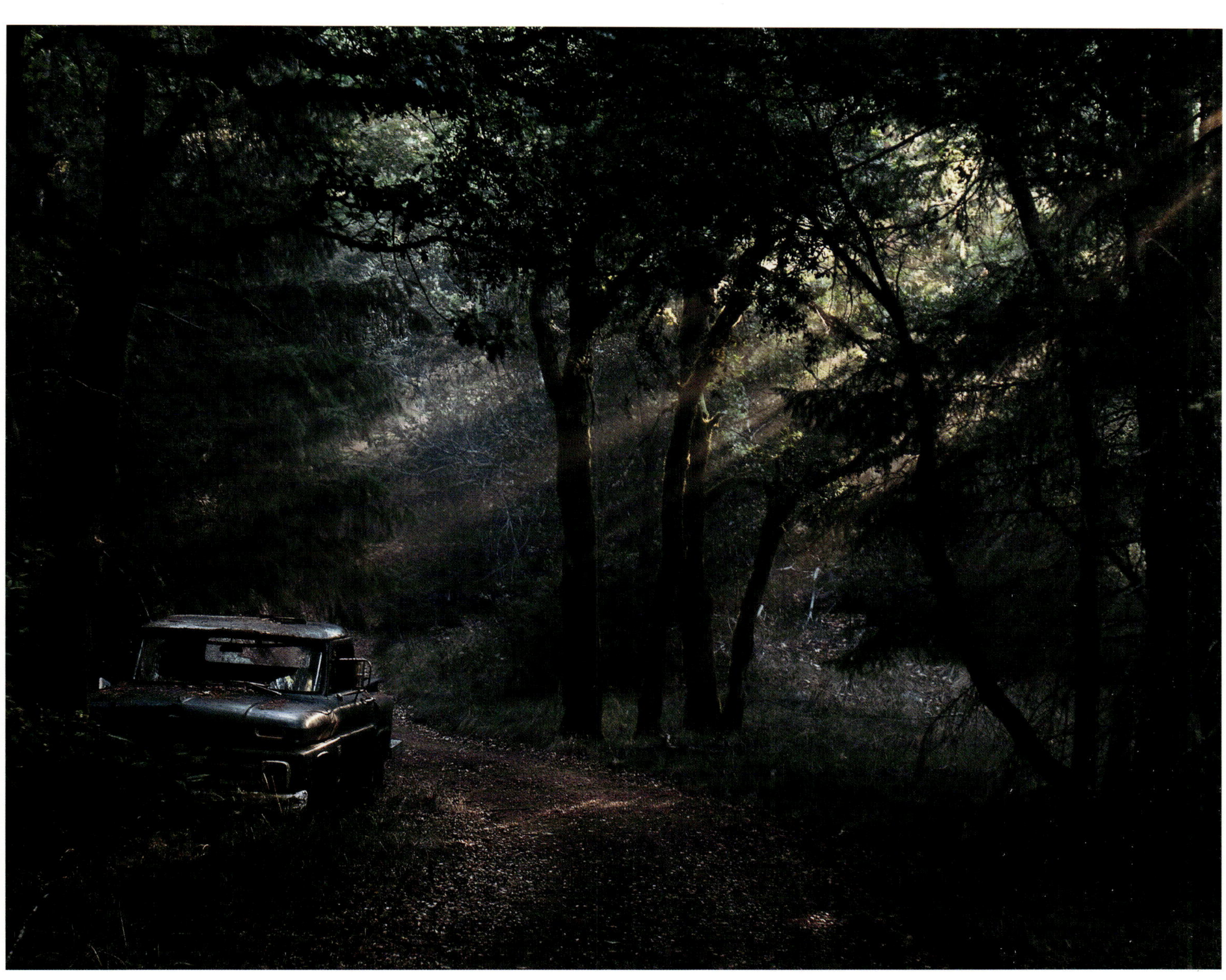

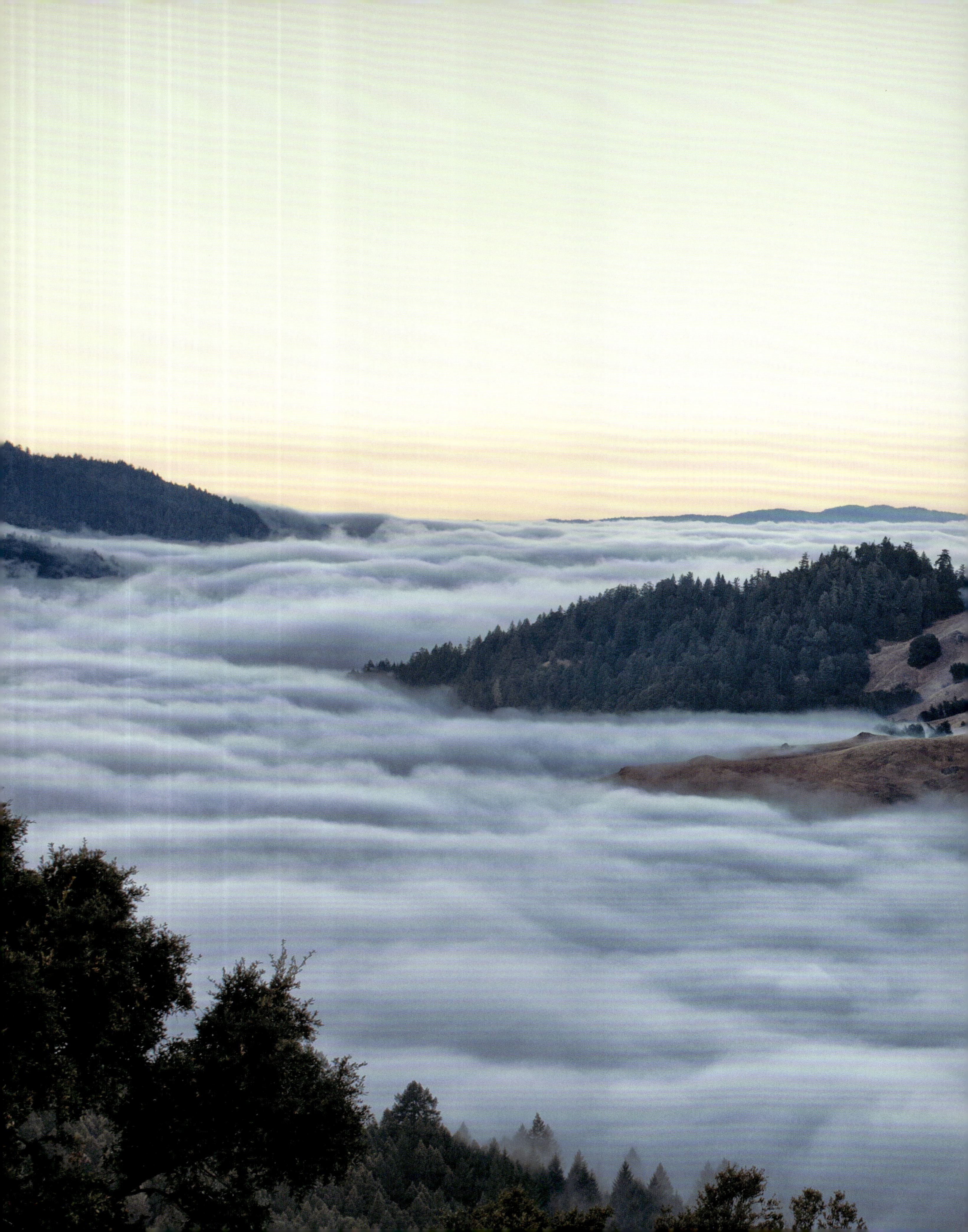

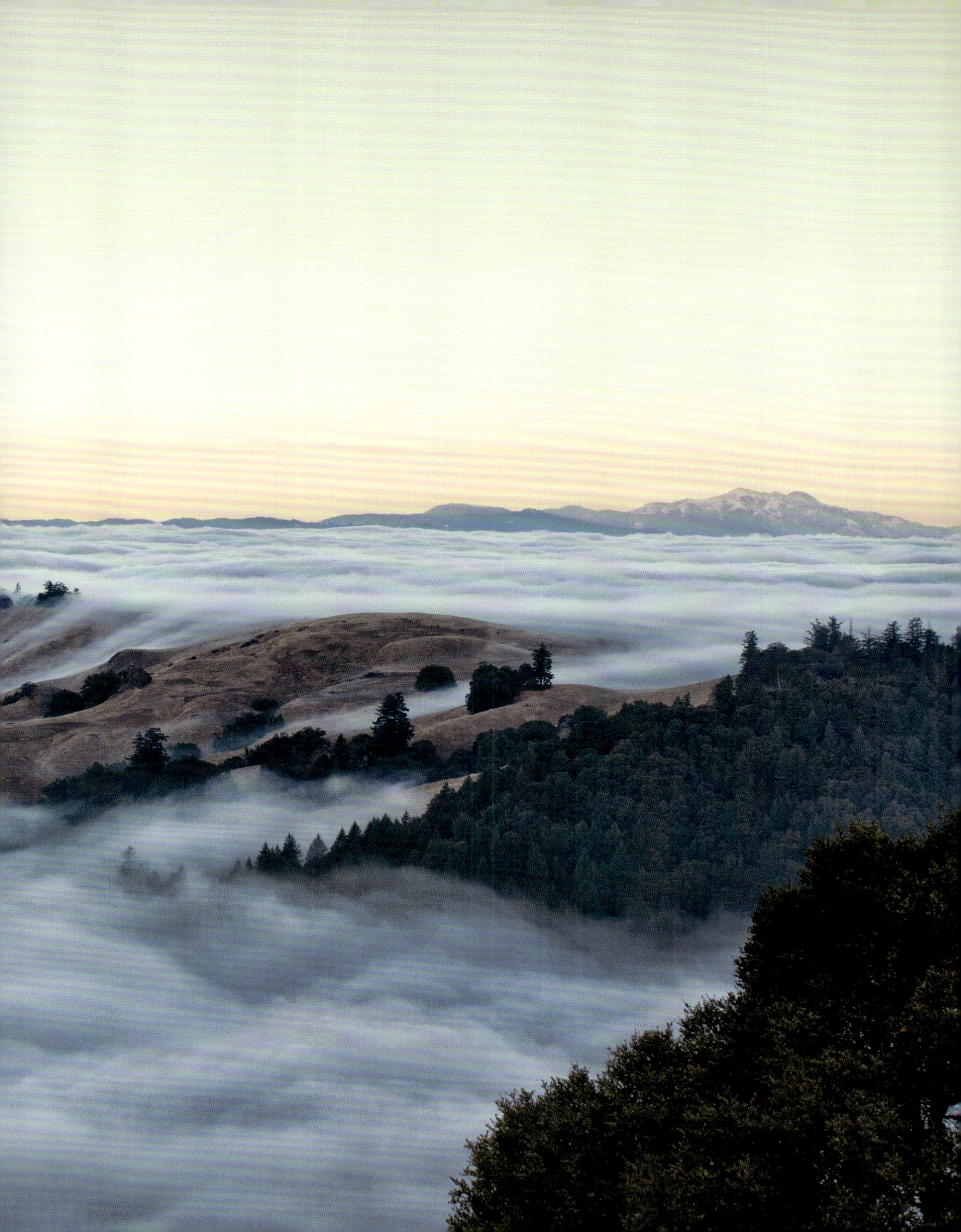

When I first arrived in Humboldt County in 2004, I expected to see acres of marijuana, like you find in the vineyards in Sonoma two hours south. I had never seen a pot plant in real life, even though I had been living in the Bay Area for a decade. And I had never heard the term "Emerald Triangle." The only thing I knew about Humboldt was that the county was home to redwood forests and a tree so big you could drive a car through it. After traversing an hour of dirt roads off the main highway, I was confident that I had arrived somewhere very much like the middle of nowhere, so I stopped the car and stepped out. I scanned the golden hillside looking for massive marijuana fields but found nothing but the vast breathtaking natural beauty of Northern California.

I don't smoke pot. I wasn't on assignment for a magazine. And unlike the thousands who flock to Humboldt County annually for harvest season, I wasn't there to make money. Romance led me to these hills—and into a secret world hidden in plain sight that few outsiders had visited.

Past road signs peppered with bullet holes, I rattled down the bumpy driveway to a padlocked metal gate, an entryway I would come to know as quintessentially Humboldt. As I clicked the combination to the lock, I was taken aback by the vista before me. Stunning and secluded, it was perfect for cultivating pot. I noticed a white speck tucked into the valley below and was soon able to make out a smattering of similar patches dotting the hillside. I later learned that these white dots were hoops of PVC tubing and plastic sheathing, which housed rows of marijuana plants big and small.

Discretion and secrecy are key elements of life in the Emerald Triangle. Droves of trailer-toting tourists winding along Highway 101 every summer are unaware that hidden just off the main road is the epicenter of America's cannabis cultivation industry. If you don't speak the secret language—billboards tout competitive prices for turkey bags (used to store dried buds) and high-tech lighting (for indoor growing)—you'd never know that you were deep in marijuana country.

The man I had come to visit had a 400-acre ranch. I was shocked to see that his entire pot garden was composed of a tiny patch of land, no bigger than a suburban backyard. I spent my first afternoon in Humboldt reading outside, while he went to a community sweat lodge ceremony. When he returned, I told him I smelled a skunk, and he laughed. Marijuana plants, I was told, had a pungent skunk-like odor. And thus began my education in the world of weed.

I spent much of the following eight years hanging around Humboldt, but for most of that time I didn't take pictures. As a journalist, I was drawn to this outlaw community with a cast of characters like none I had ever encountered. But I was an outsider, and I understood that this was a very delicate circumstance; confidentiality was a non-negotiable rule. And at first, I wasn't ready to document Humboldt. For one thing, it was dangerous. Paranoia was everywhere, and the risk of getting arrested or shot was no hallucination. Theft was a fact of life, guns were hidden behind many doors, and conversations about big busts and rip-offs traveled through the hills. But there is safety in numbers, I learned. And after opening my eyes just a bit wider, I discovered that nearly everyone living in the area was involved in the pot business in one way or another. And the mom-and-pop growers I knew, if discreet and savvy, were not really targets for the federal government.

Looking back now, I realize that my curiosity was also dampened because I had already come to conclusions: my preconceived notions about the growers' motivations, their off-the-grid lifestyles, and their involvement in the drug trade all clouded my ability to see this strange world with real clarity.

Over time, I relaxed and began to listen to the voices of this anti-establishment culture and community, and I learned more about the magical and medicinal plant that everyone seemed to love and upon which so many livelihoods depended. I came across a variety of growers—avid smokers, those who believed in legalization, city folk who came to cash in, second-generation kids who never left, those passionate for permaculture, and back-to-the-landers aiming for an alternative lifestyle who earned just enough to scrape by.

Many locals believed that pot would be legal in our lifetime, which seemed ridiculous when I arrived. But as the years passed, the laws began to loosen; the price of wholesale marijuana dropped as the number of plants increased, and I began to change in my beliefs and understand how this little-known slice of California was changing our country.

It was 2010 when I finally decided to turn my lens on the scene. It was the year that Proposition 19, an initiative to legalize various pot-related activities, appeared on the state ballot. Promising not to disclose the identities of my subjects, I was permitted access to several ranches and homesteads, and I documented a year of outdoor cannabis cultivation from harvest to harvest. In 2013 I returned for a week and discovered that, in just two years, the scale of cultivation had increased remarkably: pot plants were growing taller and more out in the open, the white greenhouse hoops that were once hard to spot were now an eyesore on the endless horizon, and the towns north of San Francisco were crawling with backpackers and 20-somethings who were migrating in increasing numbers for the fall trim season. The Emerald Triangle and the marijuana industry were not the only things that had expanded. As America had become more aware—and tolerant—of this once highly secretive underground culture, so had my own perception shifted: I found myself walking through town without judgment. The place had come to feel like a home of sorts. I felt a deep respect for the risks these farmers took as they struggled to carve a living out of the landscape, along the way changing the shape of our nation's culture and history.

—H. Lee, Humboldt County

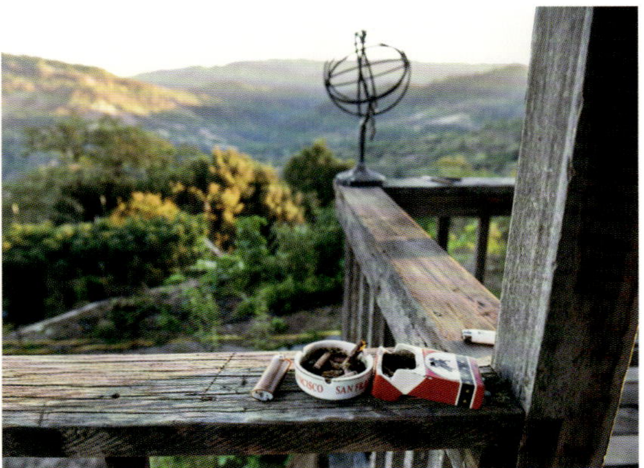

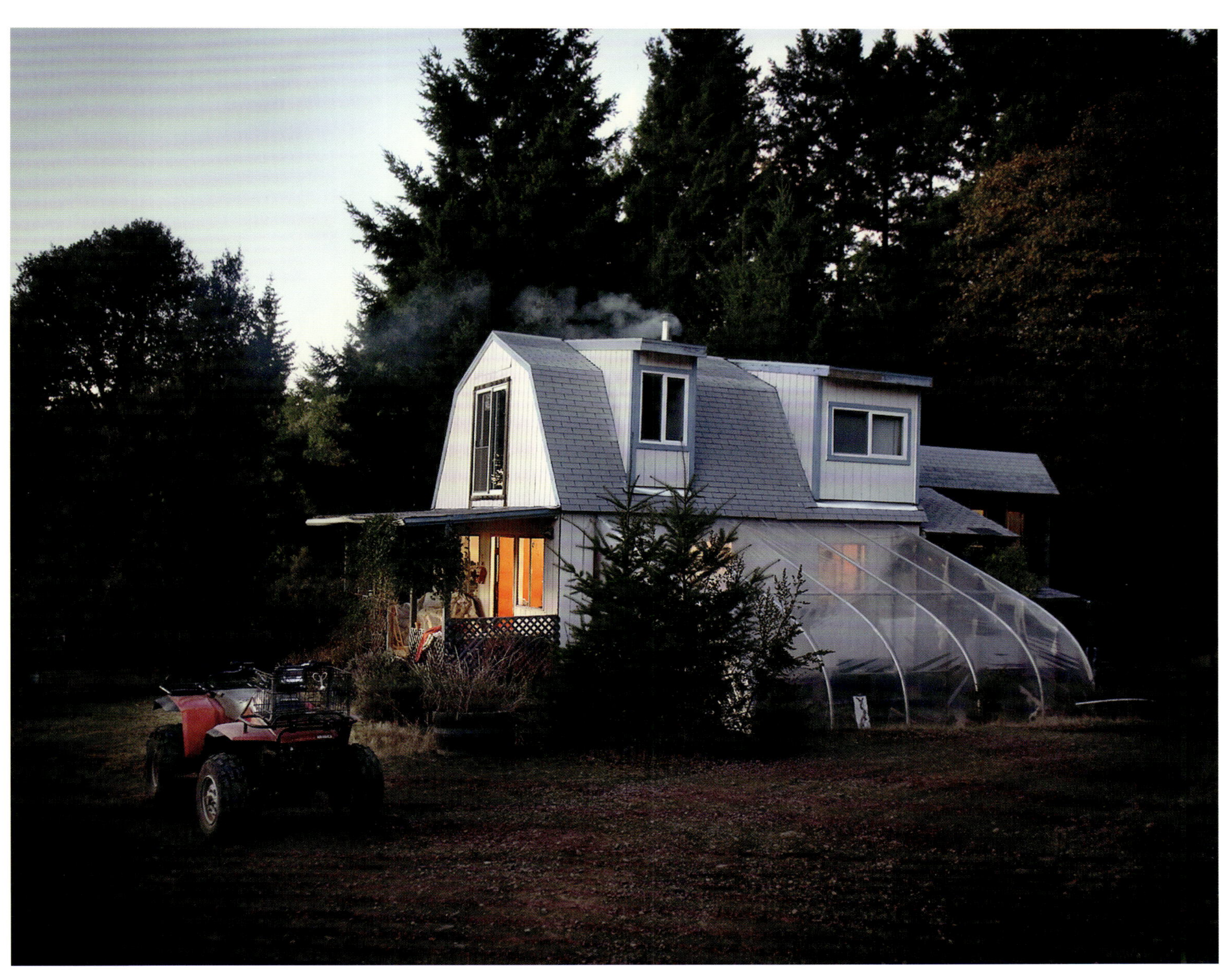

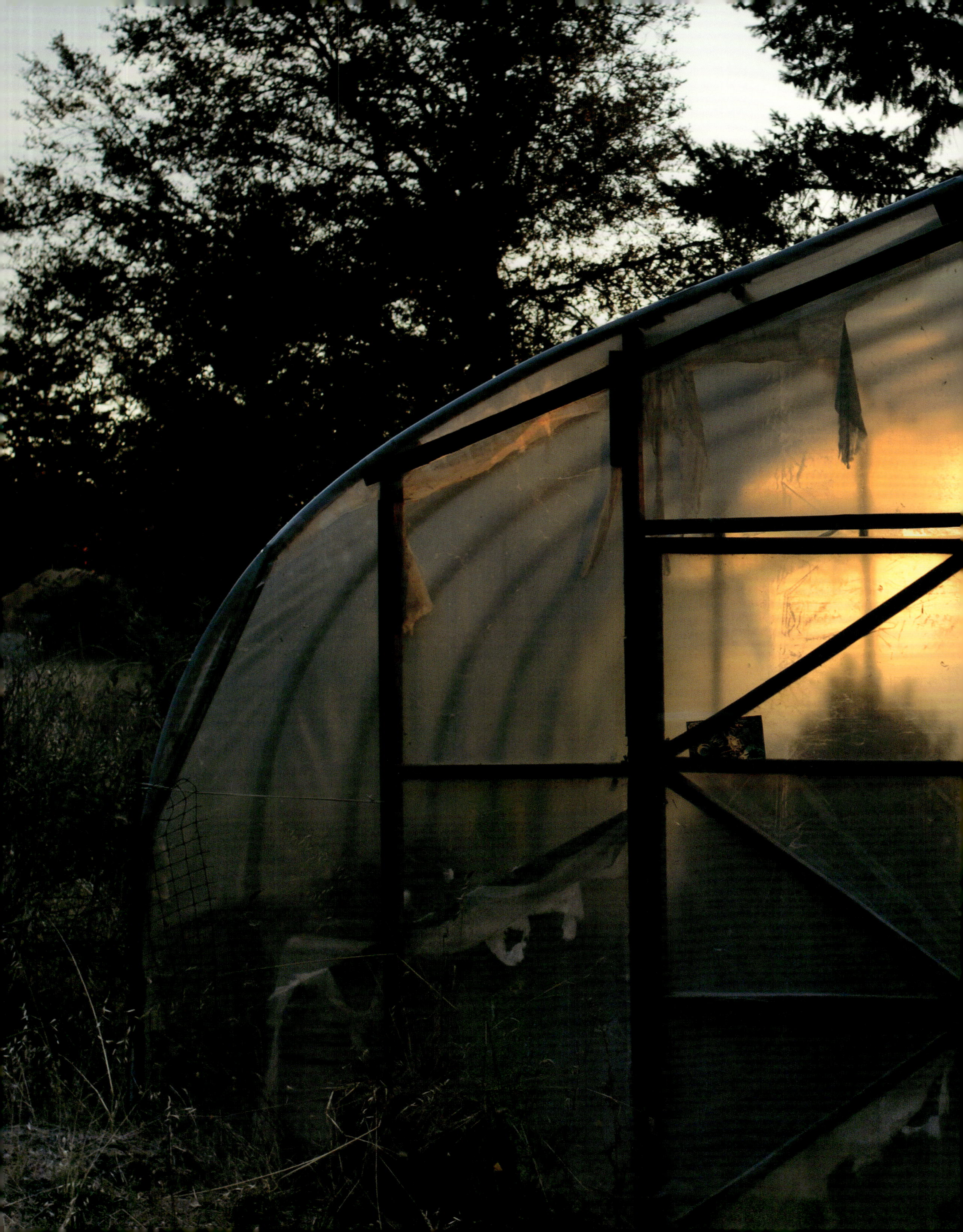

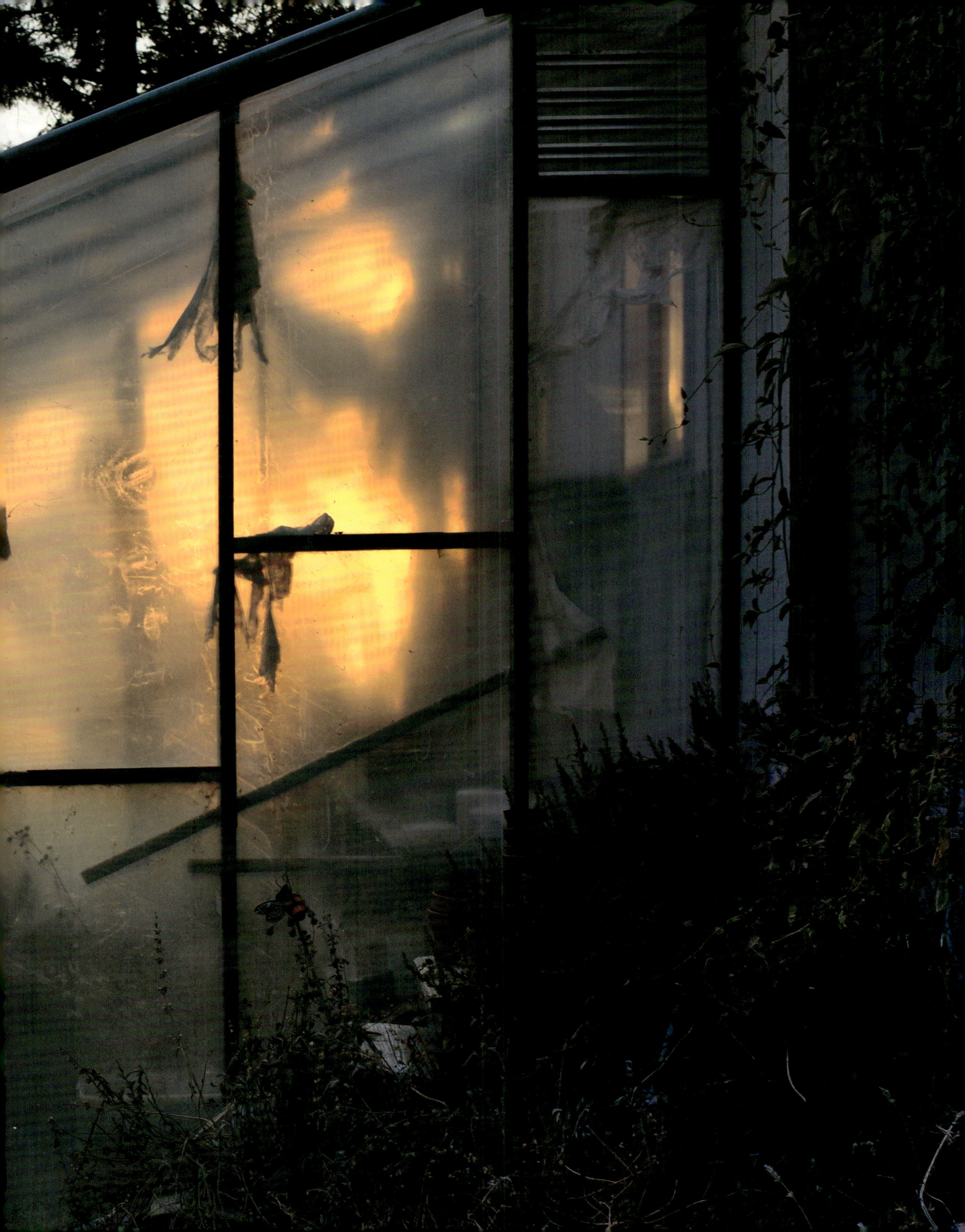

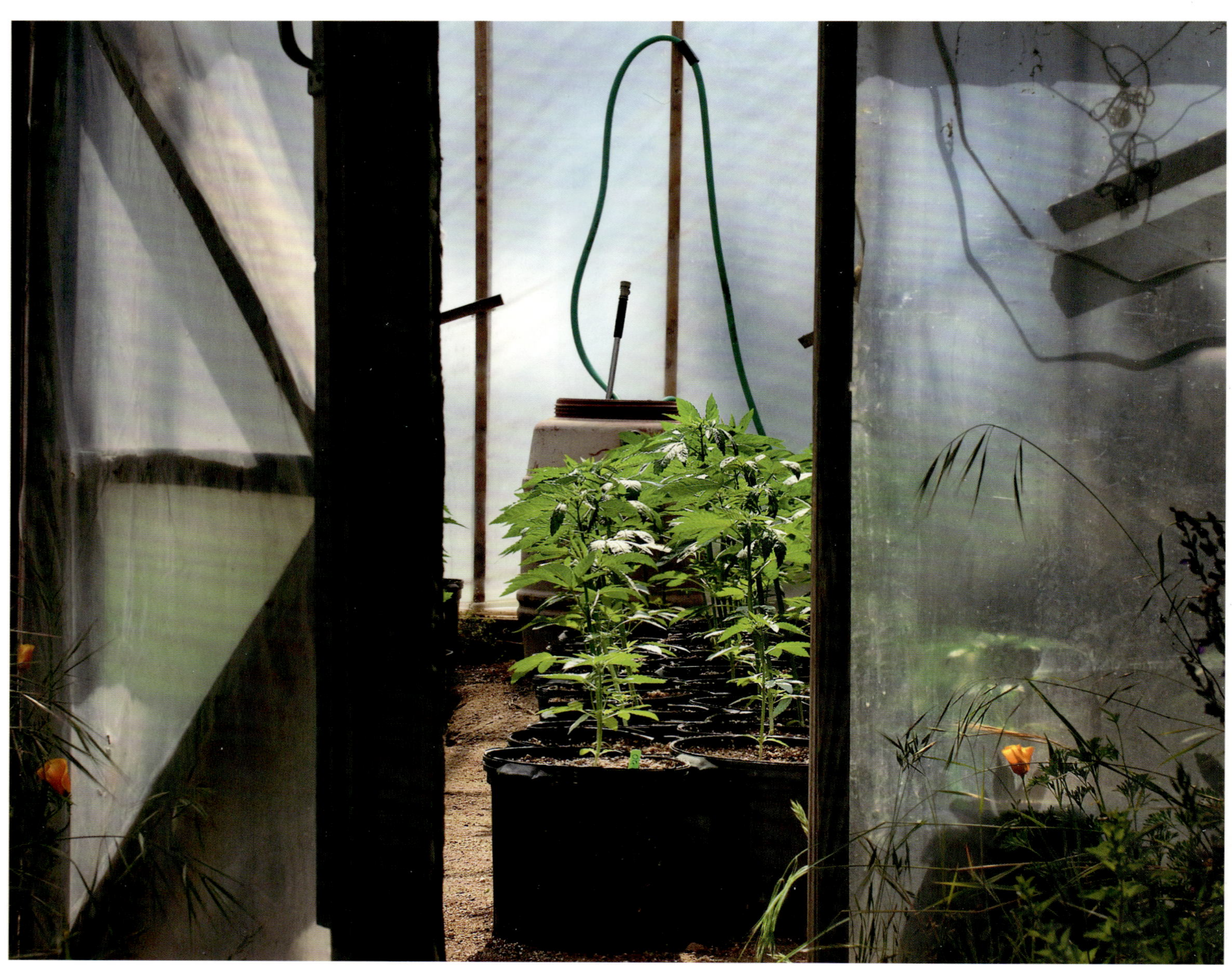

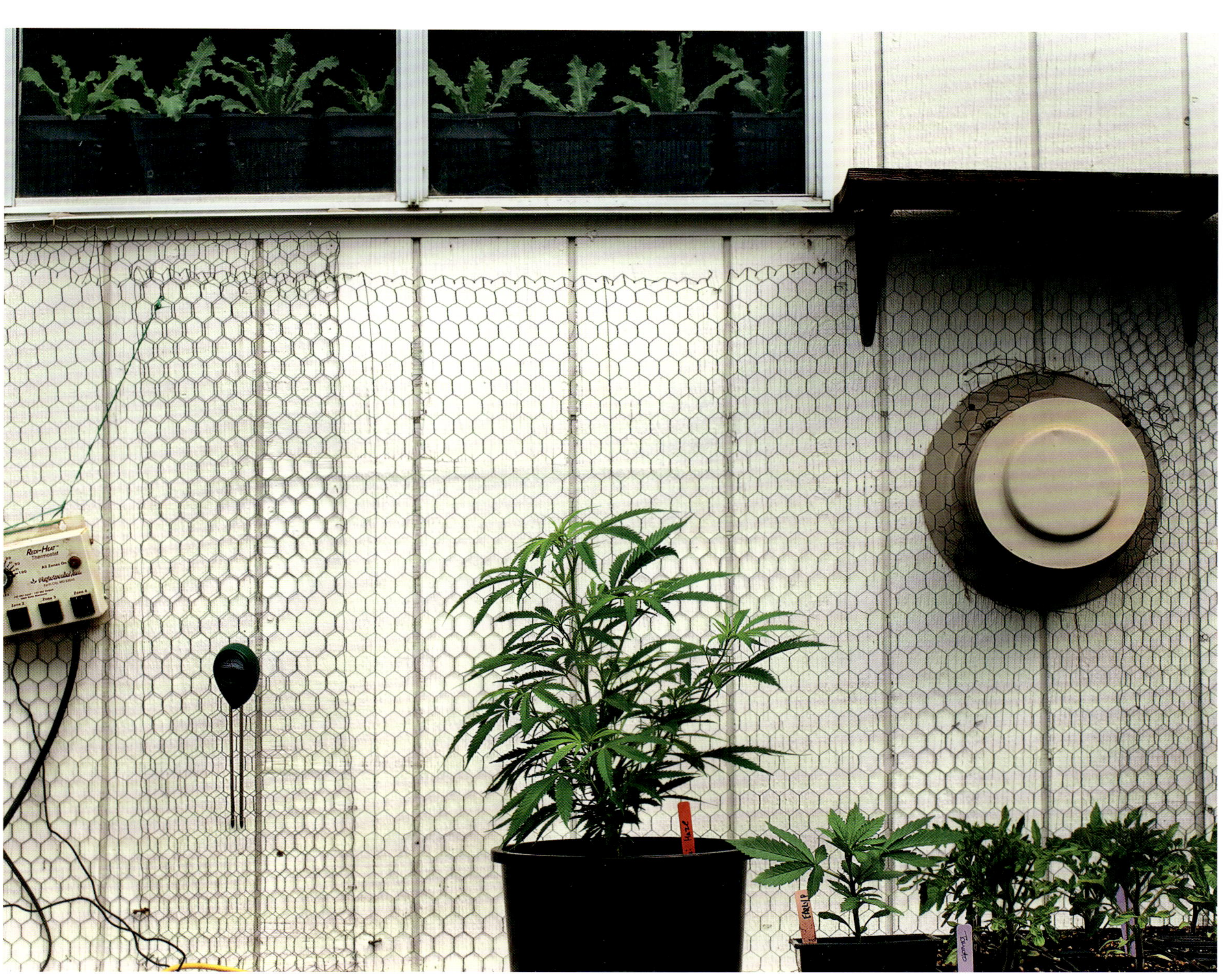

Redi-Heat™ Thermostat
All Zones On
Zone 2
Zone 3
Zone 4
Haze
Early P
Tomato

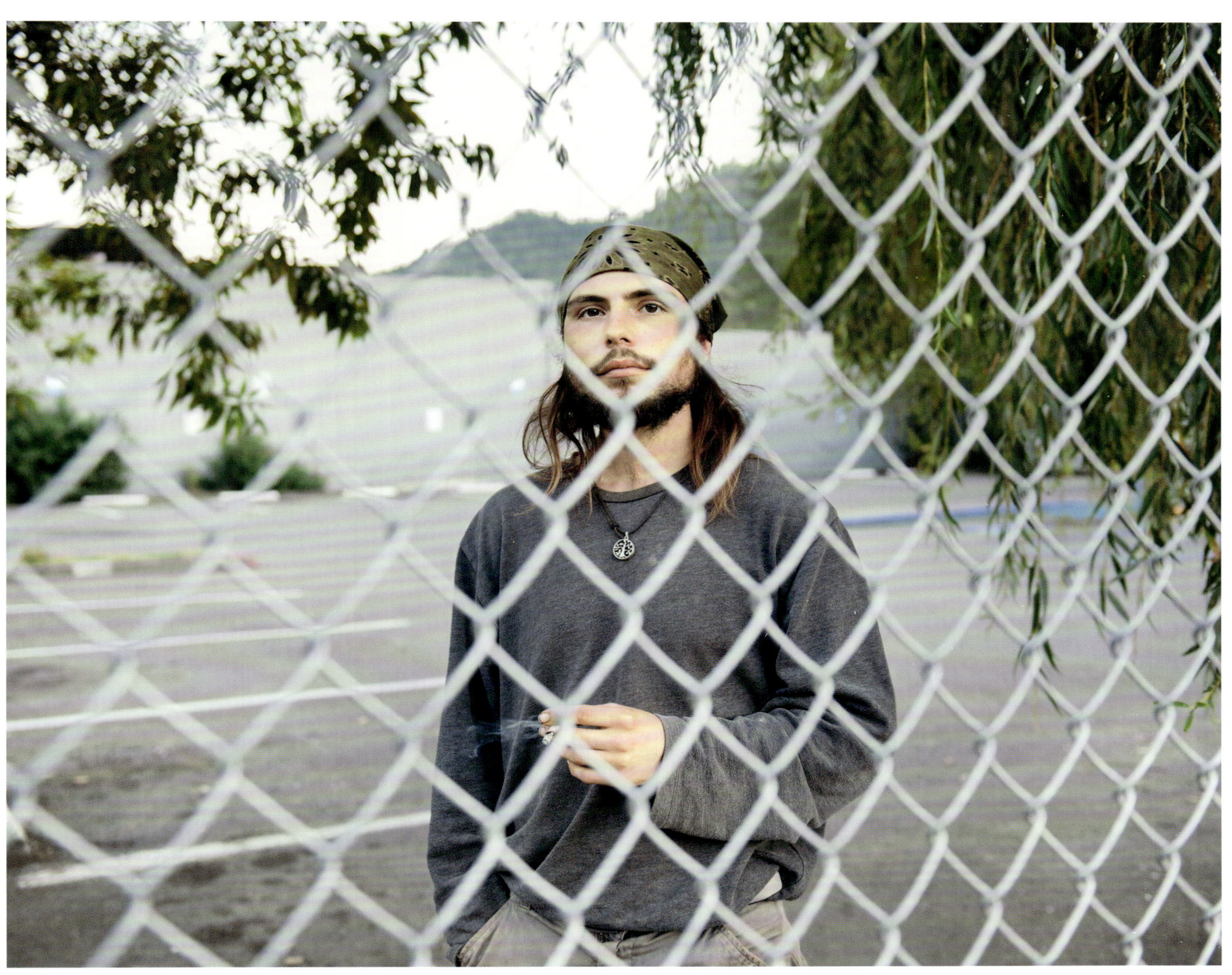

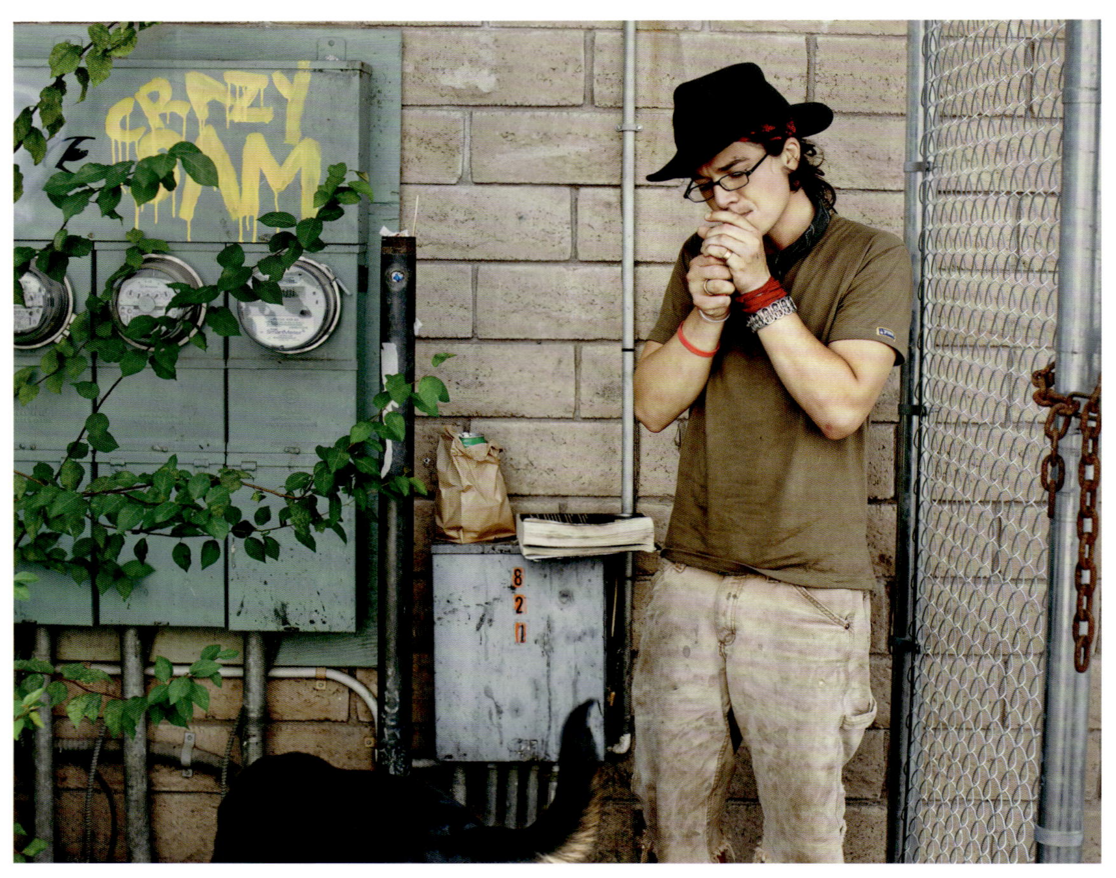
CRAZY
AM
8 2 1

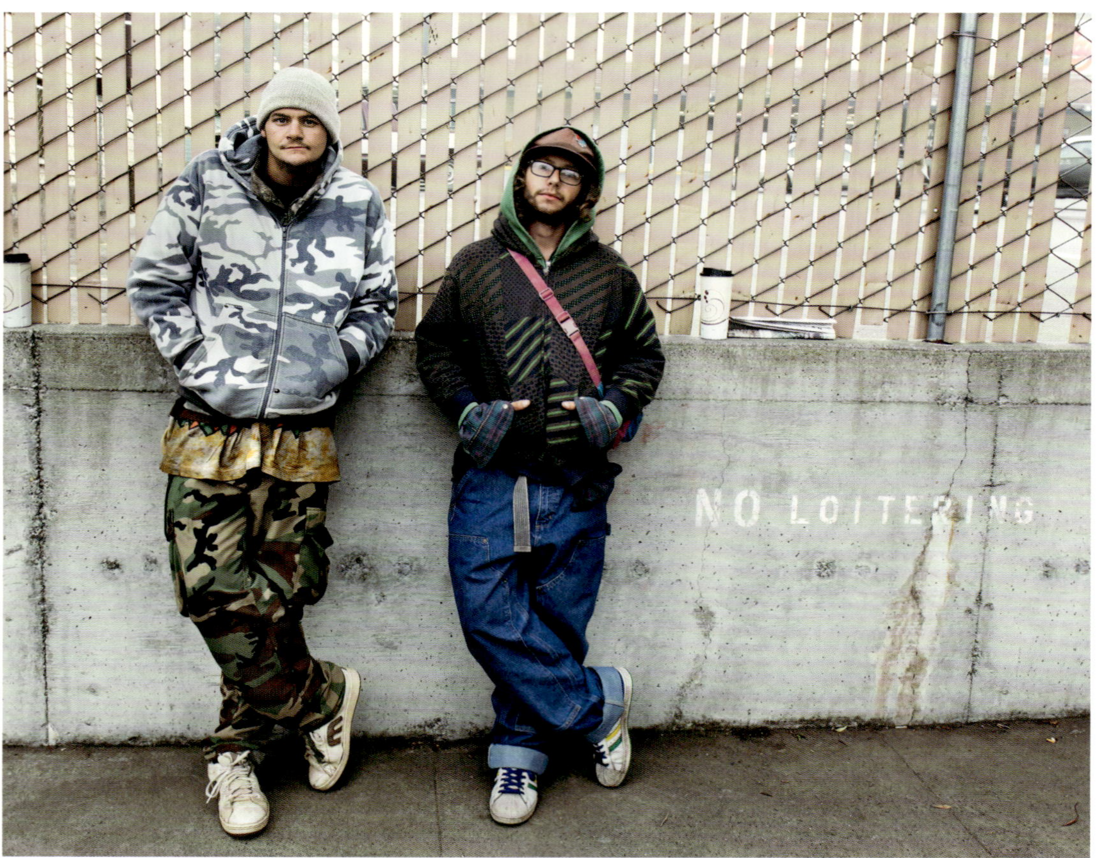
NO LOITERING

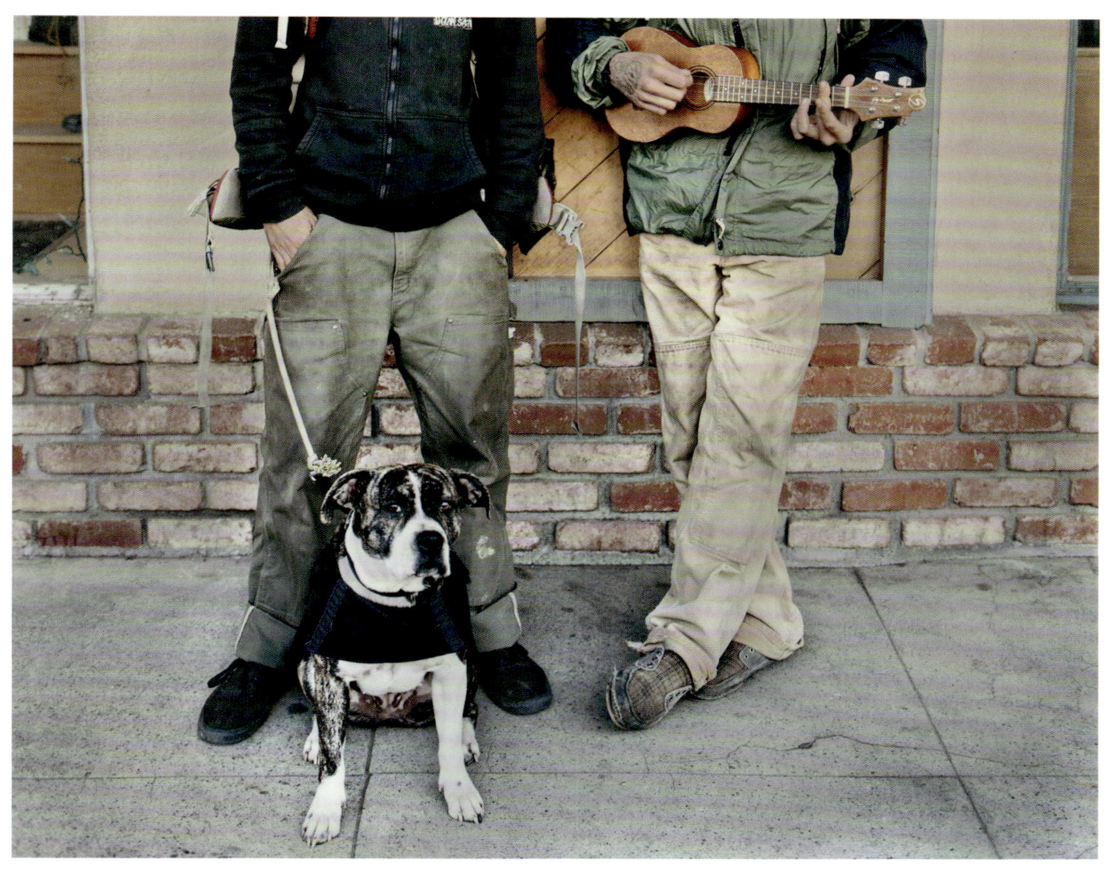
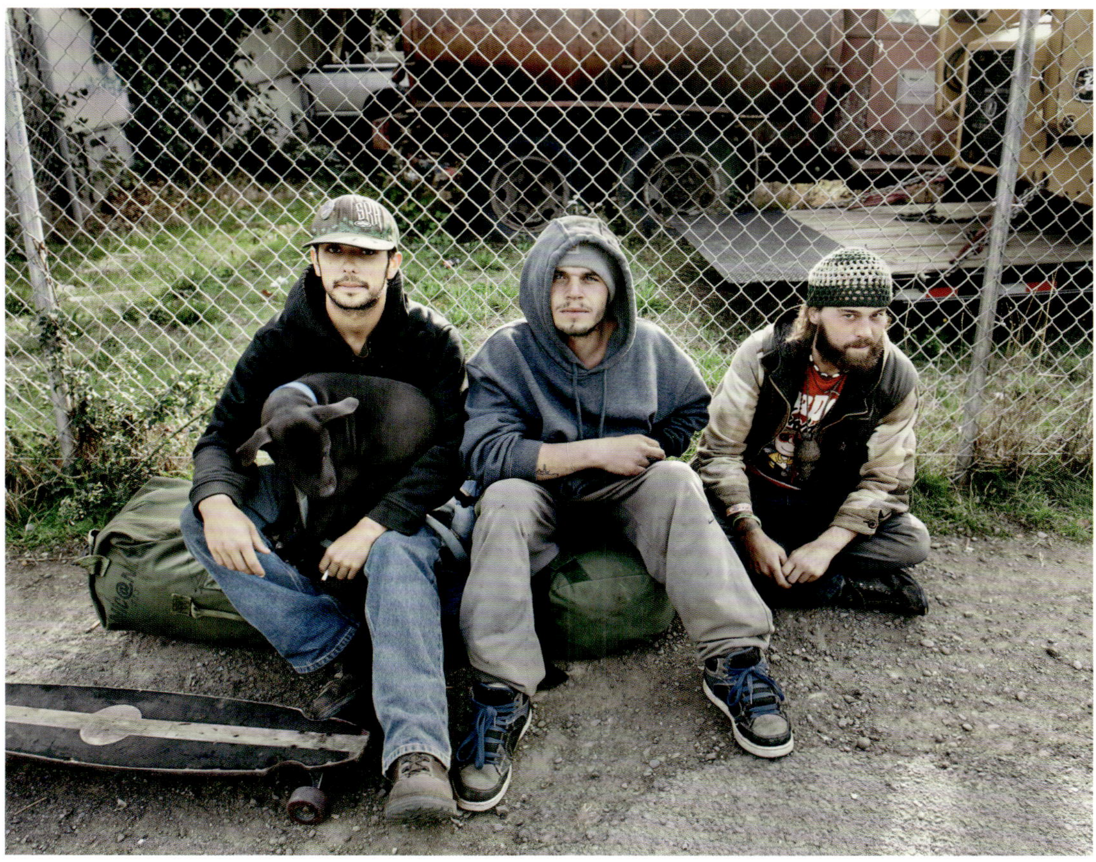

We were sitting in a parked car on Main Street in Garberville in southern Humboldt County. The car was covered in a coat of dust so thick it looked like it had just crossed the Black Rock Desert. Most of the cars and trucks parked next to us had a similar layer of dust, a telltale sign of journeys up dirt roads to secret gardens behind locked gates.

It was late in the summer of 2010, and the woman in the driver's seat next to me was explaining the importance of secrecy and trust. I was new to the community, an outsider who had arrived by chance and had become so captivated by the story I found that I had decided to stick around and write a book about it. At this point I was still trying to understand what the secrecy was all about, why people weren't strutting around proudly in "I'm a weed farmer" T-shirts and owning their history. It had been 14 years since California passed the nation's first medical-marijuana law, and in a few months voters would head to the polls to consider legalizing pot outright. Yet in Humboldt, people who had been in the marijuana business for years lived in fear that outsiders would discover what they did for a living. Meanwhile, newcomers in places like Los Angeles and San Francisco were appearing on TV and in the papers, dominating all the attention pot growing and dispensaries were receiving. I didn't get it. The woman grew quiet for a moment and then turned and looked me straight in the eye.

"Can I trust you?" she asked.

In time, I came to understand and appreciate her fear. By trusting me with the secret that she grew marijuana for a living, she risked ending up in prison or having her children taken away. It is still a federal crime to possess, grow, or distribute marijuana, and while state laws were evolving, after decades of distrust of authorities it was hard for growers in Humboldt to realize that the world really was changing around them, that it didn't have to be a secret anymore.

It also took me a while to understand that the question "Can I trust you?" wasn't one she was asking me. She was asking herself. She had to decide if she trusted me, because that is how it worked in this community. When you work outside the law, you can't sue your business partner when something goes wrong. When you risk jail time by telling the wrong person what you're growing in your greenhouse, everything comes down to trust.

Trust is what H. Lee earned of her subjects in order to bring us the beautiful images in this book. The hidden world that she documents is one that has been able to survive outside the mainstream for so long thanks to its culture of secrecy and its underground economy, which ensured that for decades the marijuana growers of southern Humboldt County were among the most prosperous small farmers in America. The world she takes us into is one of great natural beauty, where fog settles in wisps across the tops of the world's tallest trees, the Pacific coast redwoods, and the grassy hills turn the color of straw during the summer months. The lifestyle is one of almost total independence. Many homes were built by hand, and electricity comes from the solar panels or a windmill, not the electric grid. It is a place where the clock ticks to the cycle of the marijuana-growing season. Seeds are sprouted in the spring, and plants grow so tall in the summer that some growers need ladders to reach the top branches. Come harvest time, in the fall, the hands of farmers and trimmers become covered in a sticky brown coat of resin. Colas, or marijuana branches, are hung to dry and then cured and stored in paper bags before they are trimmed. The place truly is Grassland. But it wasn't always this way.

To understand Humboldt County and how it became the heartland of America's marijuana industry, it's important to know that it was very much a story of chance. In the late 1960s and early 1970s, there was an exodus of young people from America's cities. They headed out into the countryside of states such as New York, Vermont, and, of course, California. They arrived in VW Beetles and painted vans. Some hitchhiked. They were driven by a desire to live independently and free. It was known as "back-to-the-land," and it was a pioneer movement of sorts.

These young folks who first arrived in Humboldt (and the two adjacent counties, Mendocino and Trinity, which would eventually be collectively known as the Emerald Triangle) arrived in the first wave of idealistic youth, and they were always quick to remind me that they didn't move there to grow pot. At the time, most of the pot smoked in the United States came from Mexico. They moved to Humboldt, a sparsely populated and mountainous county about four hours north of San Francisco, because the land was cheap and beautiful. They lived on communes, in teepees, and in ramshackle cabins. Times were tough. Humboldt was a county that loggers built, but by the late 1960s most of the magnificent old-growth redwoods had been destroyed, and with them the local economy. A brief culture clash ensued between the old-timers, who were mainly ranchers and loggers, and the new arrivals, who wore their hair long and didn't seem to have two nickels to rub together. But these young folks soon discovered something that bridged the divide.

Driven by independence and poverty, many of these new people grew their own food, and, as everyone including Nixon knew, these young members of the counterculture liked to smoke pot. Marijuana that came from Mexico contained seeds, and it was only so long before people started fishing the seeds out of their stashes and planting them in their gardens between the summer squash and the raspberry bushes. It turned out that their friends back in the city liked to smoke the pot that they grew and were willing to pay a little money for it. And then, sometime in the early to mid-1970s, no one remembers exactly when, they discovered how to grow that pot without seeds. It was called sinsemilla. It was stronger and more potent than anything anyone had ever smoked before, and their friends back in the city were willing to pay a whole lot of money for it.

By the mid-1970s, sinsemilla growing became widespread and not just among the counterculture. Many of the old-timers quickly realized they could make a living at it too. Word slowly trickled out, and outsiders began trickling in to try their luck at growing what would become Northern California's cash crop. By 1979 the secret was out. That year a story appeared in *The New York Times* about how the marijuana crop had "revived" the area—pot prices were up, Main Street in Garberville was bustling, and deputies had confiscated more pot that year than the year before. The reputation of the "marijuana moonshiners," as one back-to-the-lander I wrote about liked to call them, was firmly established.

How was this able to continue for so long in our backwoods while we waged the War on Drugs on inner-city American streets and in the highlands of Colombia? Why didn't the cops shut it down? They certainly tried. Early efforts at eradicating marijuana grows in Northern California began in the late 1970s with Operation Sinsemilla. Newspapers of the day featured photos of law enforcement standing in front of felled plants. By 1983 efforts had become more organized, and the Campaign Against Marijuana Planting, or CAMP, a multi-agency task force bent on wiping out marijuana production, began scouring the hills of Humboldt every fall in helicopters, searching for marijuana gardens to destroy.

But this crackdown had an unintended consequence: the price of pot soared. With a black-market product, precise price points are difficult to pinpoint, but here's an example: In the early 1980s, one farmer I met earned $1200 per pound for her outdoor, organically grown weed. That price jumped during the "Just Say No" 1980s. At times, marijuana was worth more per ounce than gold. By the early 1990s, that same farmer was earning $6000 per pound for her crop. People weren't able to grow in the full sun then, like they do today. Some Humboldt growers moved their plants indoors and under lights, or planted them under meticulously pruned tree canopies, which would let in just enough sunlight while hopefully avoiding prying eyes. Some even took to growing pot in the trees themselves, and stuck plants on platforms and ran waterlines up them. Others grew their crops on public land or on large swaths of private land to reduce the chances of getting caught. The risks were great, but so were the profits. As folks in Humboldt like to say, marijuana prohibition was the greatest government price-support program in U.S. history.

And with the gardens, a culture grew. Marijuana culture. The back-to-the-landers spent part of their earnings building the foundation of their community, which now includes a radio station, a health center, a community center, and various community schools. It was a family-friendly culture. People threw fundraisers for friends who got sick or got busted. These gentler aspects of the place were far from the image of the gun-toting grower popularized in the press. Of course, the occasional shooting or rip-off did occur, and people were shocked and horrified, but sadly it became an accepted part of the business.

And somewhere along the way, this method of earning a living that was stumbled upon by chance became the only way many people in the community could see to make ends meet. In a trend that might seem counterintuitive to an outsider, when the legalization vote was cast in California in 2010, the majority of people in Humboldt and, indeed, in the entire three-county Emerald Triangle, voted against it. There were a few reasons. Many were scared the government would take the industry away, like what happened to the bootleggers after alcohol prohibition. Others who were in it just for pure profit wanted to continue reaping the inflated prices of the black market. Still others wondered how they would make a living in the backwoods without it, and how they would pay their mortgage and feed their kids.

The night of the vote, I was standing in a bar of a southern Humboldt restaurant called The Brass Rail. It was a bordello for loggers that had been converted into a steakhouse. As the CNN journalist announced the news on the screen—"Marijuana won't be legal in California, not today"—shouts of joy filled the bar, and from the back of the room came this victorious cry: "We won't be a ghost town!"

That cry summed up the feelings of so many.

In the years since the vote, life in Humboldt has continued much as it did before. Much of the economy and way of life still revolves around the marijuana-growing industry and looks exactly as H. Lee captured it in this book. Heavy flower clusters are still hung to dry every fall, industrious hands still become coated with resin, the occasional rip-off still occurs, and the natural beauty of the place remains breathtaking and wild.

But there have been changes too.

Newcomers continue to pour into the county hoping to strike it rich with weed while there is still a lucrative black market. So many of them have entered the industry that the movement has been dubbed the "Green Rush," after the Gold Rush of old. Meanwhile, growers who have been at it for decades are finding that they need to grow more to earn what they did the year before. All of this has put an enormous strain on the environment. Stories about rodenticides used by growers poisoning forest creatures, and local rivers and streams being sucked dry to water thirsty plants have received much attention in the national and international press.

Meanwhile, beyond the tree-lined borders of Grassland, a broader cultural shift continues. Medical-marijuana laws are spreading across the country, and the majority of Americans are now finally in support of recreational legalization, with the states of Washington and Colorado paving the way. All of this means that someday, in the not-too-distant future, the biggest change of all will finally come to pass. And when it does, these images will become historical documents of the rugged individualism of the American West and of an industry and a culture at a crossroads.

—Emily Brady, San Francisco

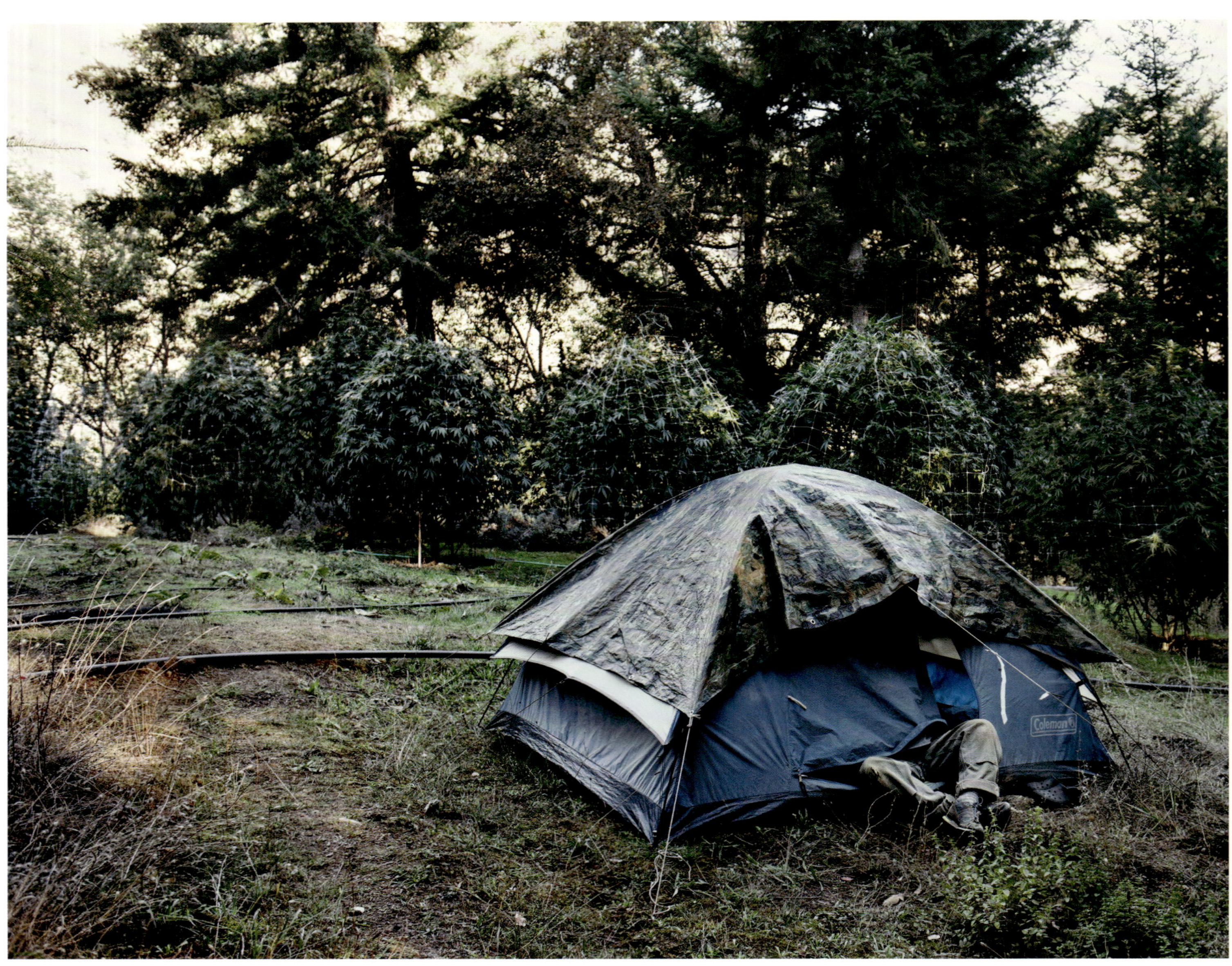
Coleman

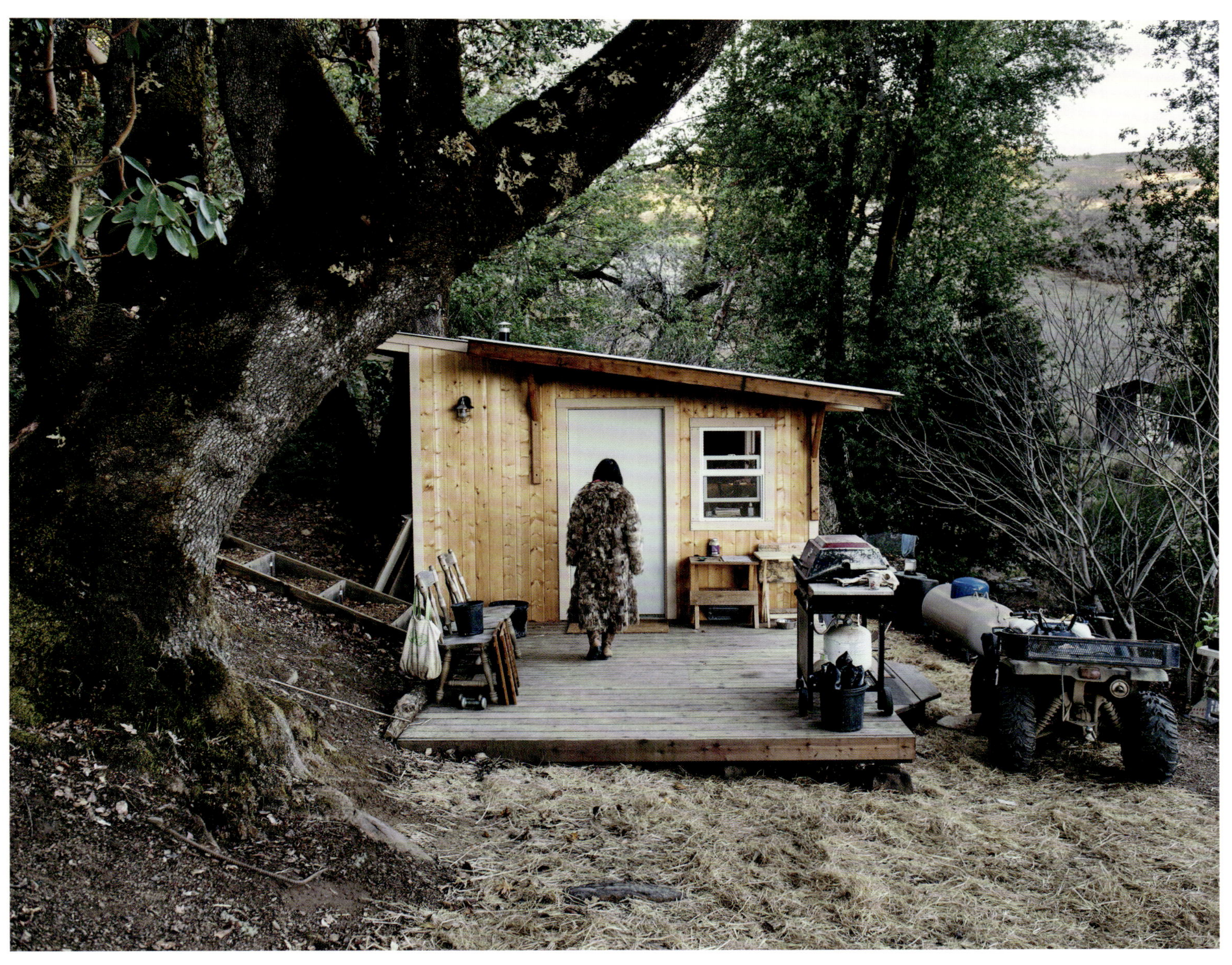

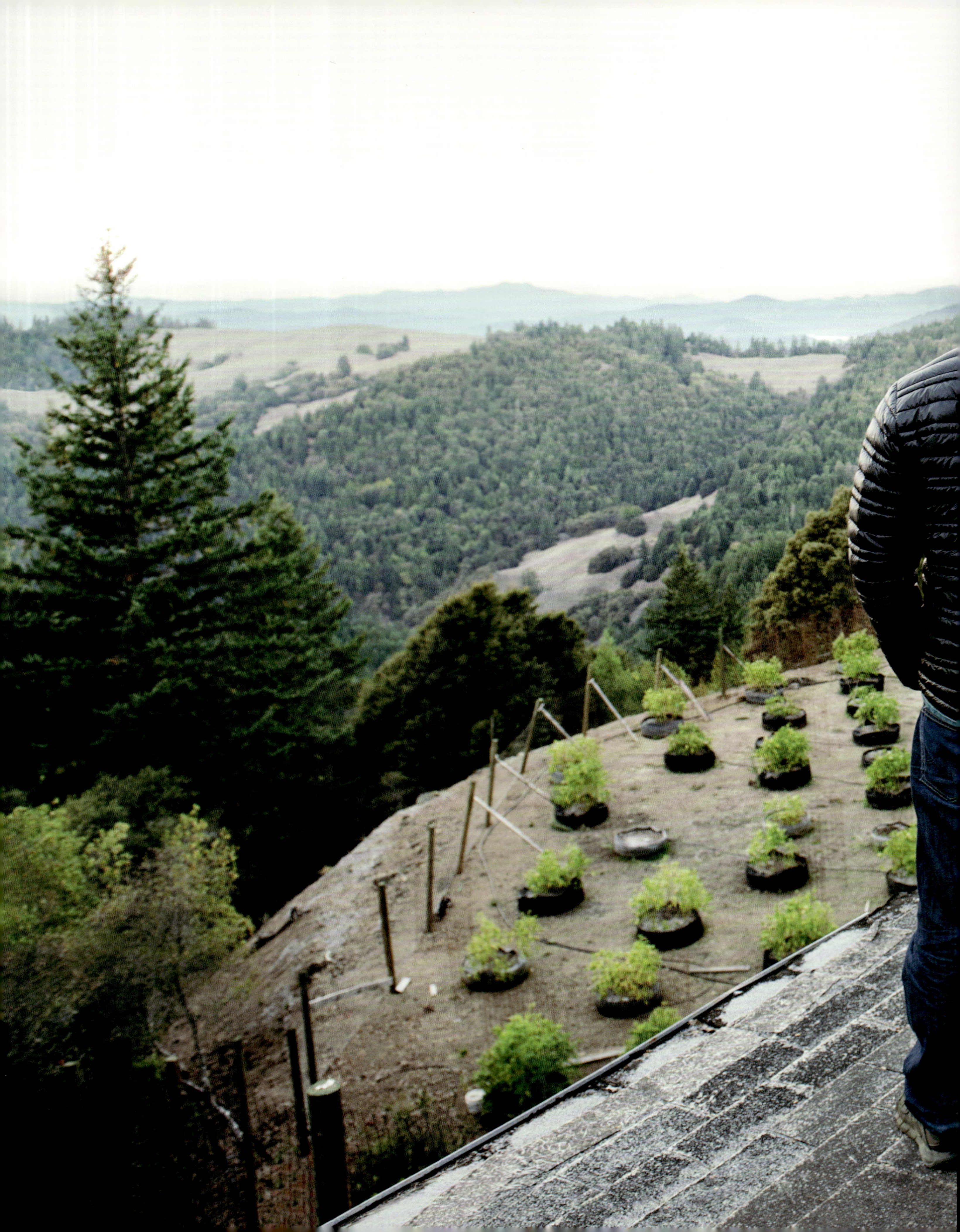

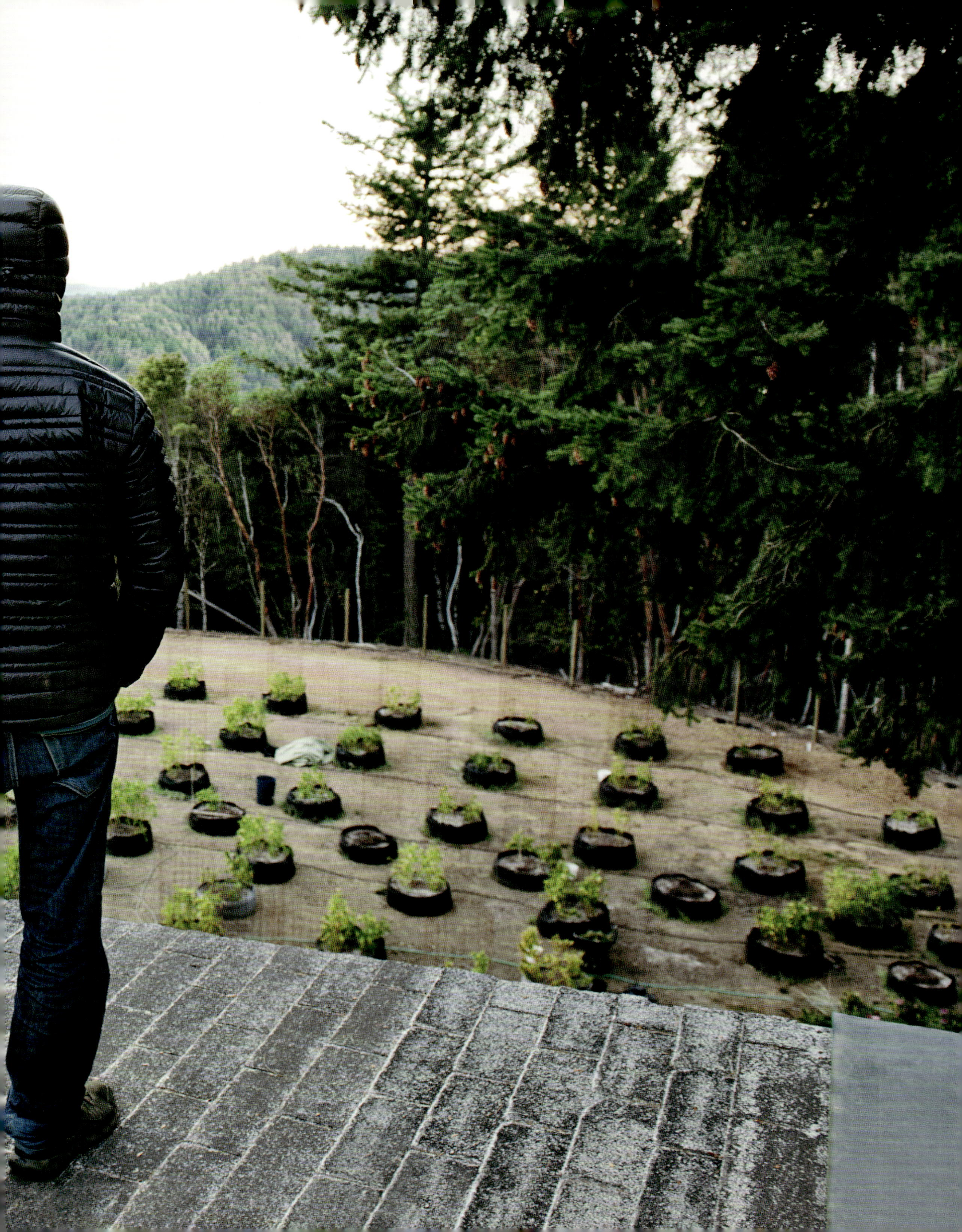

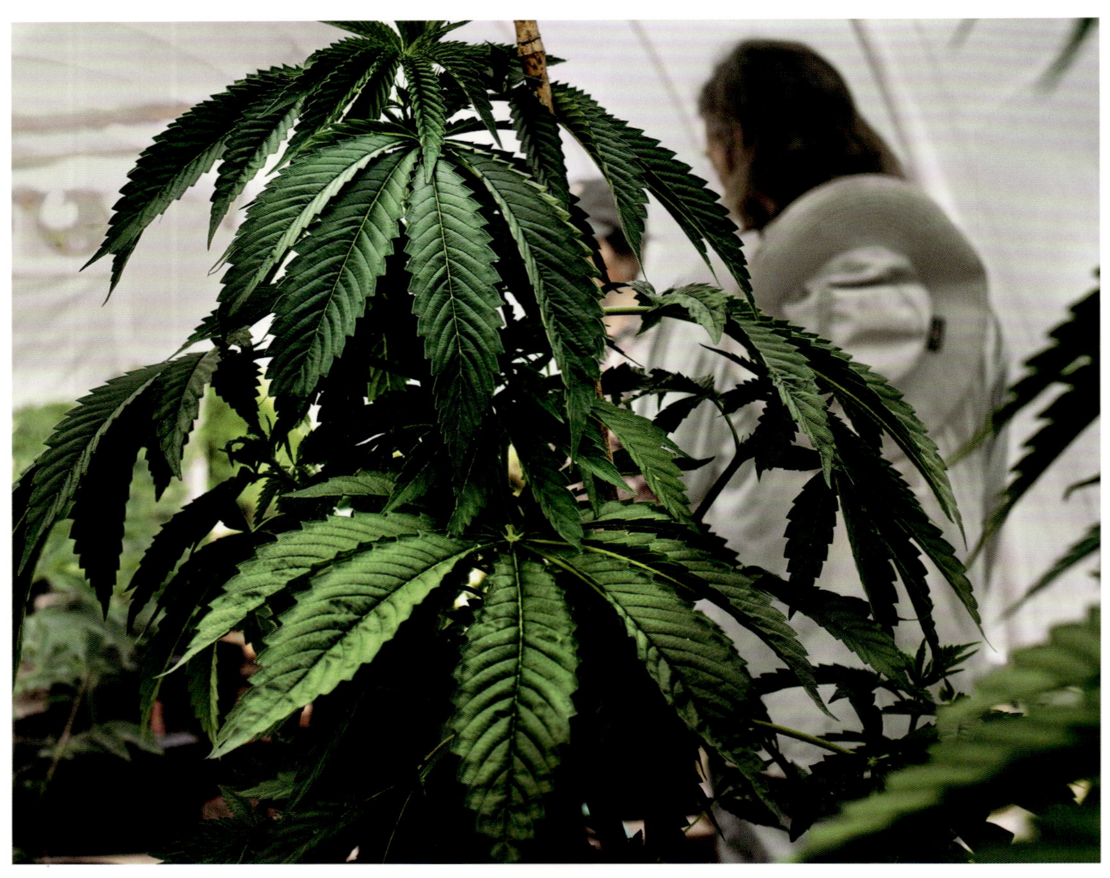

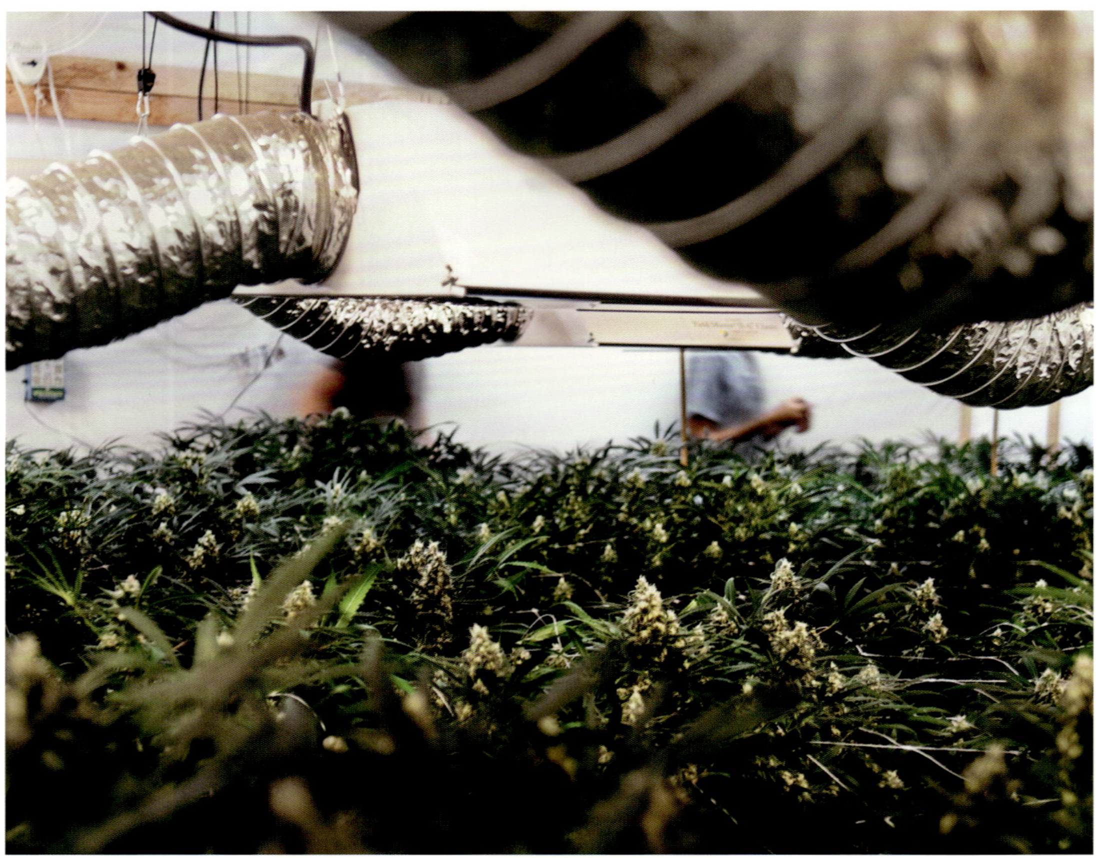

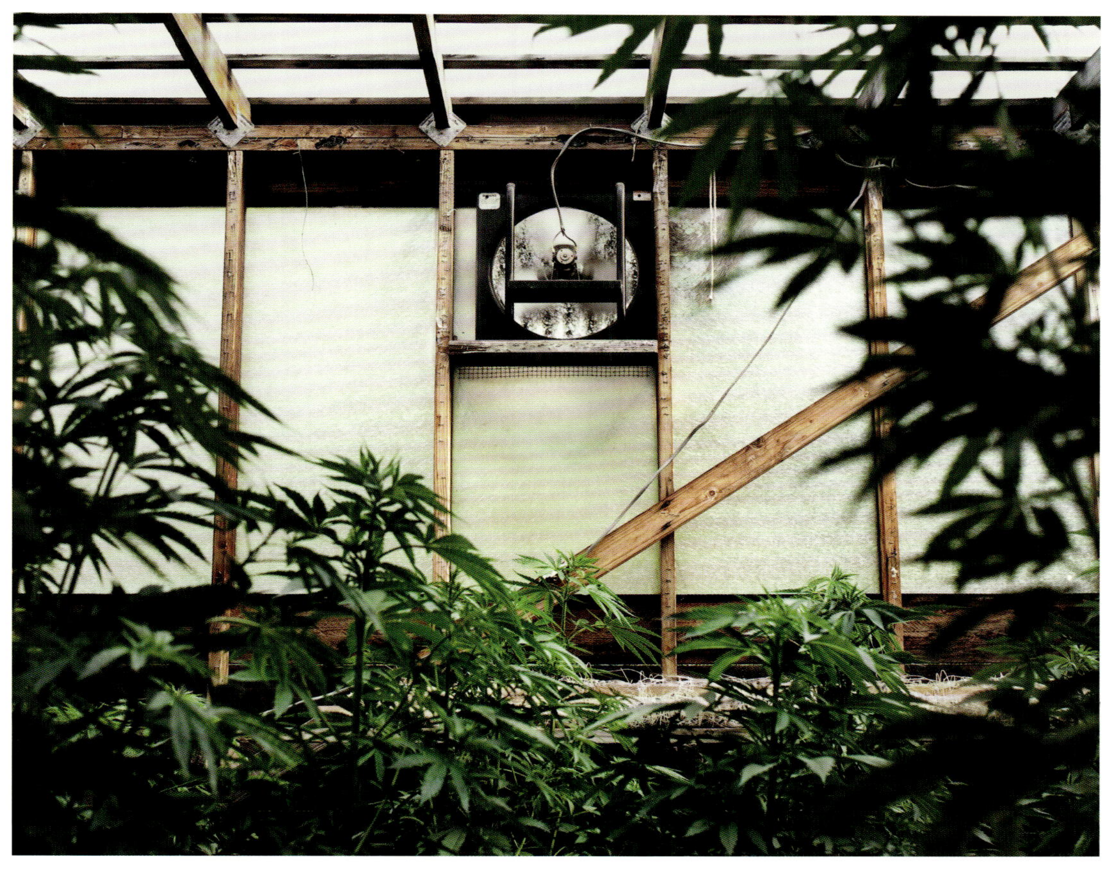

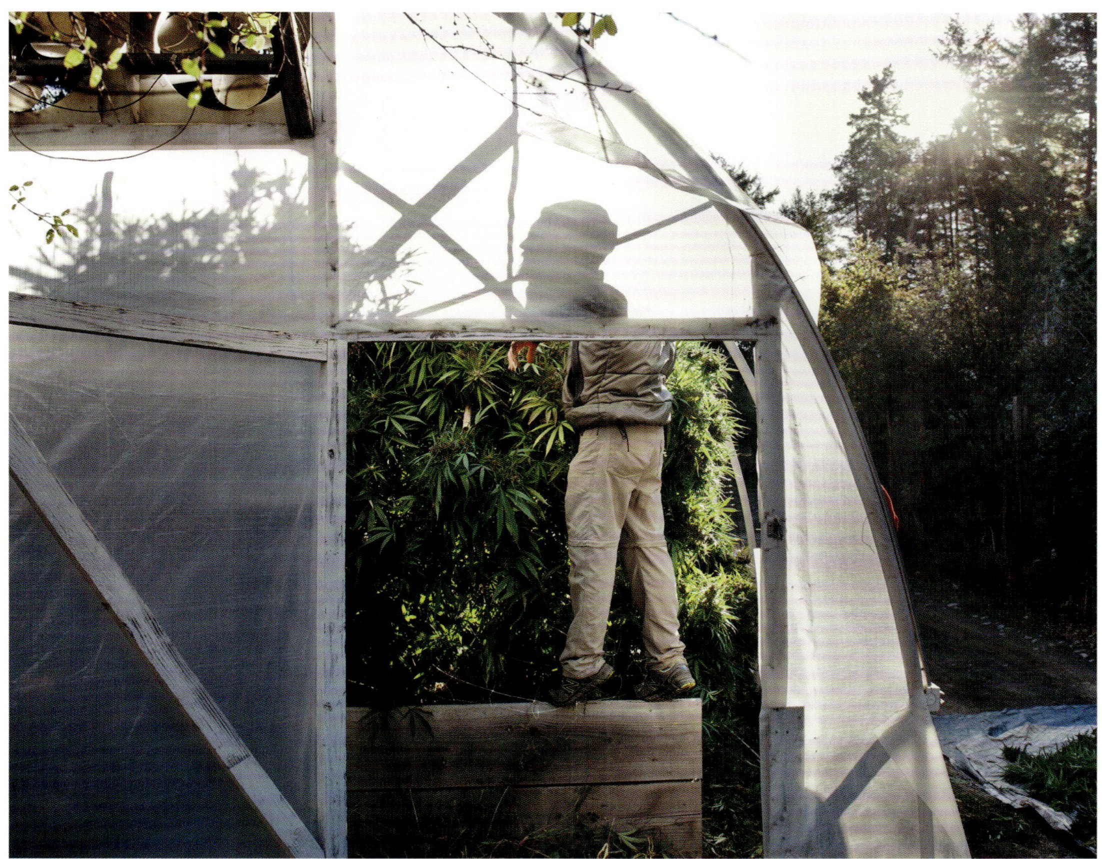

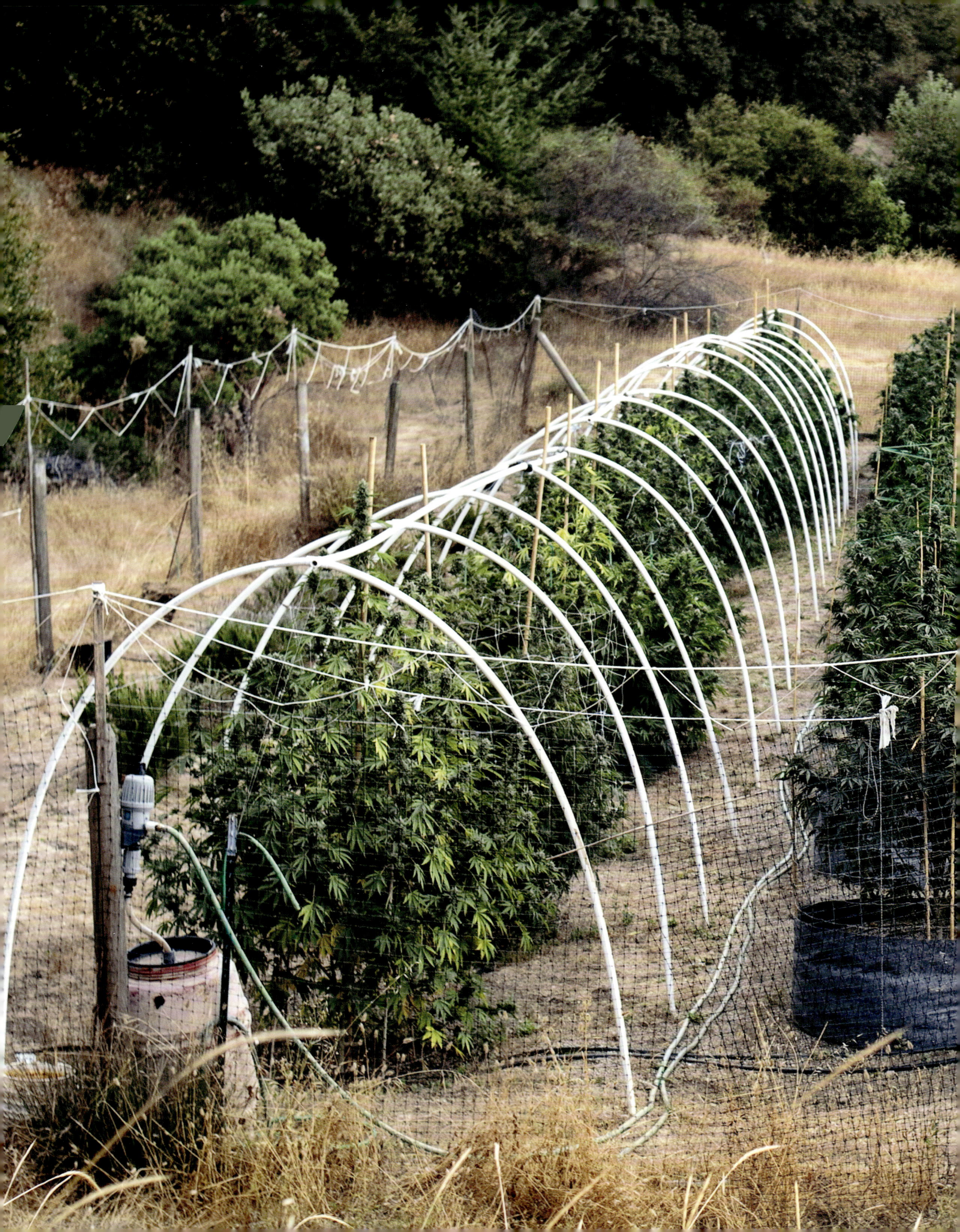

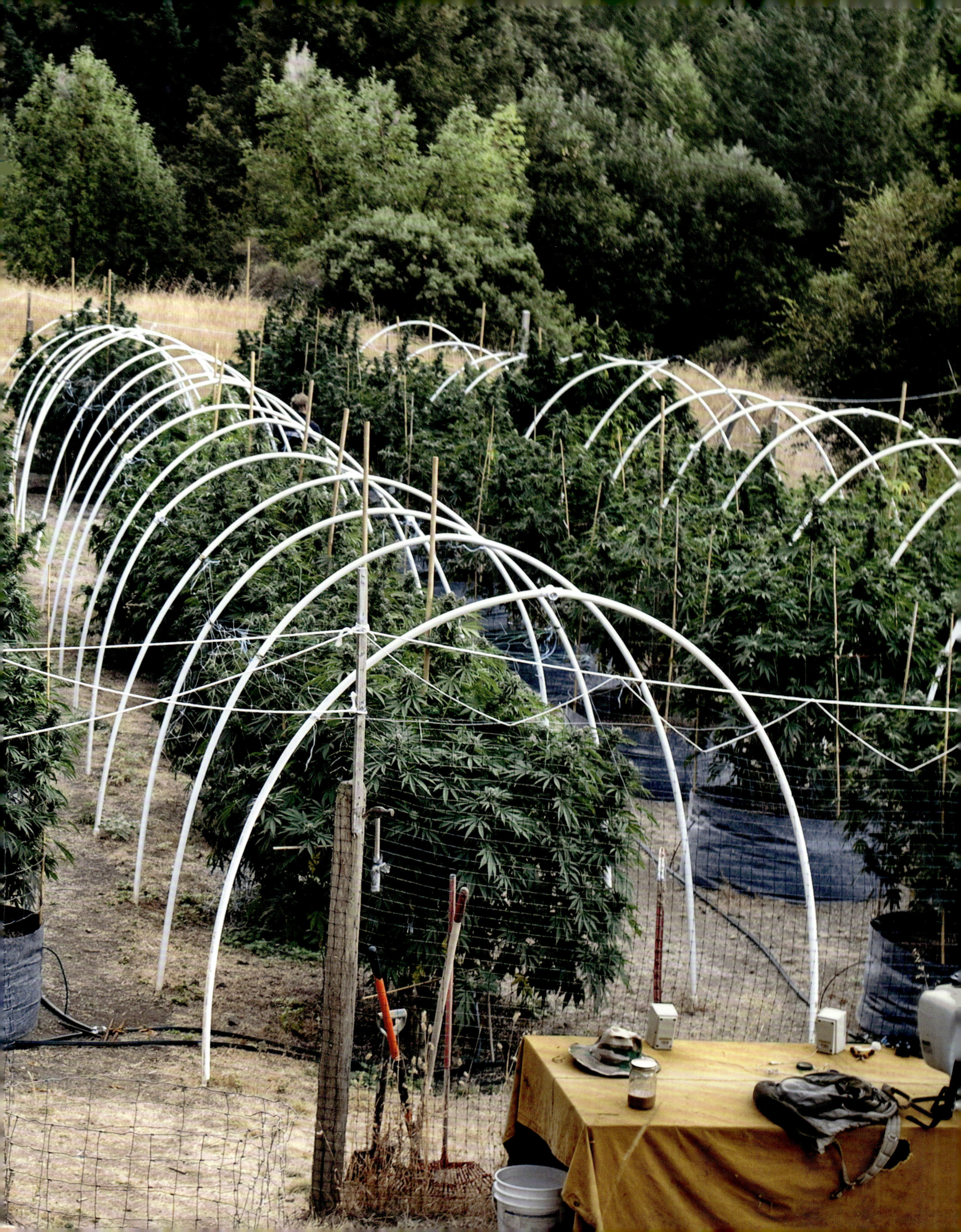

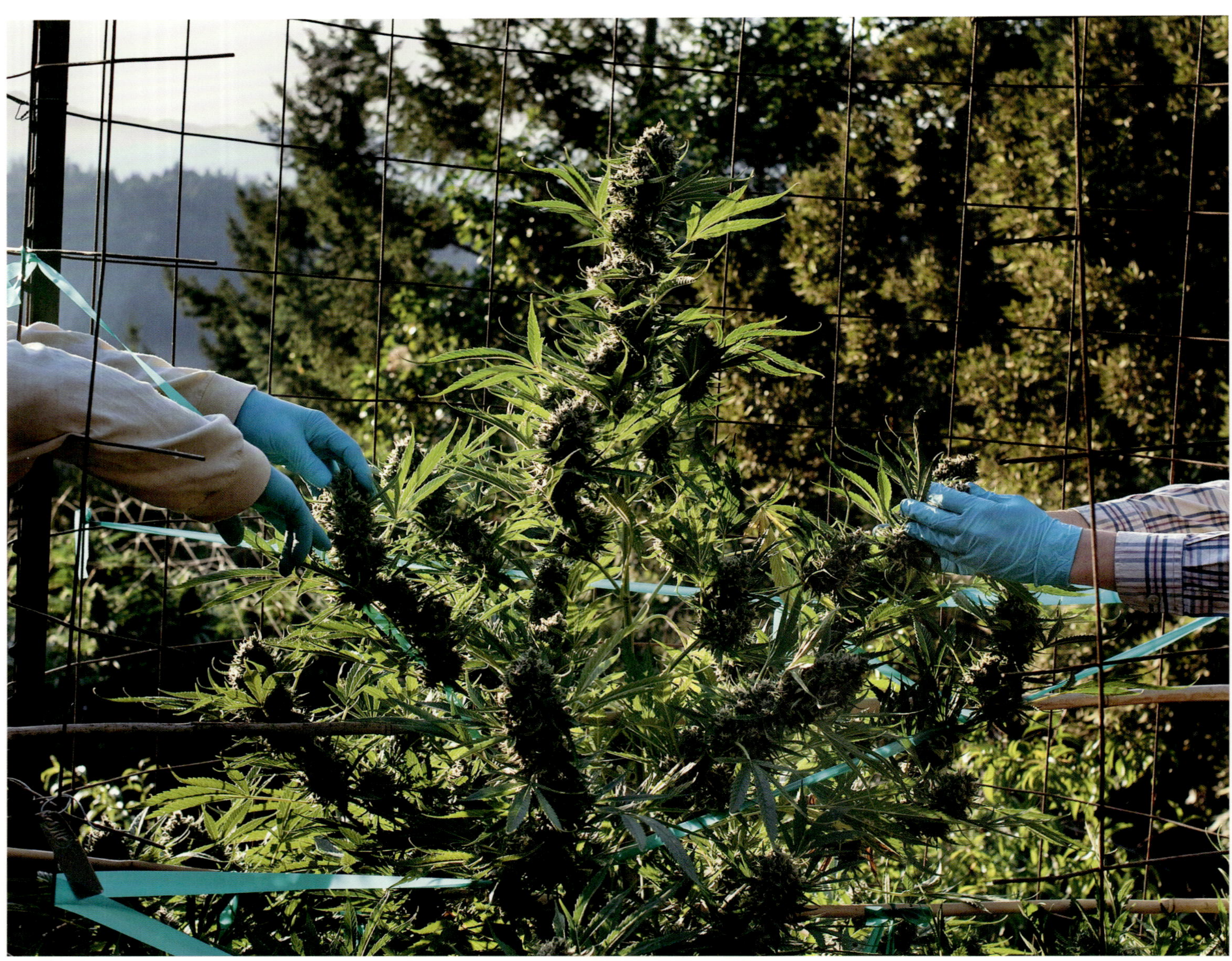

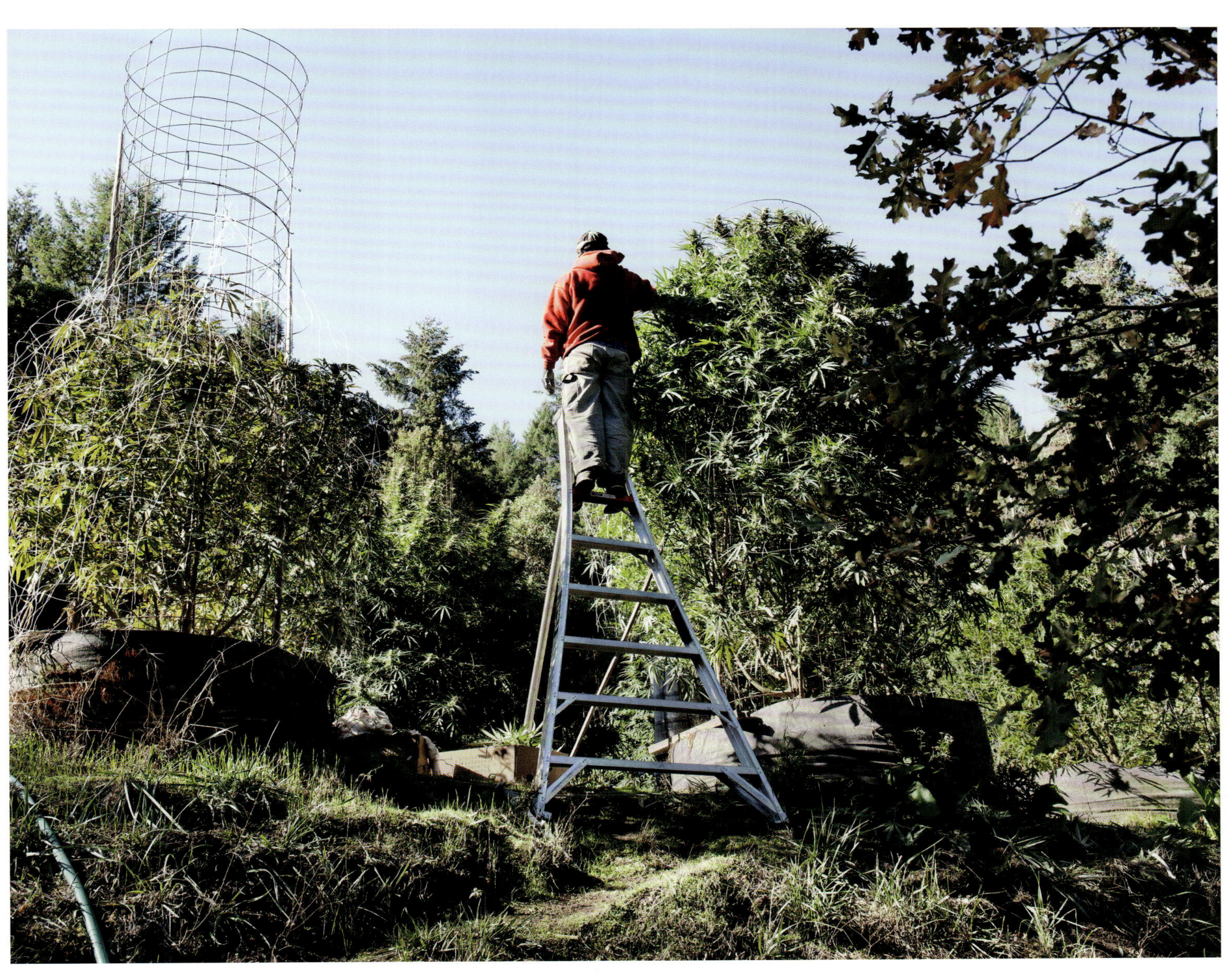

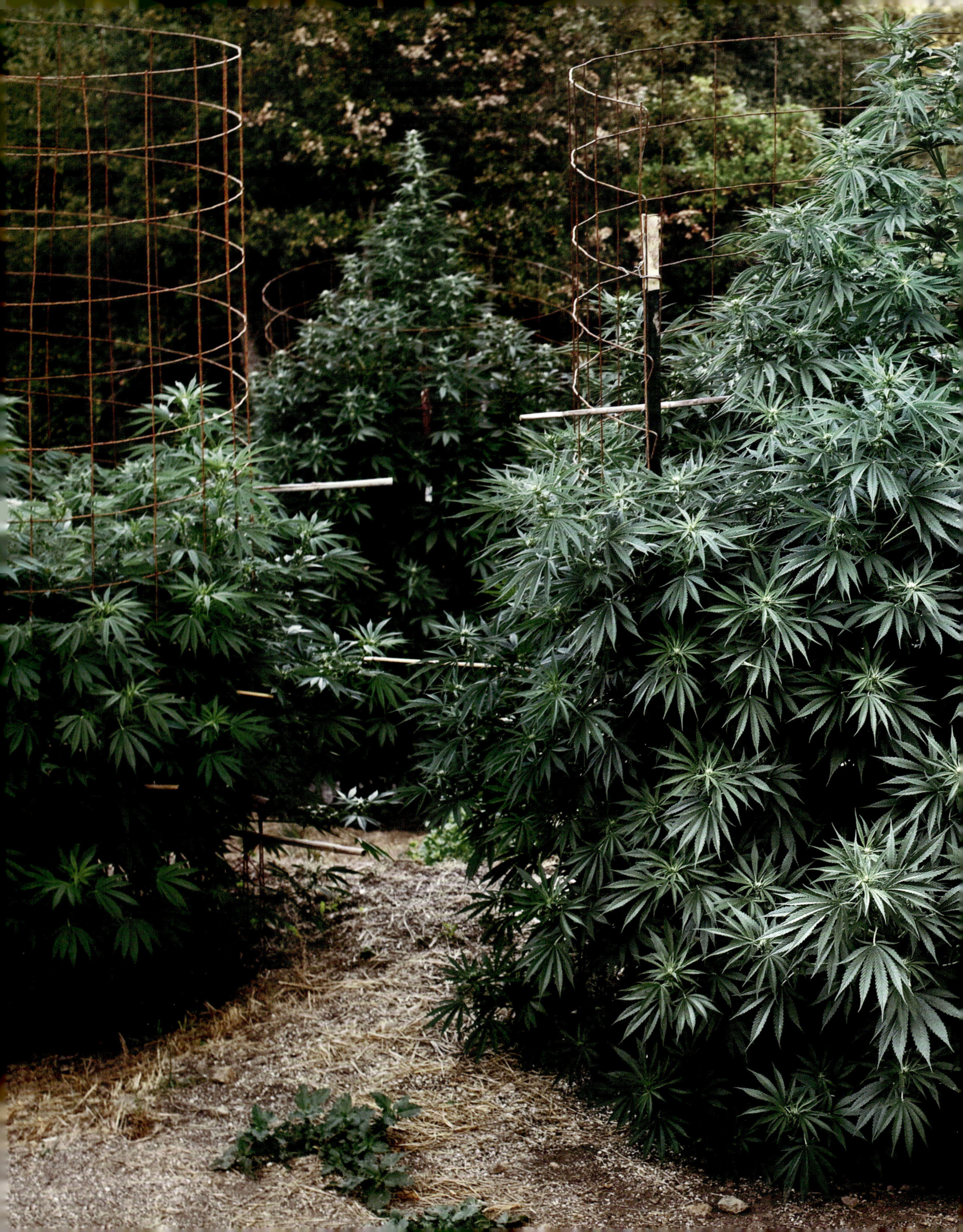

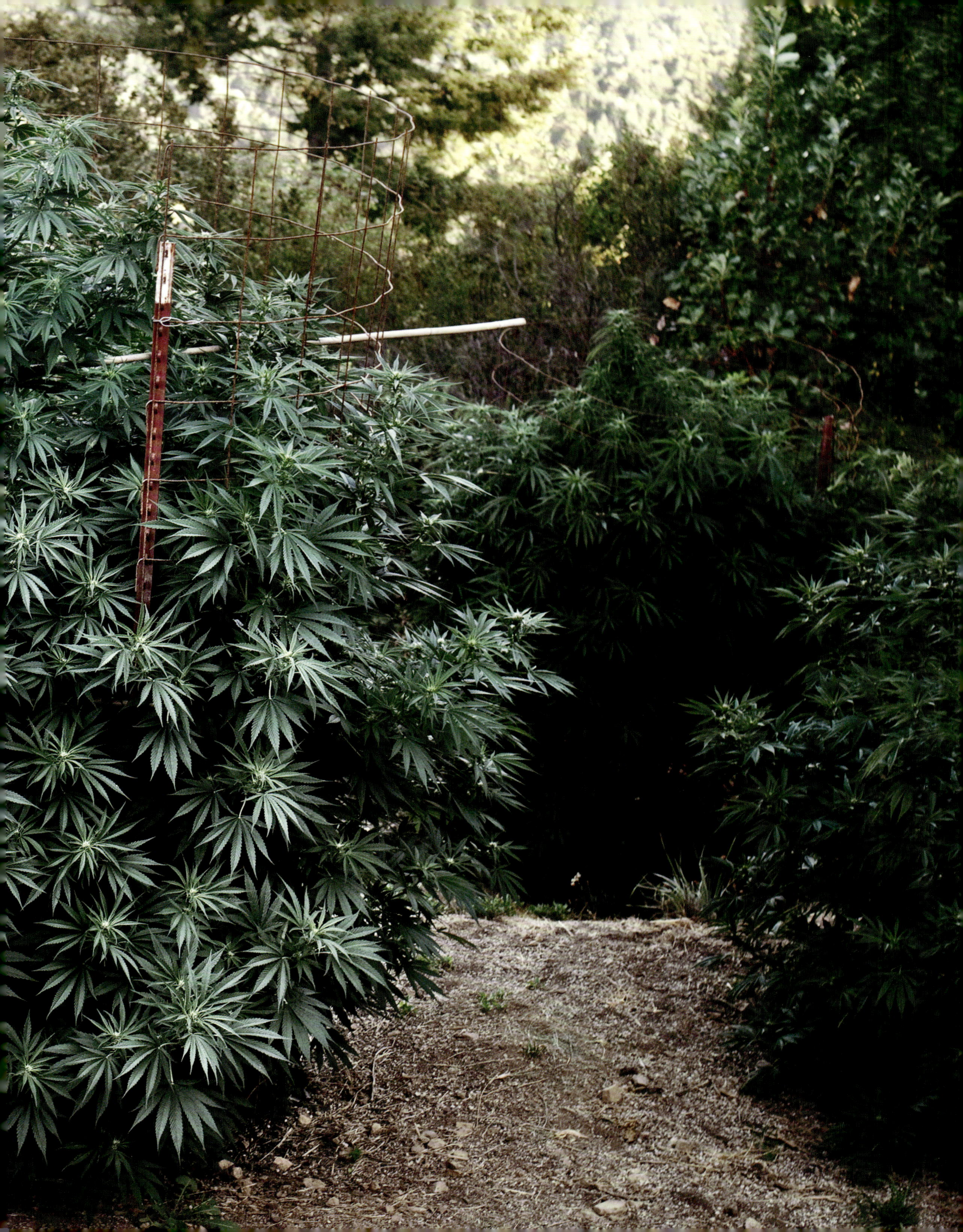

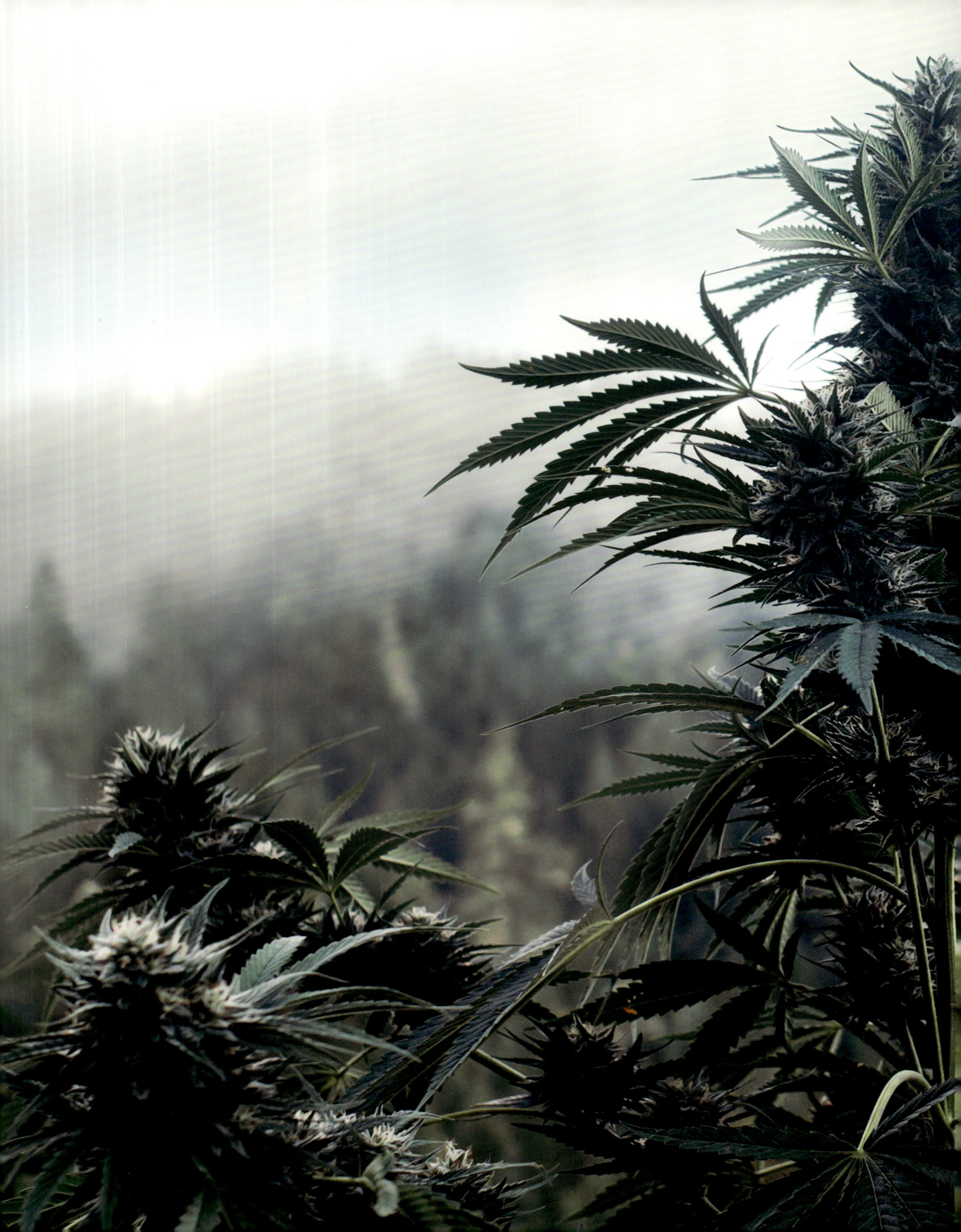

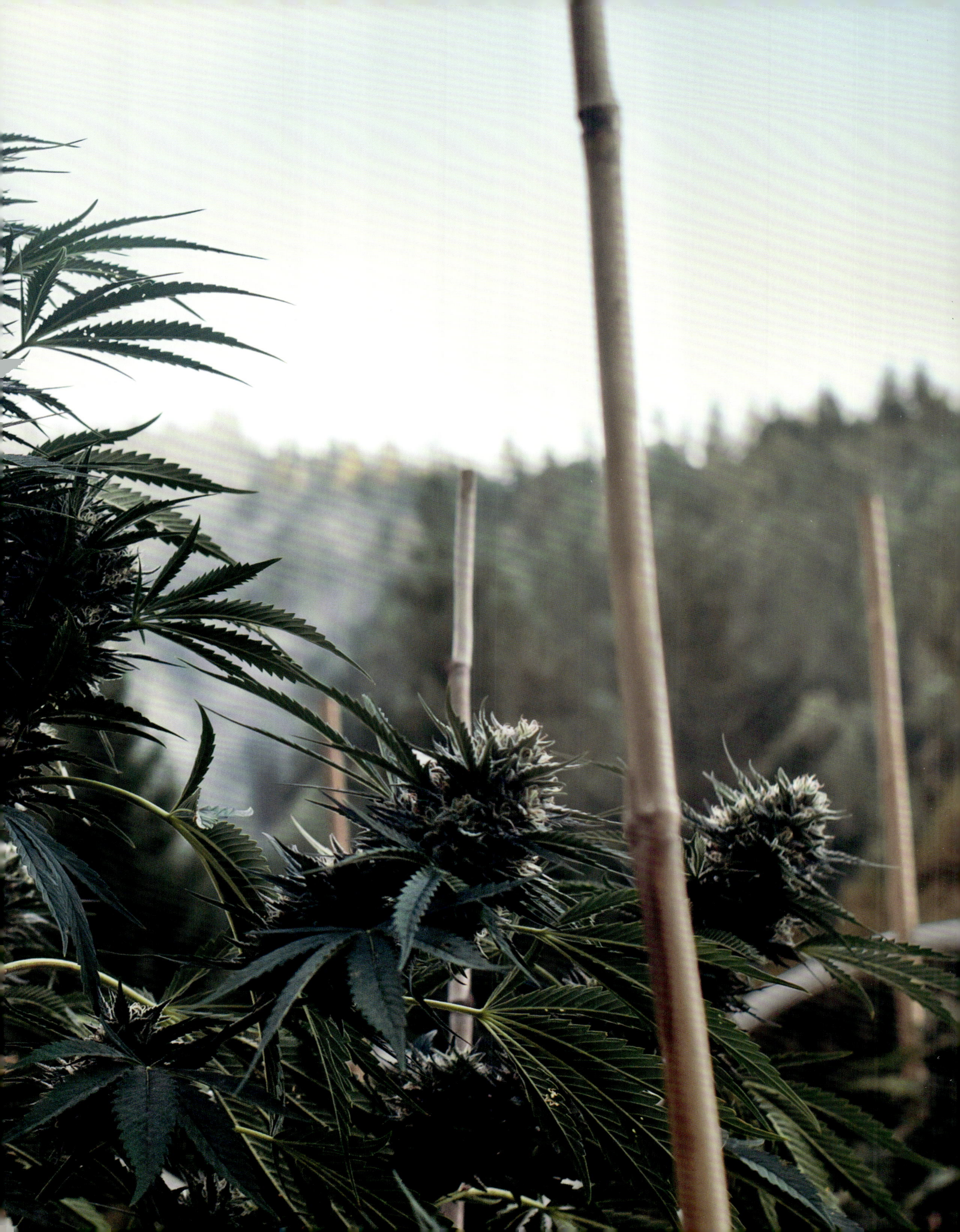

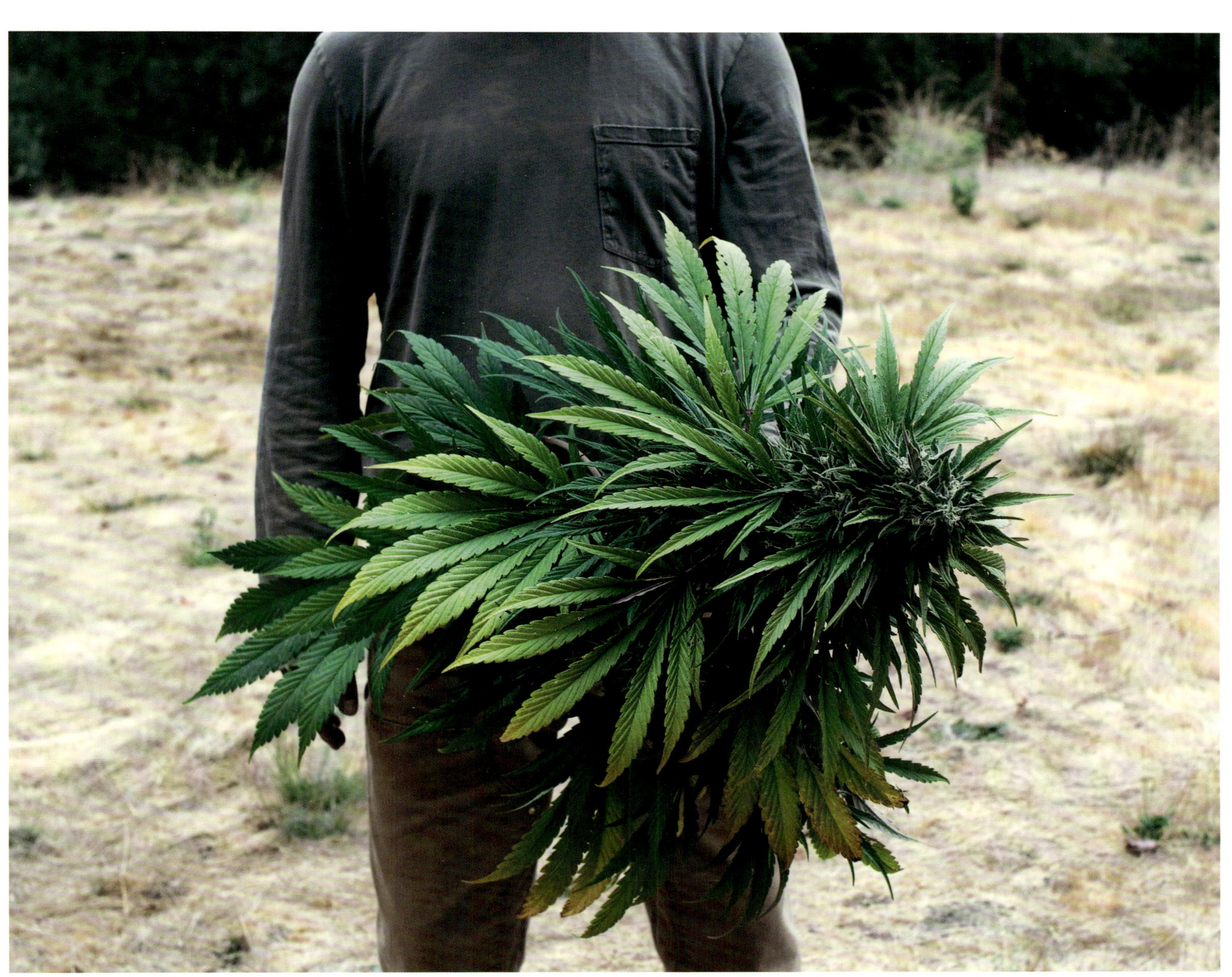

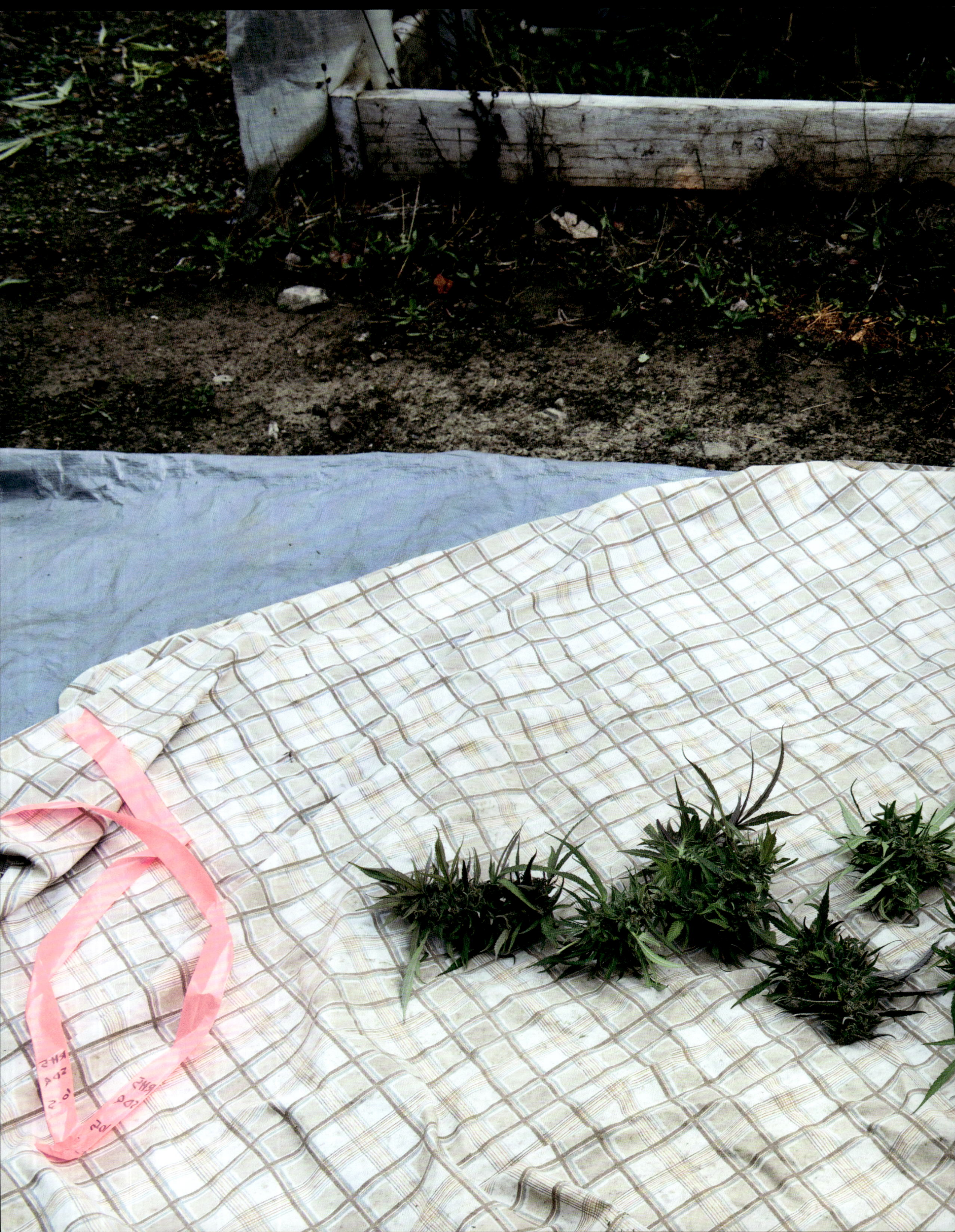

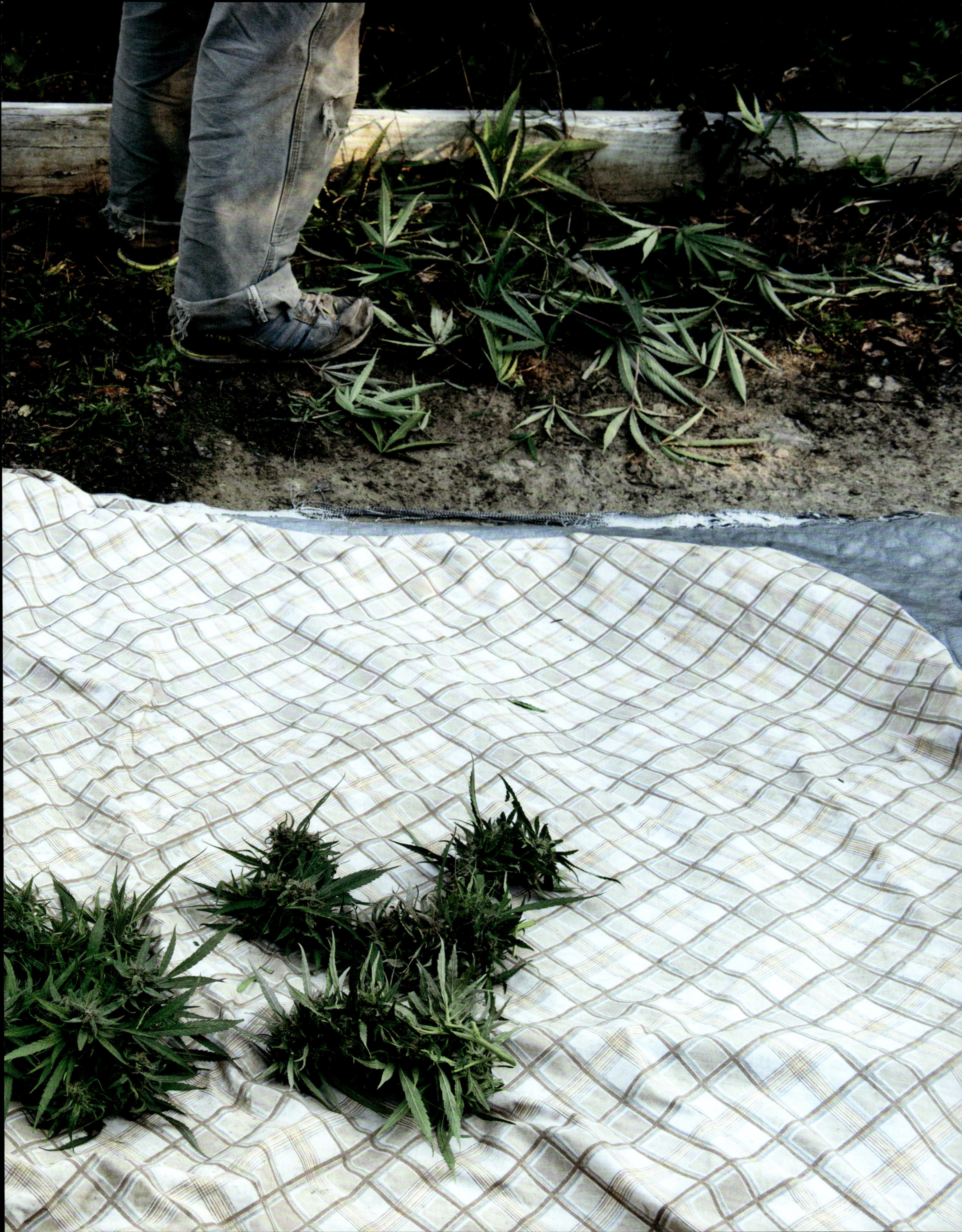

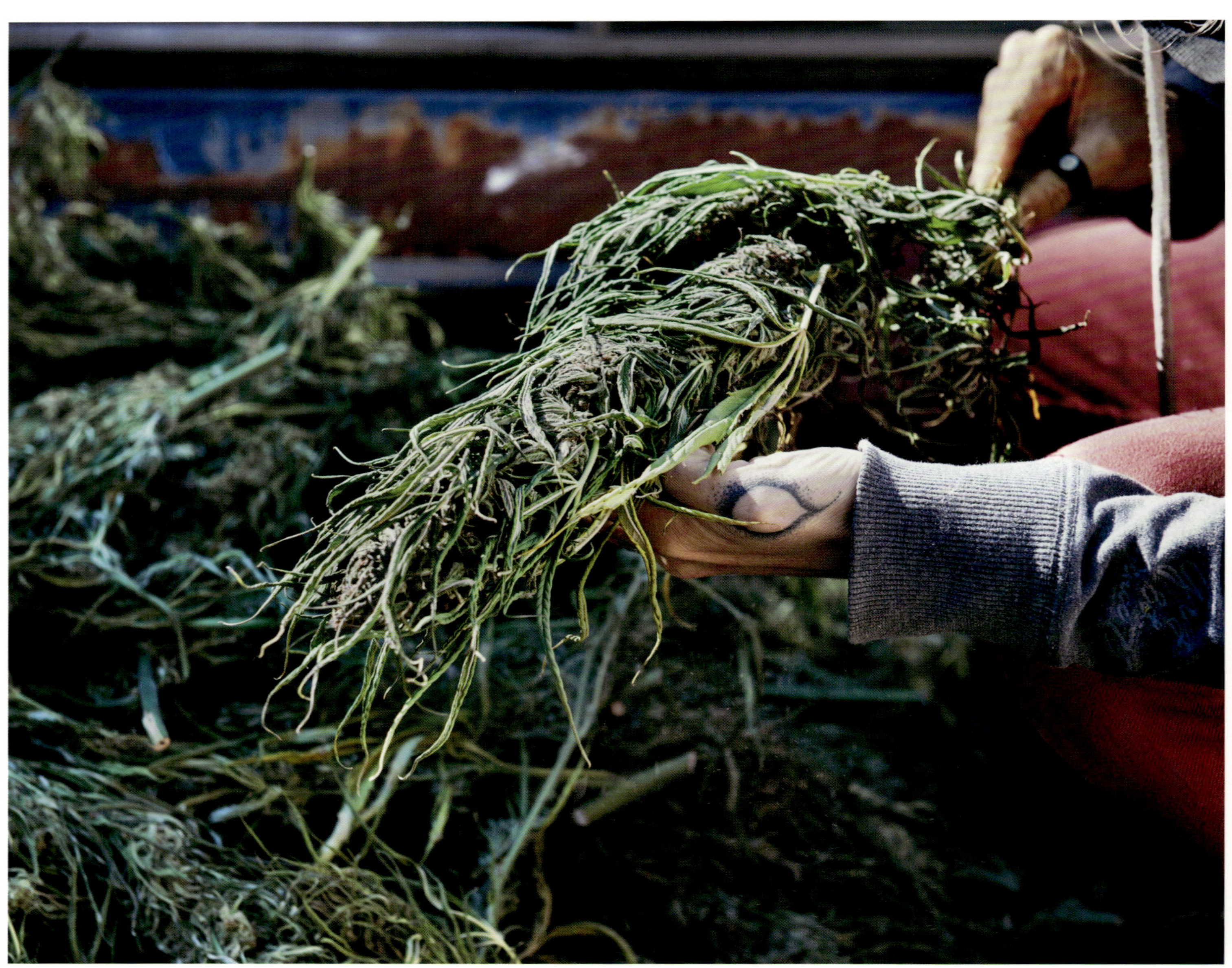

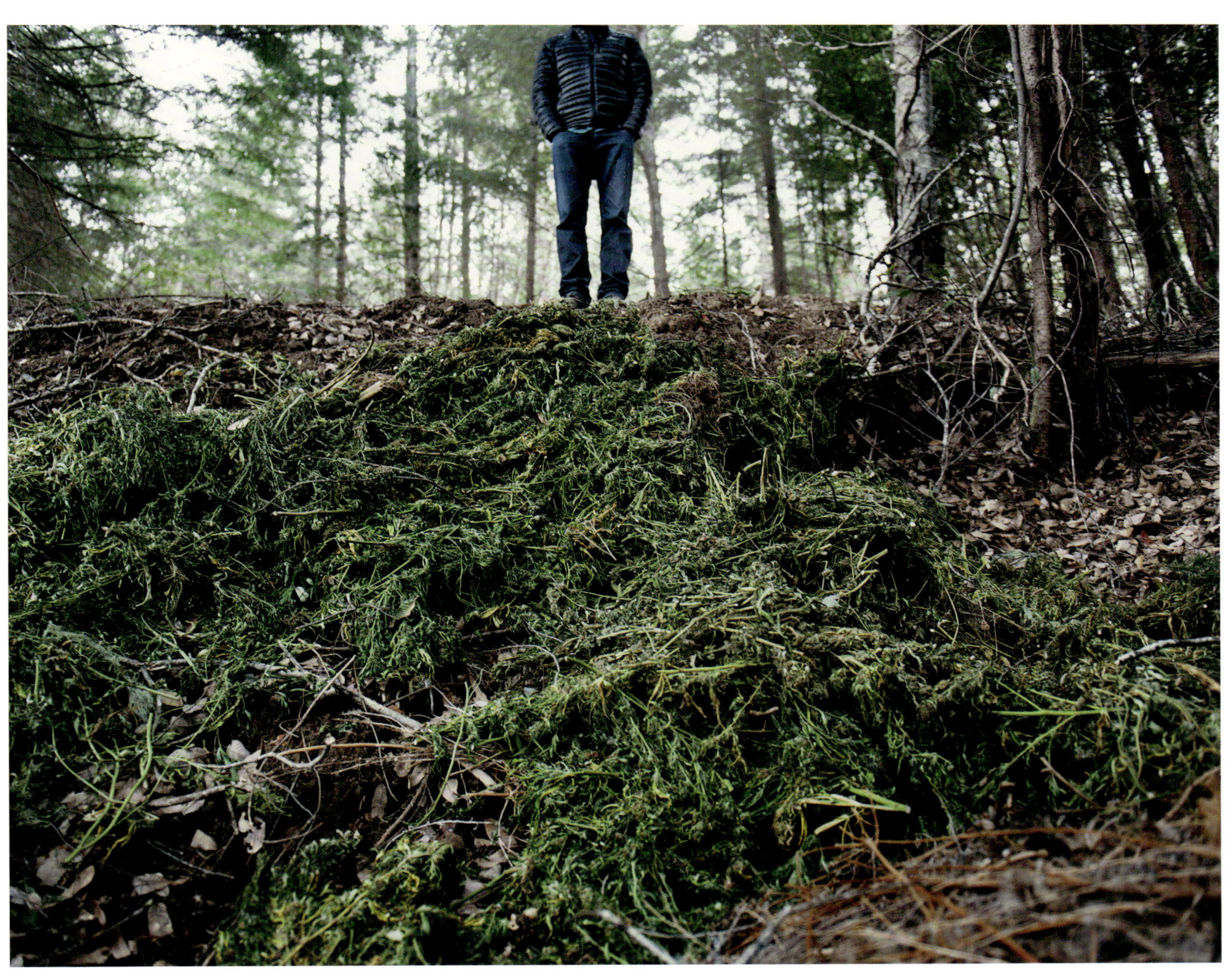

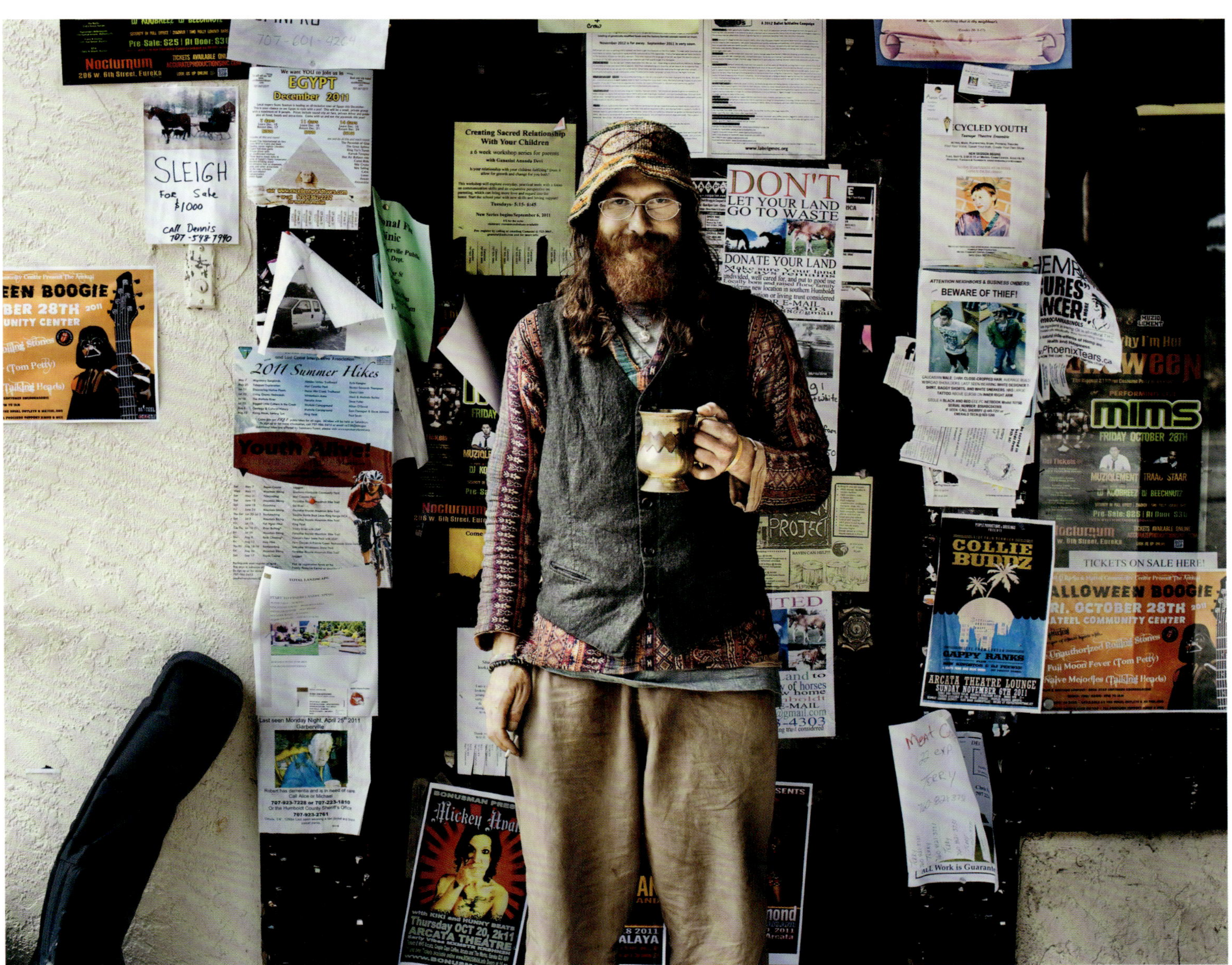

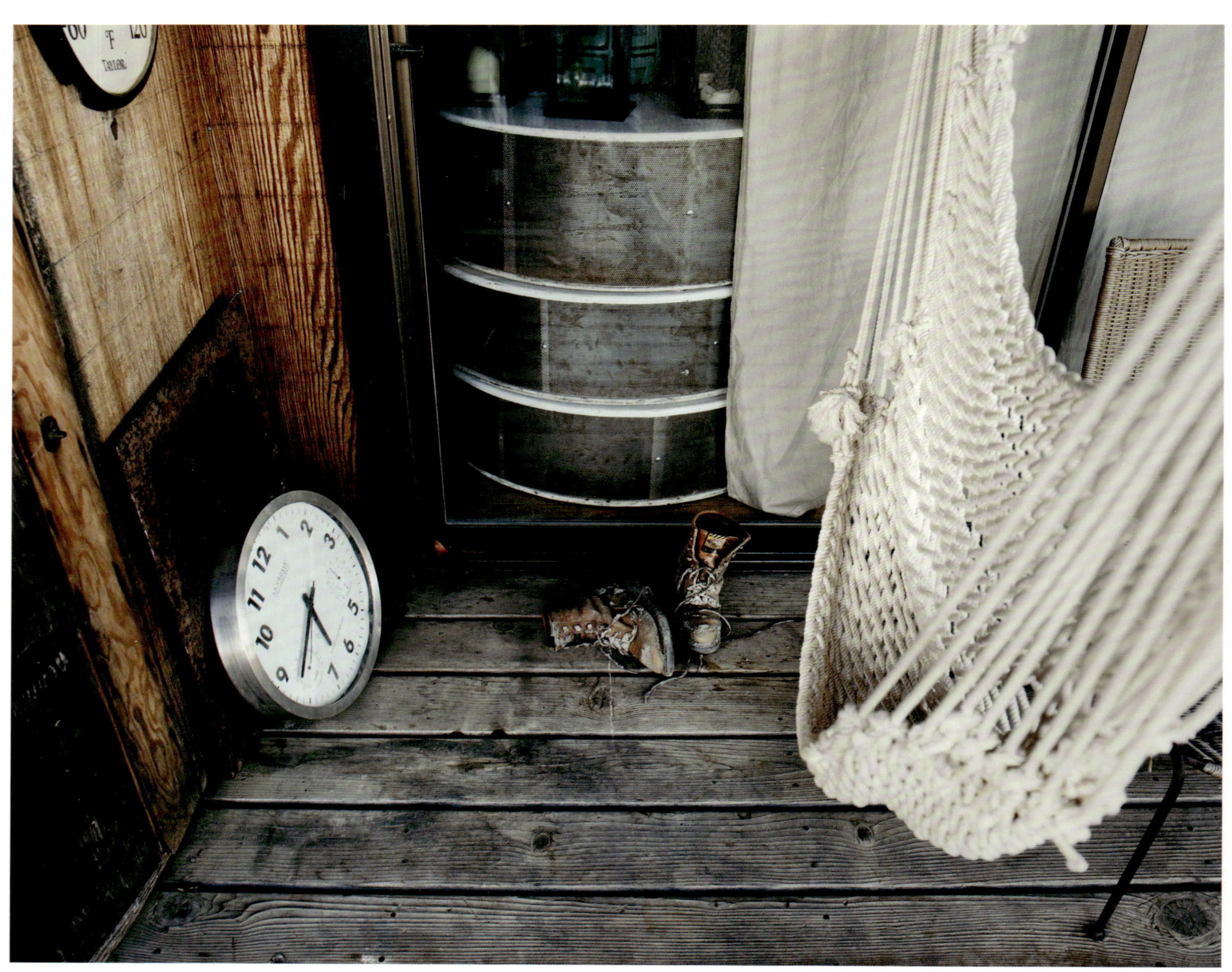

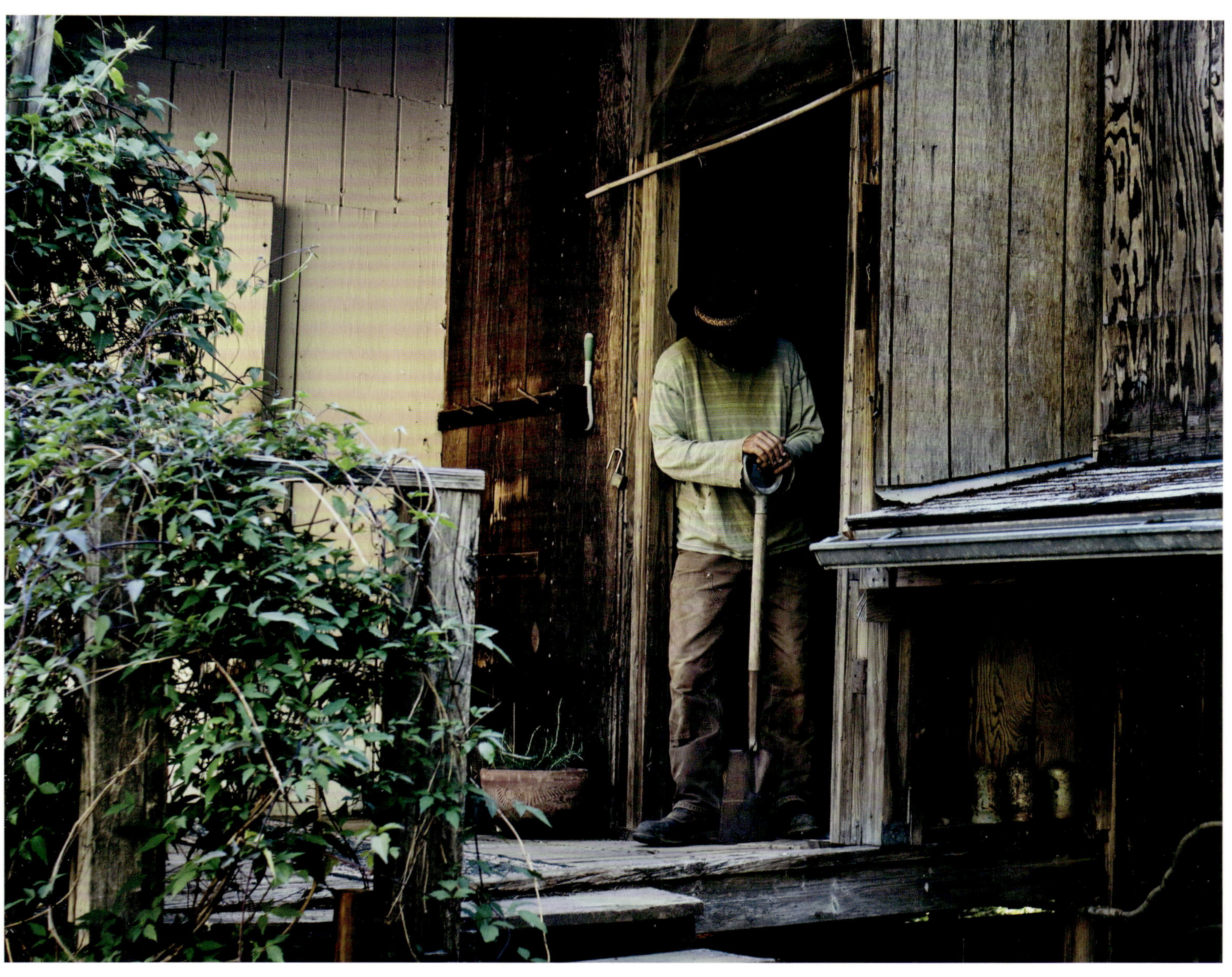

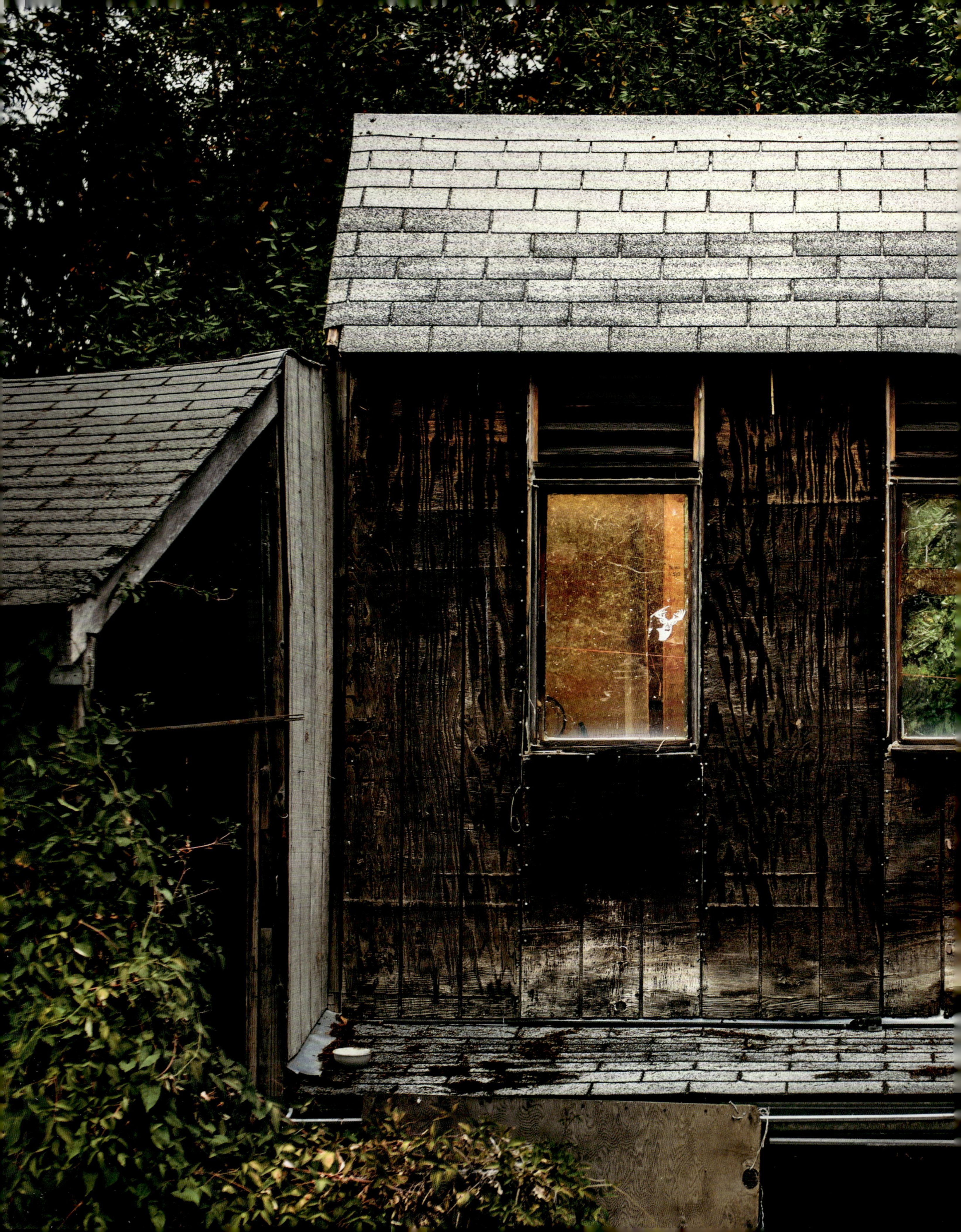

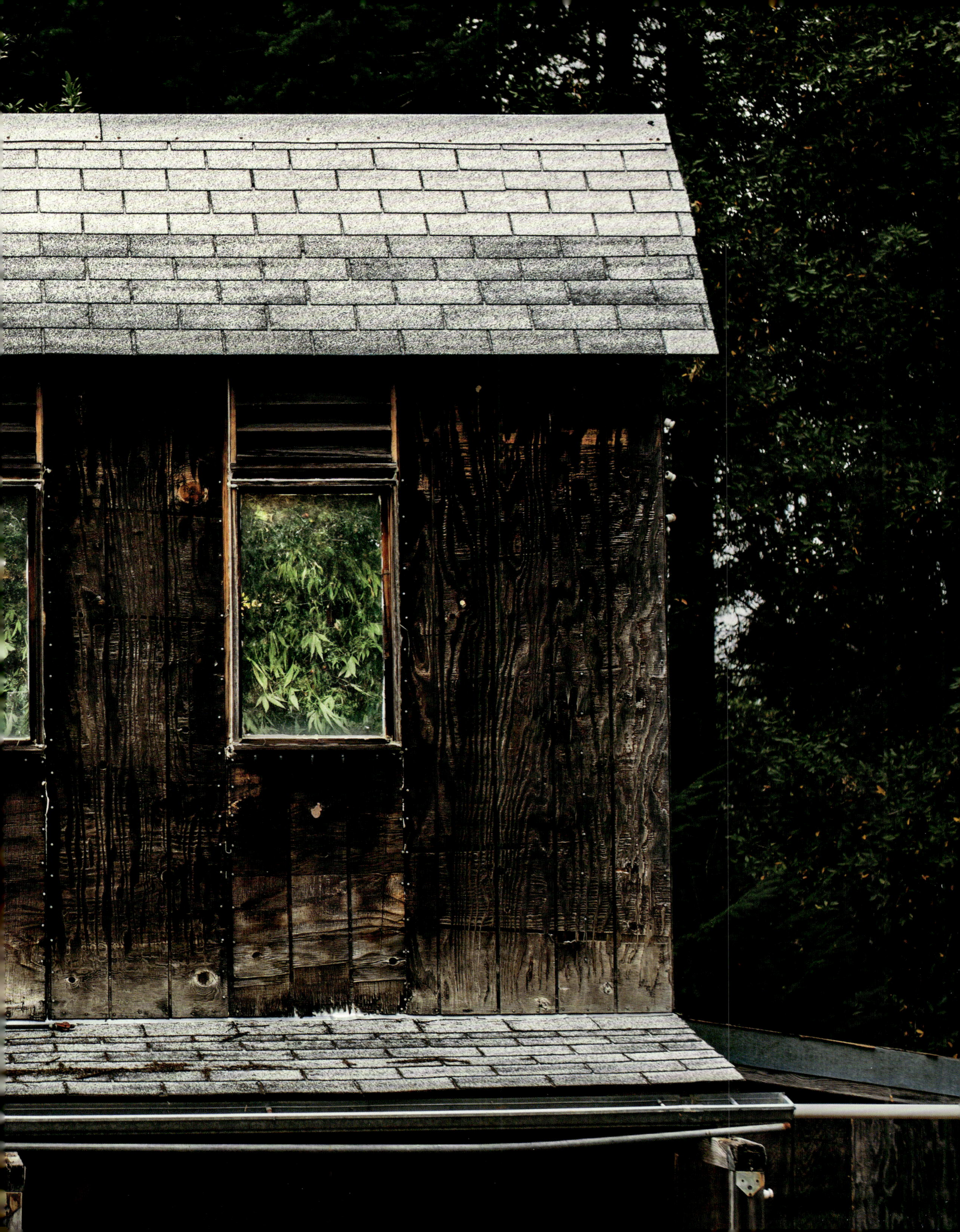

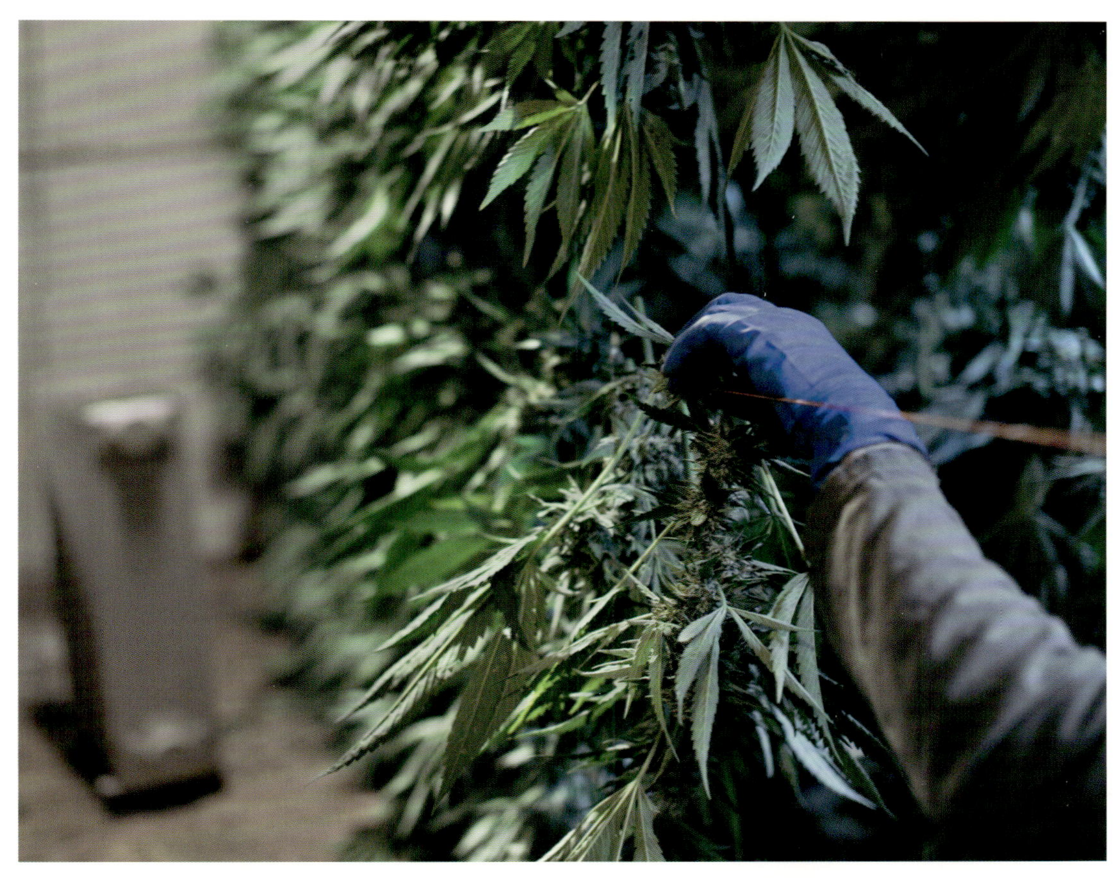

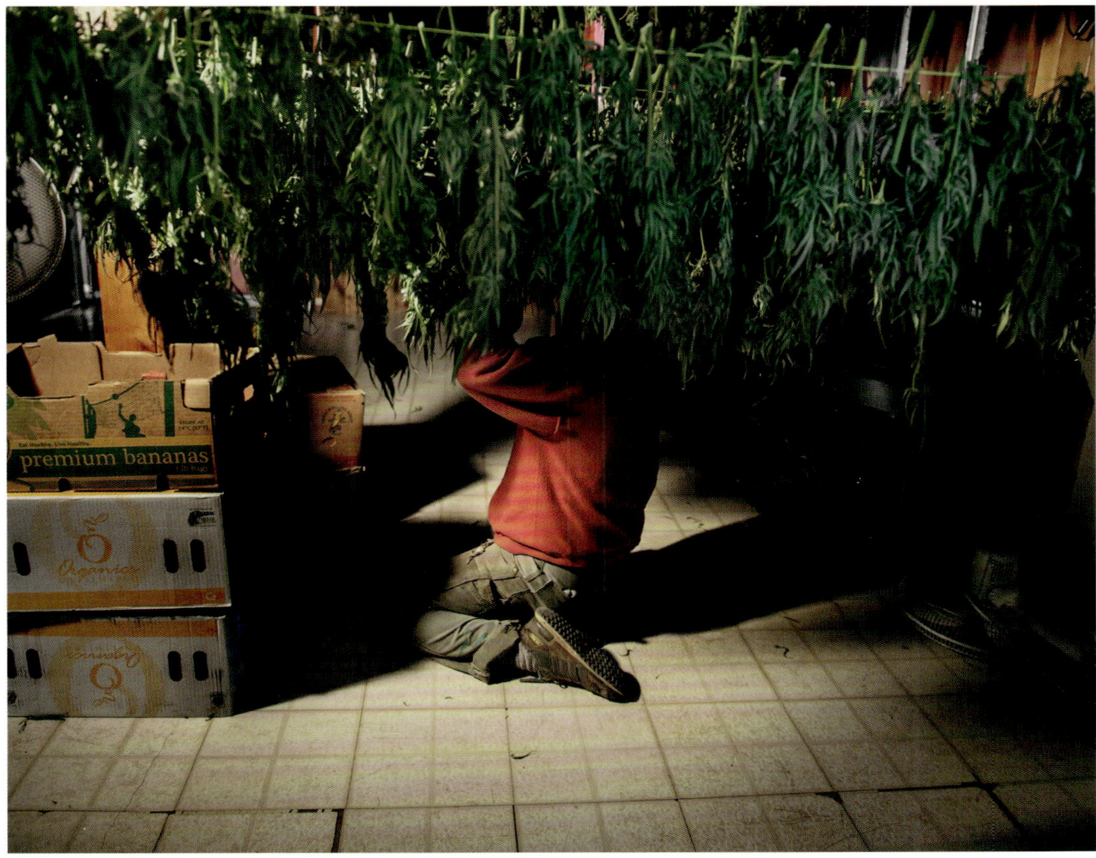

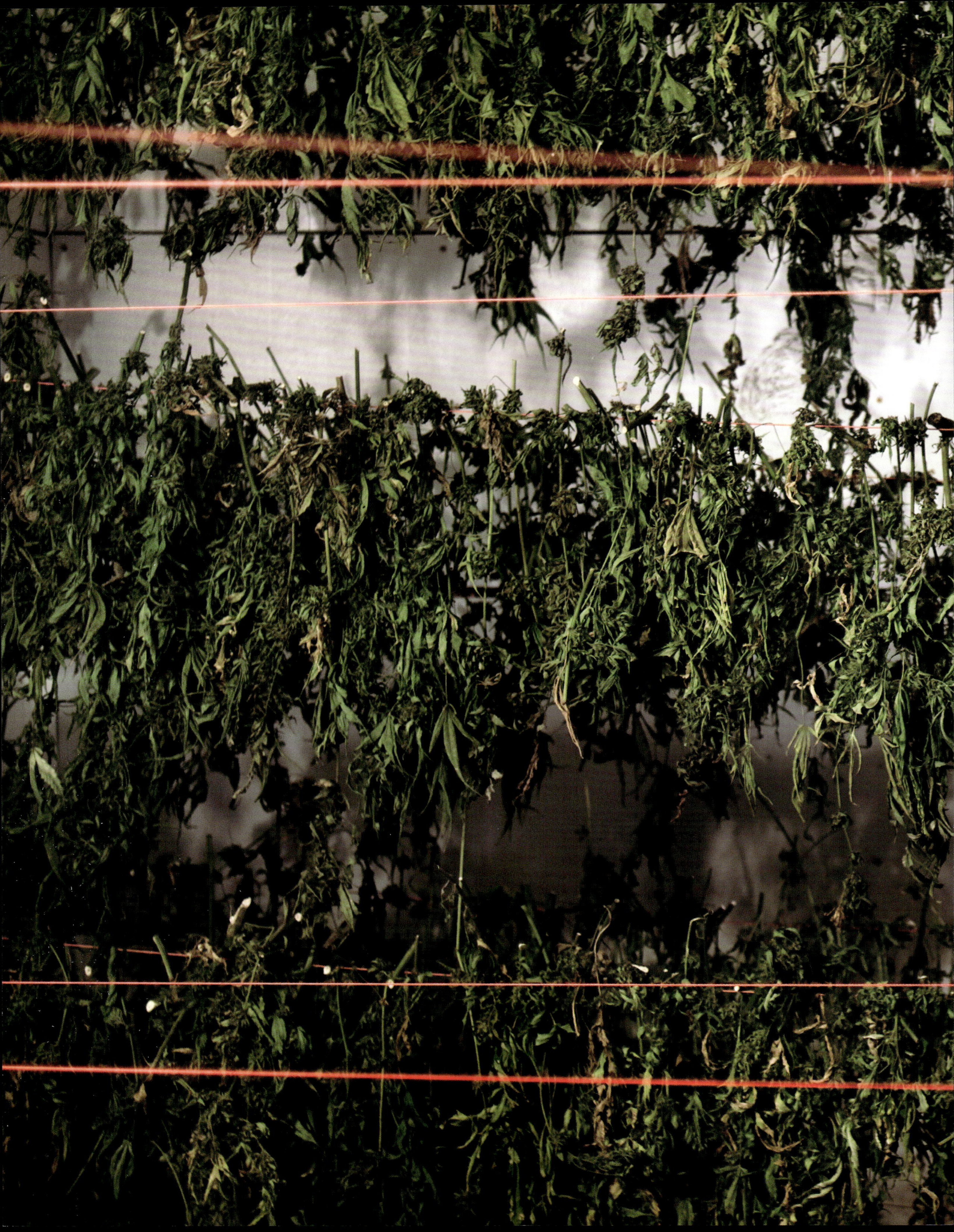

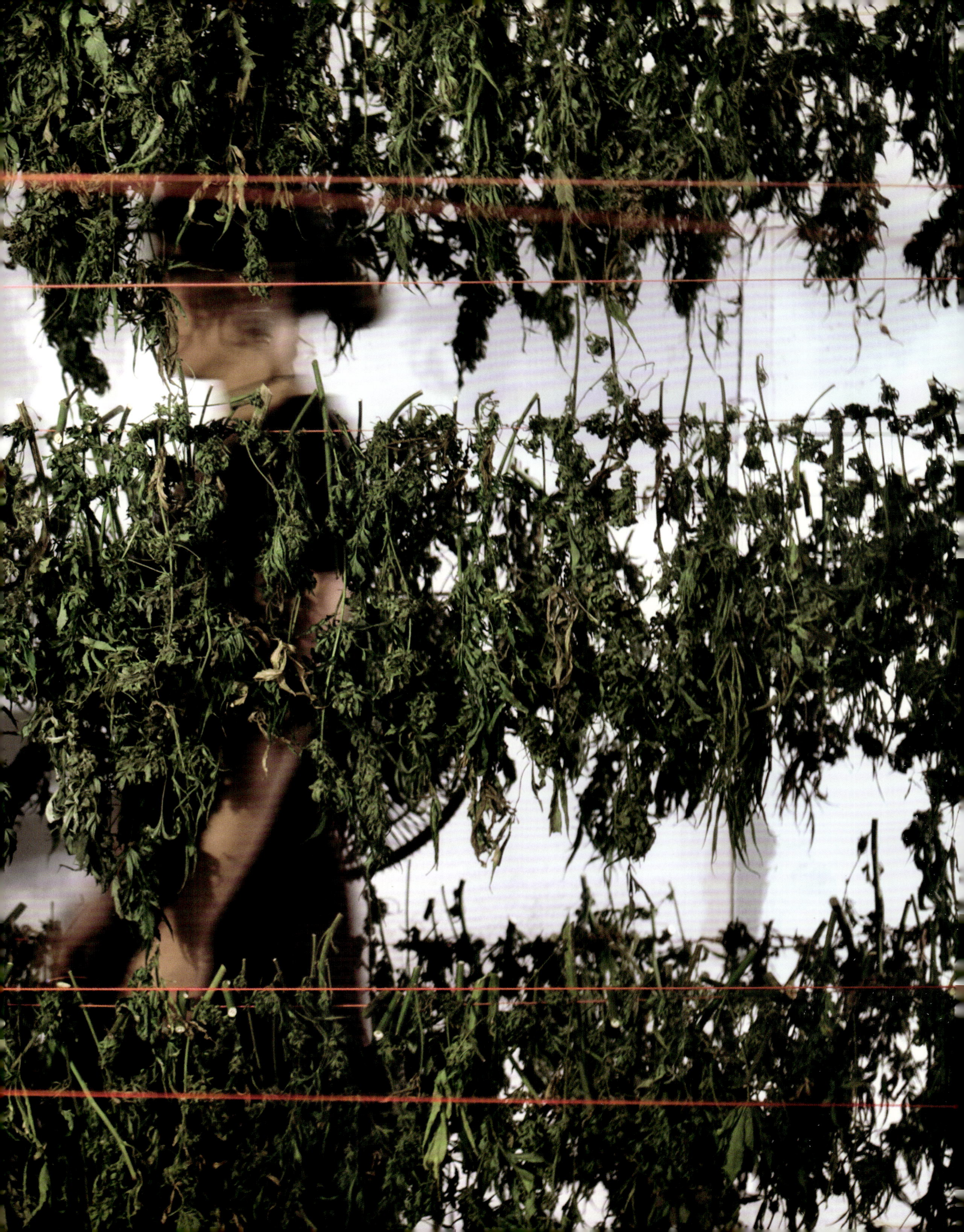

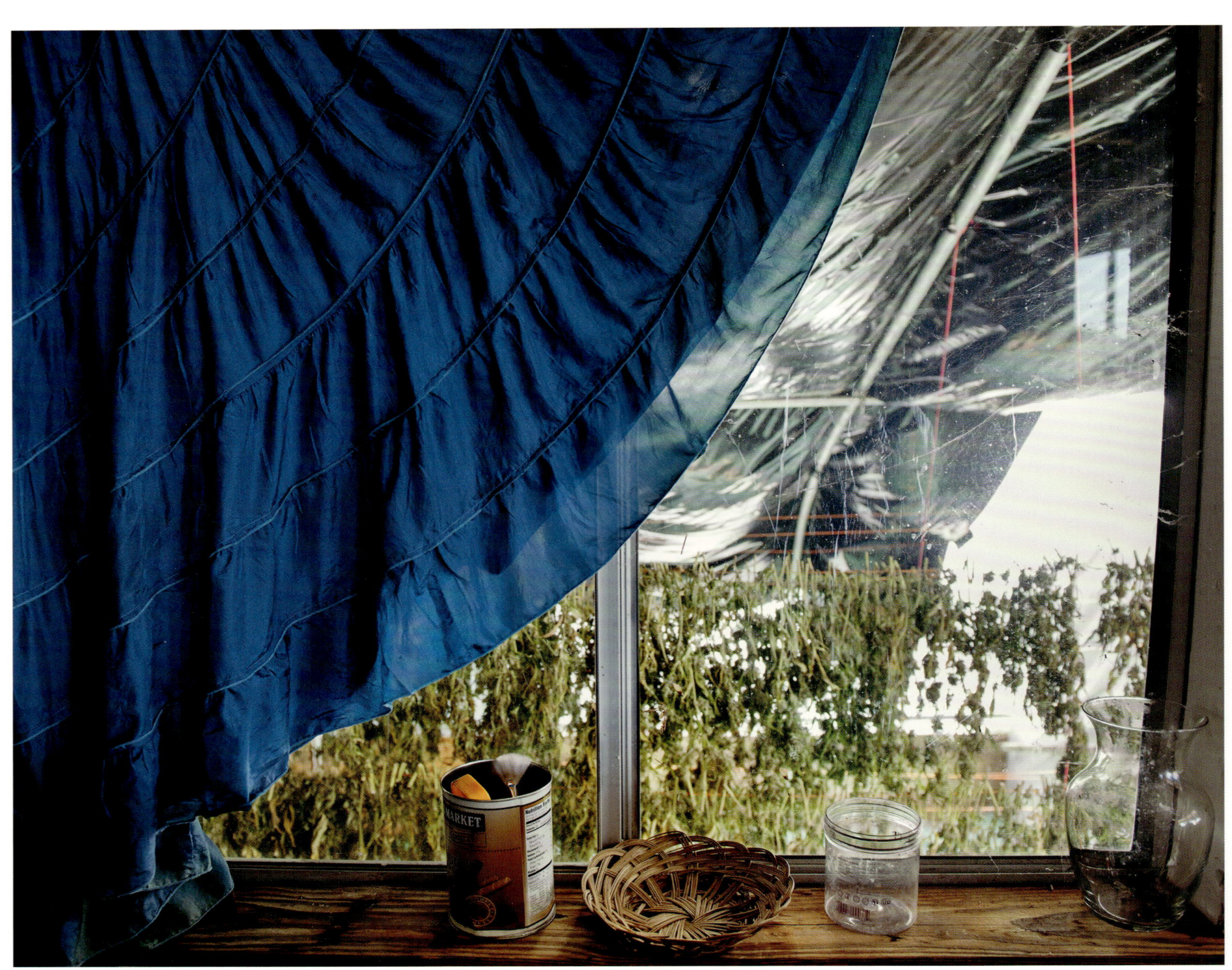

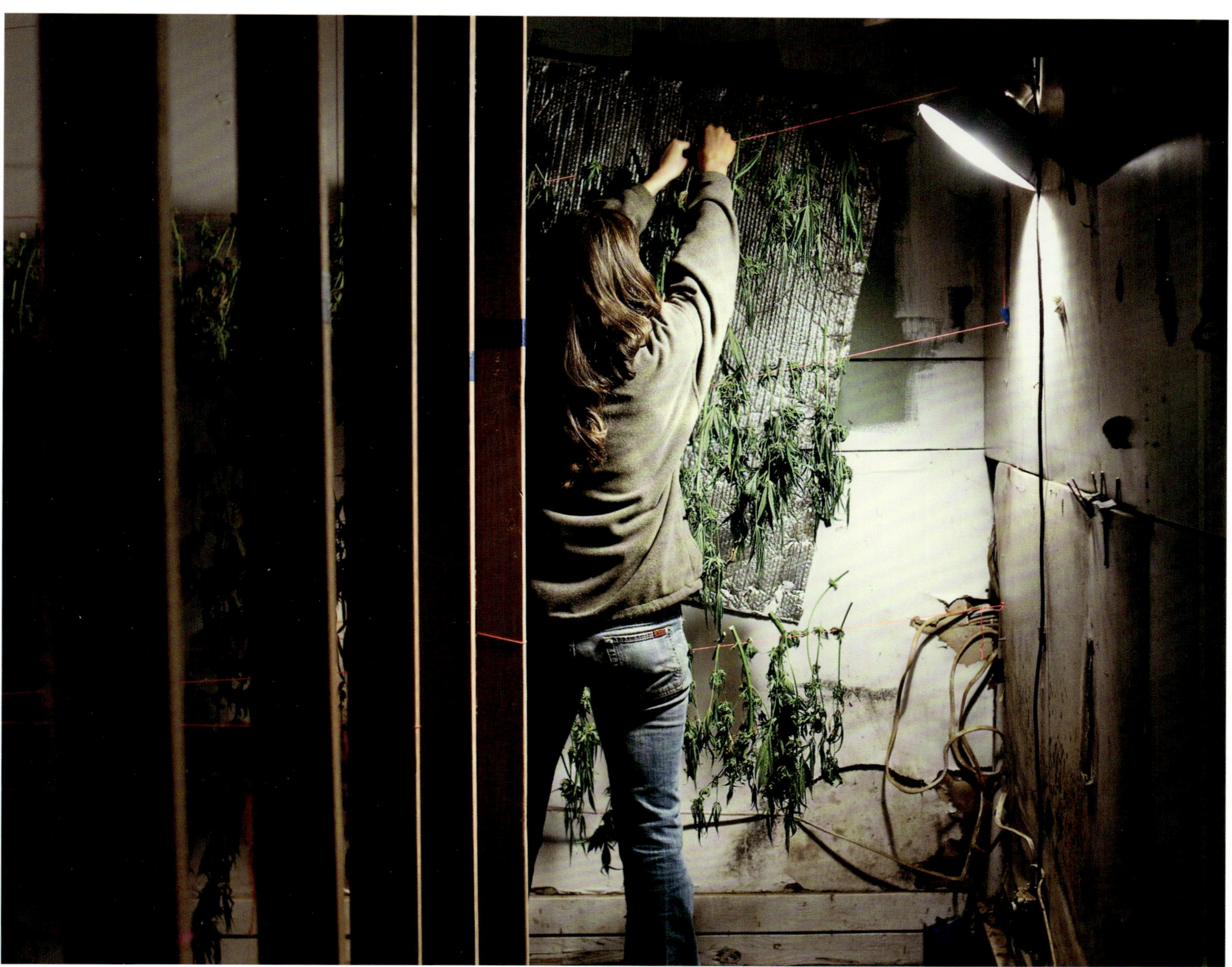

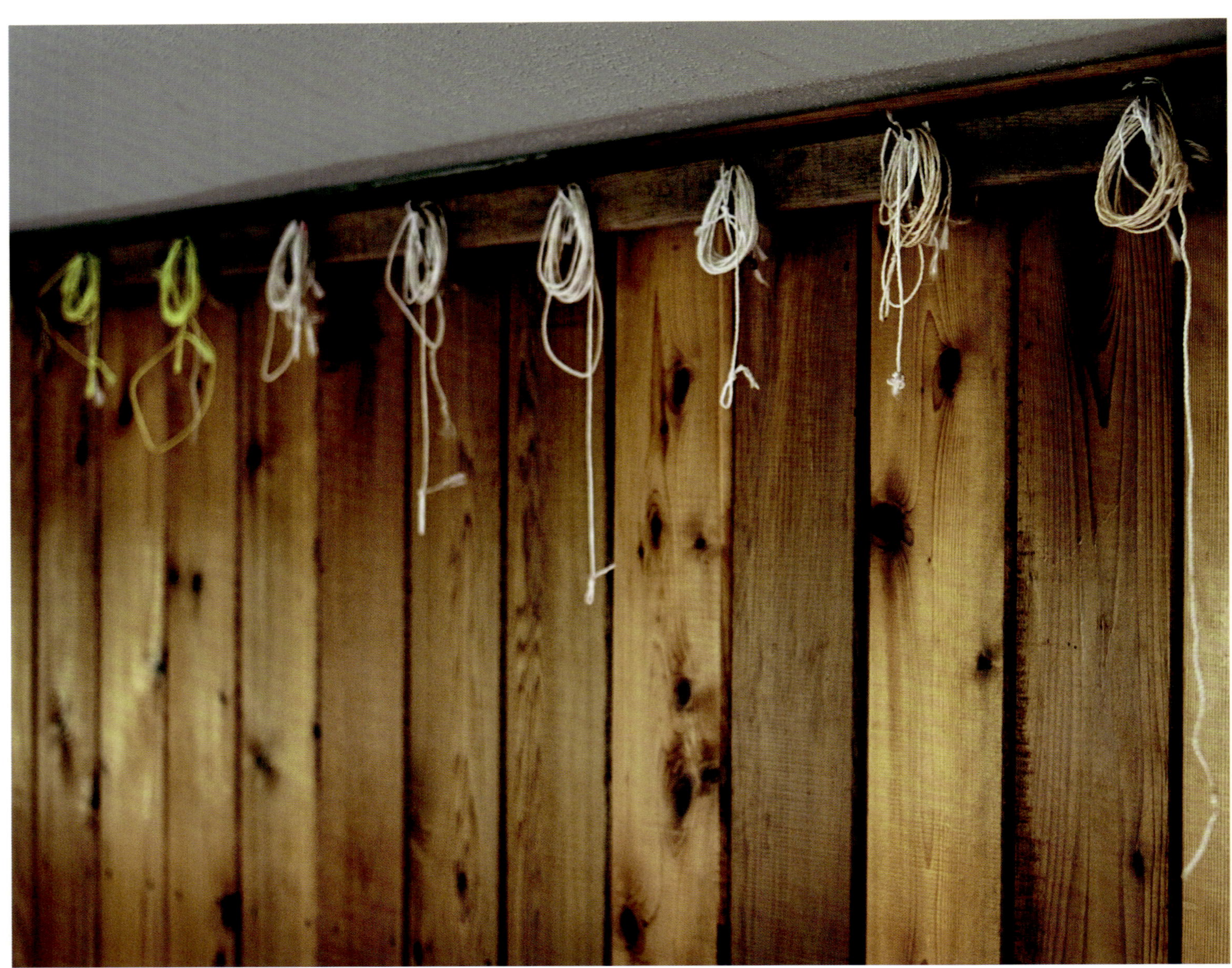

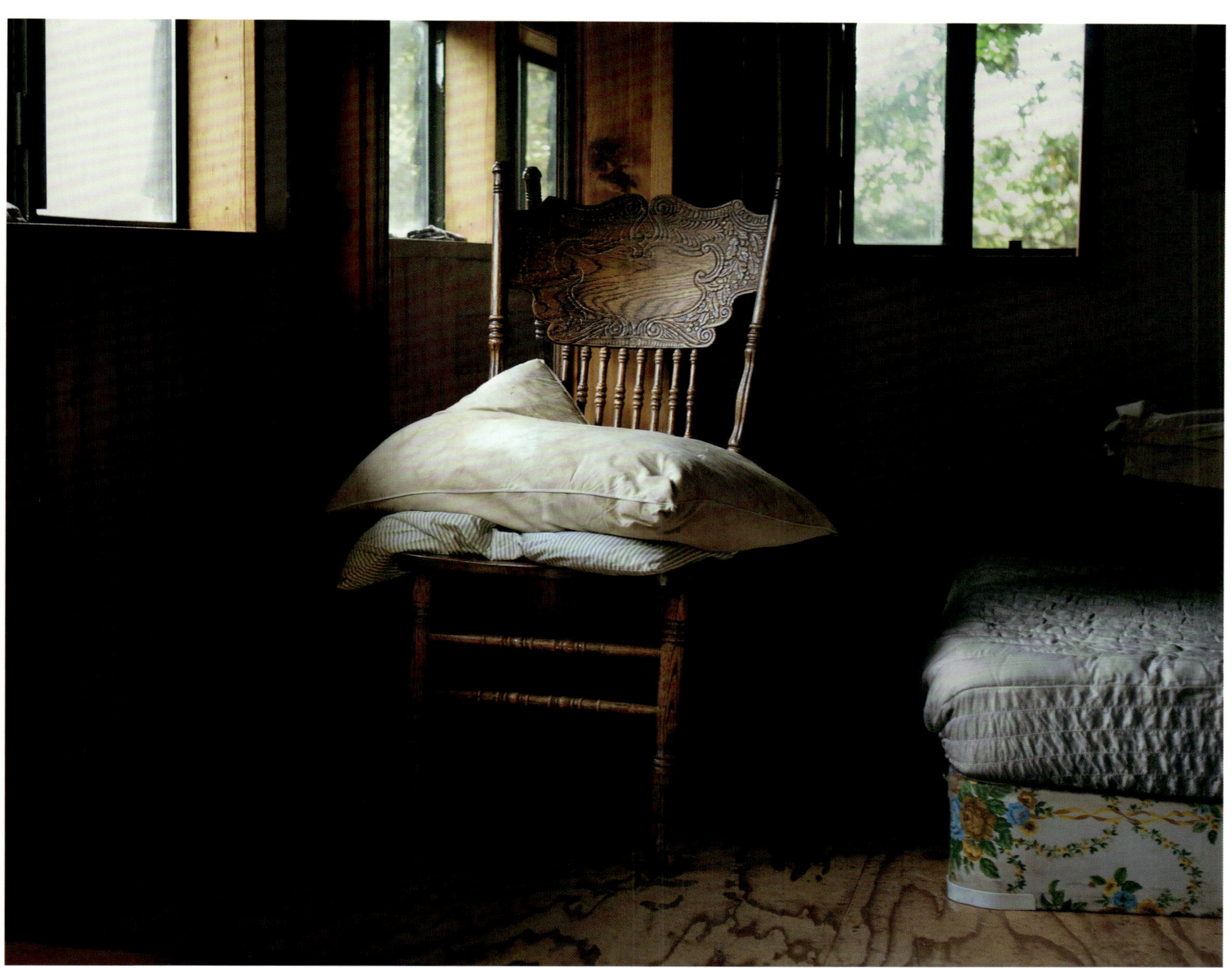

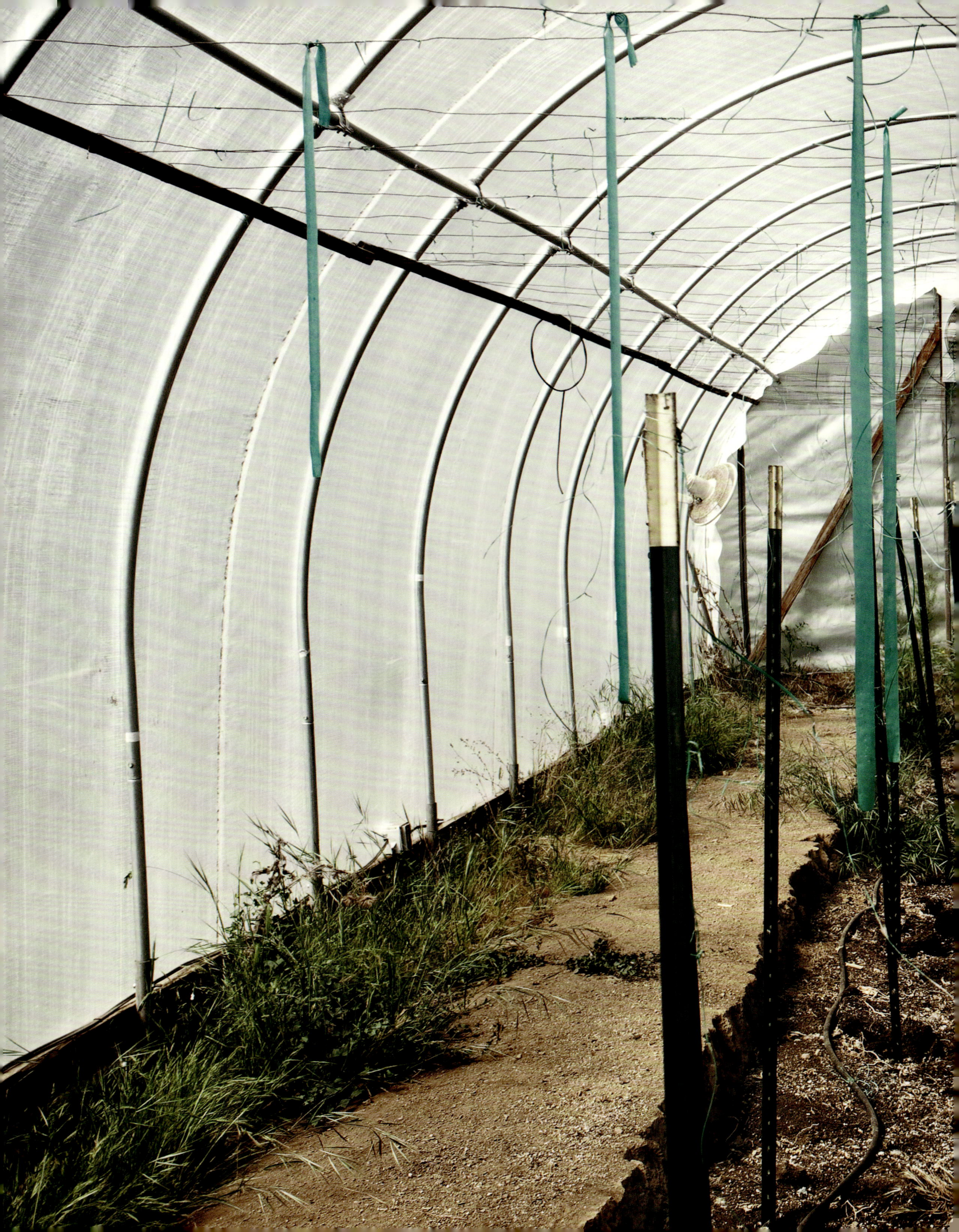

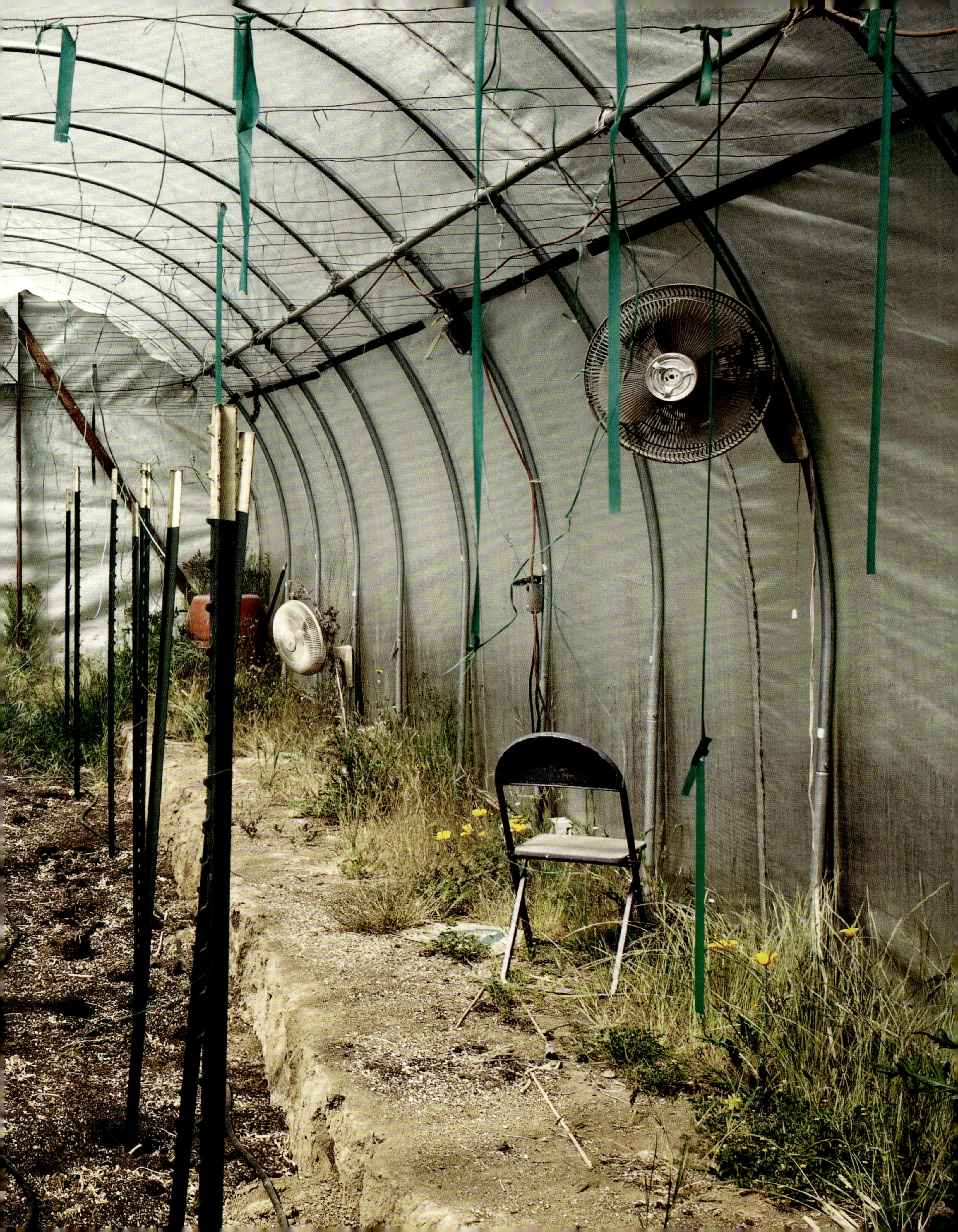

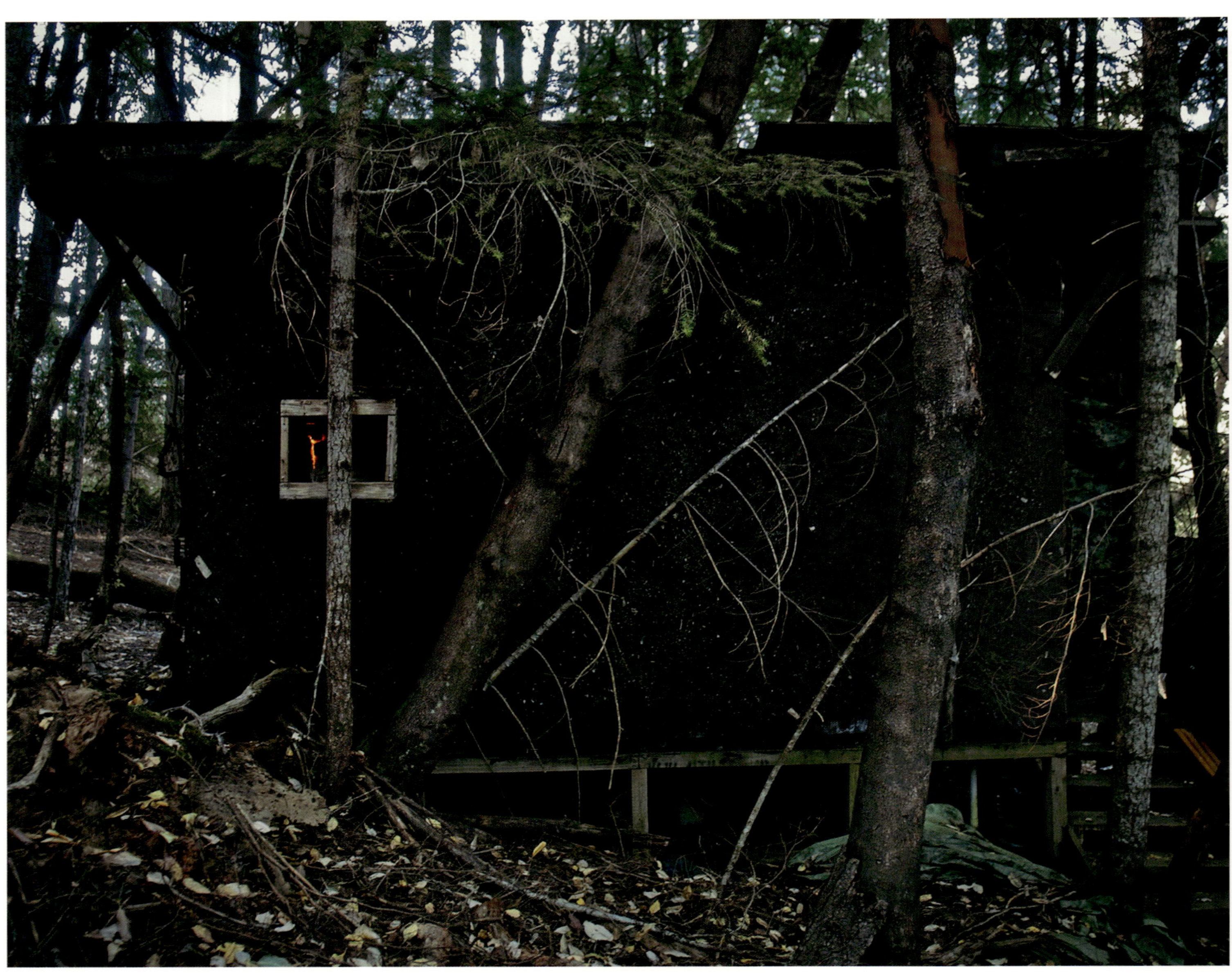

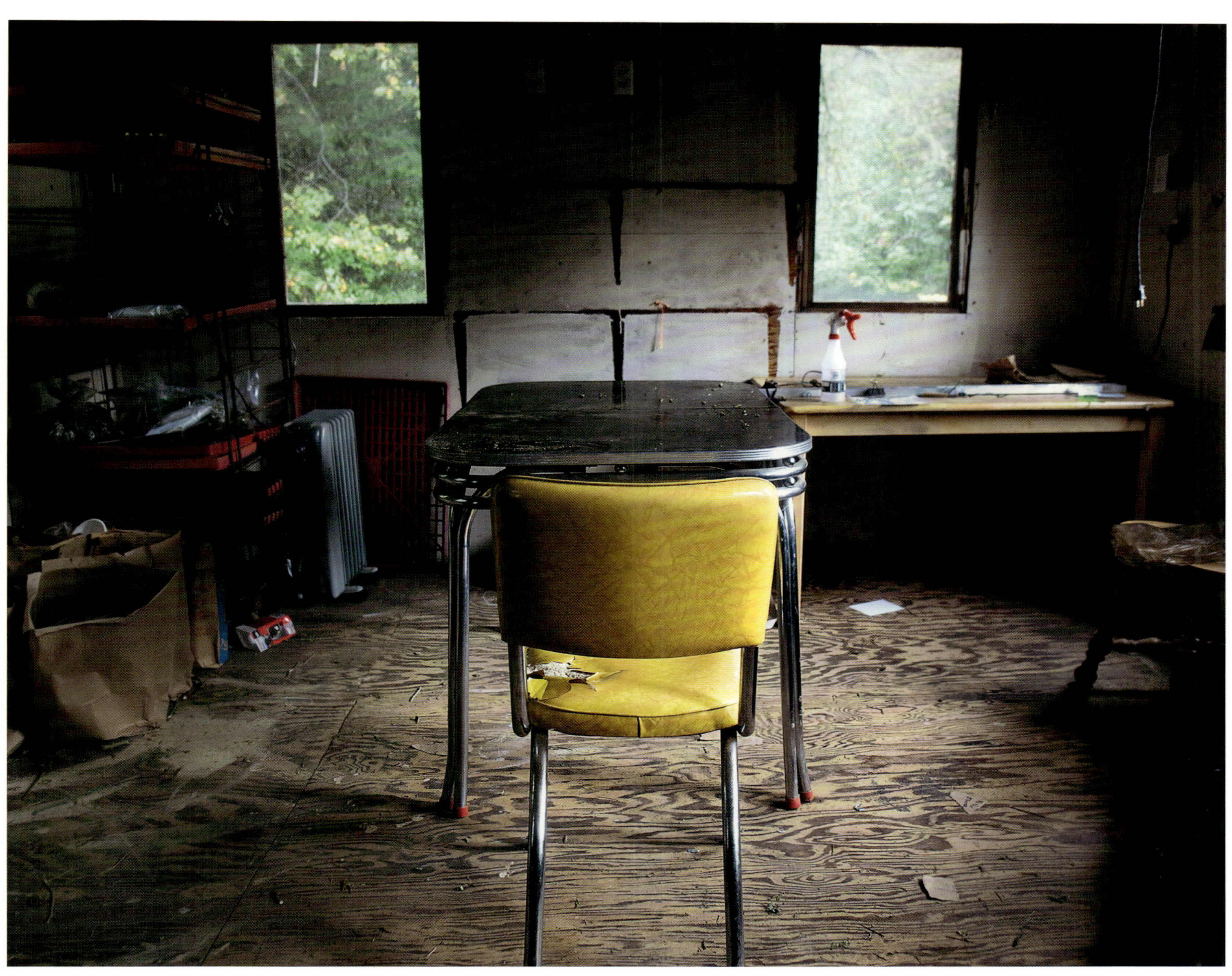

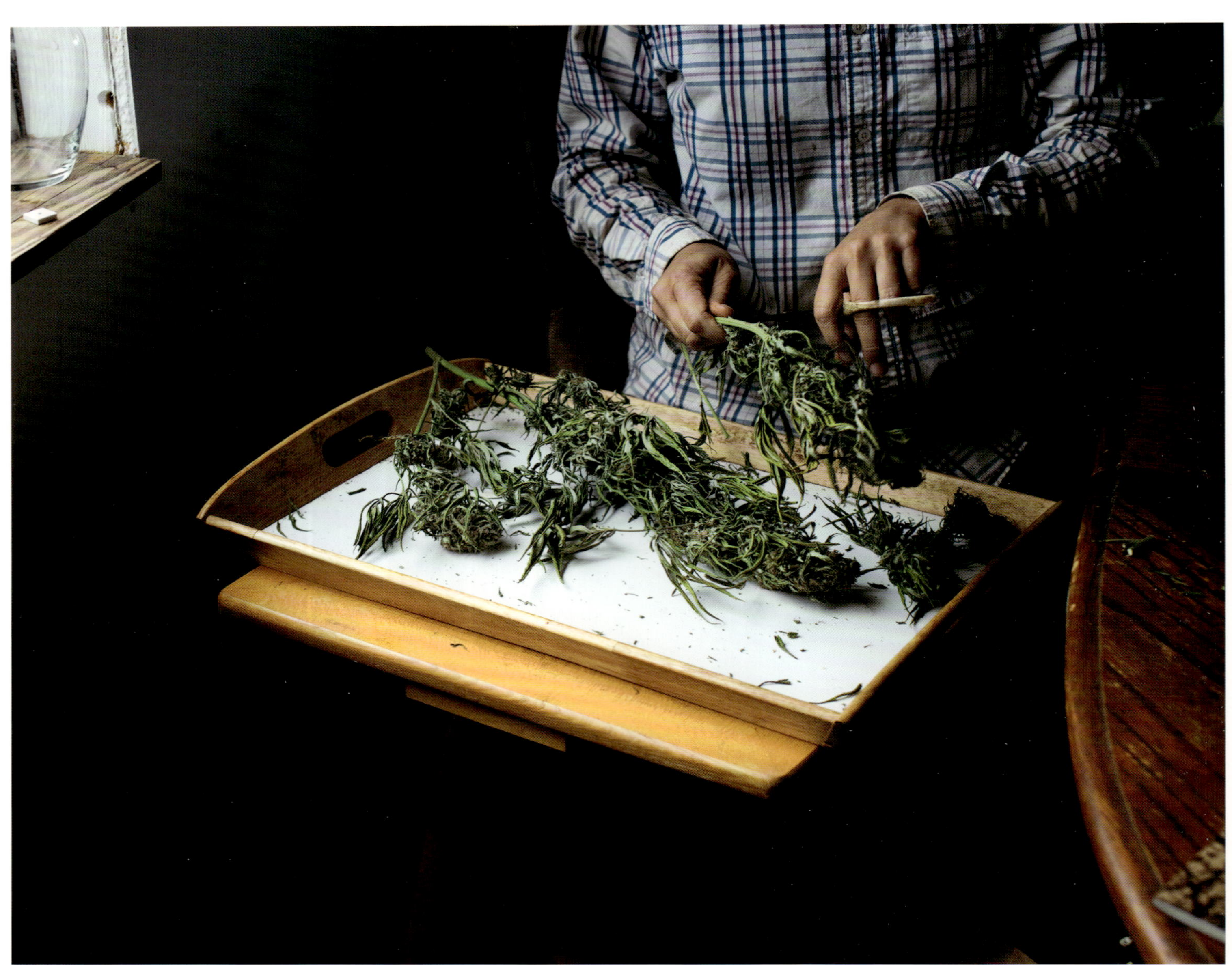

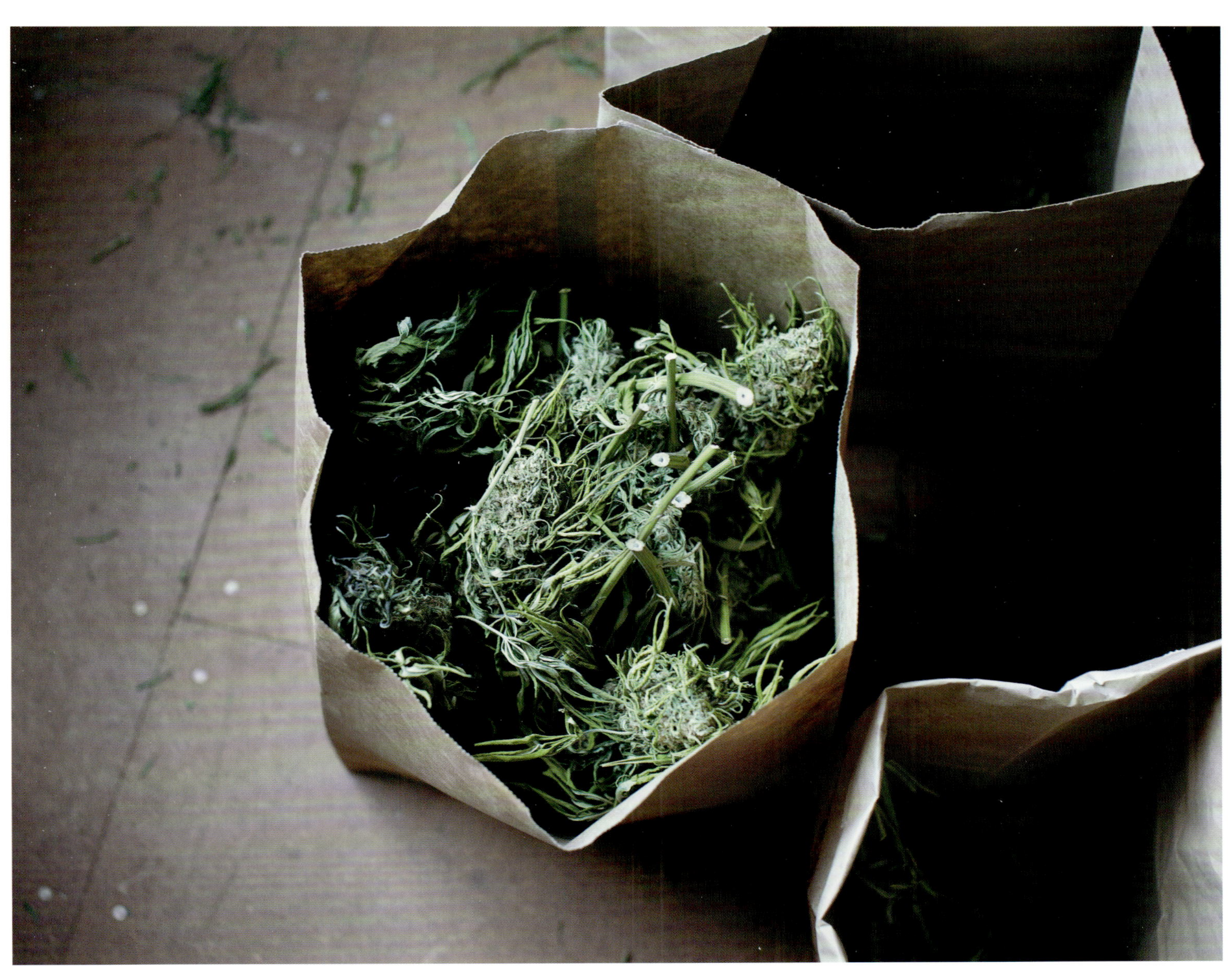

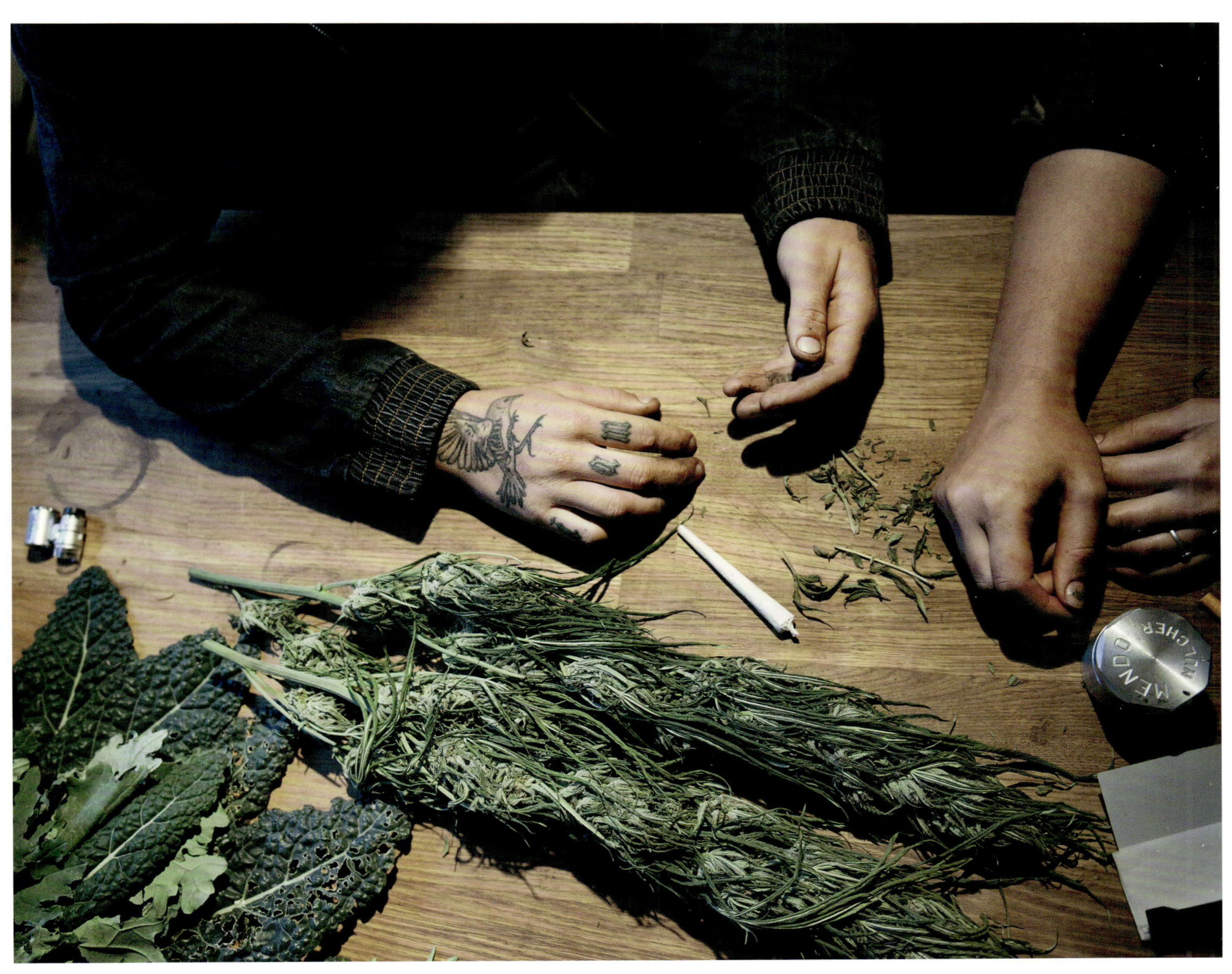

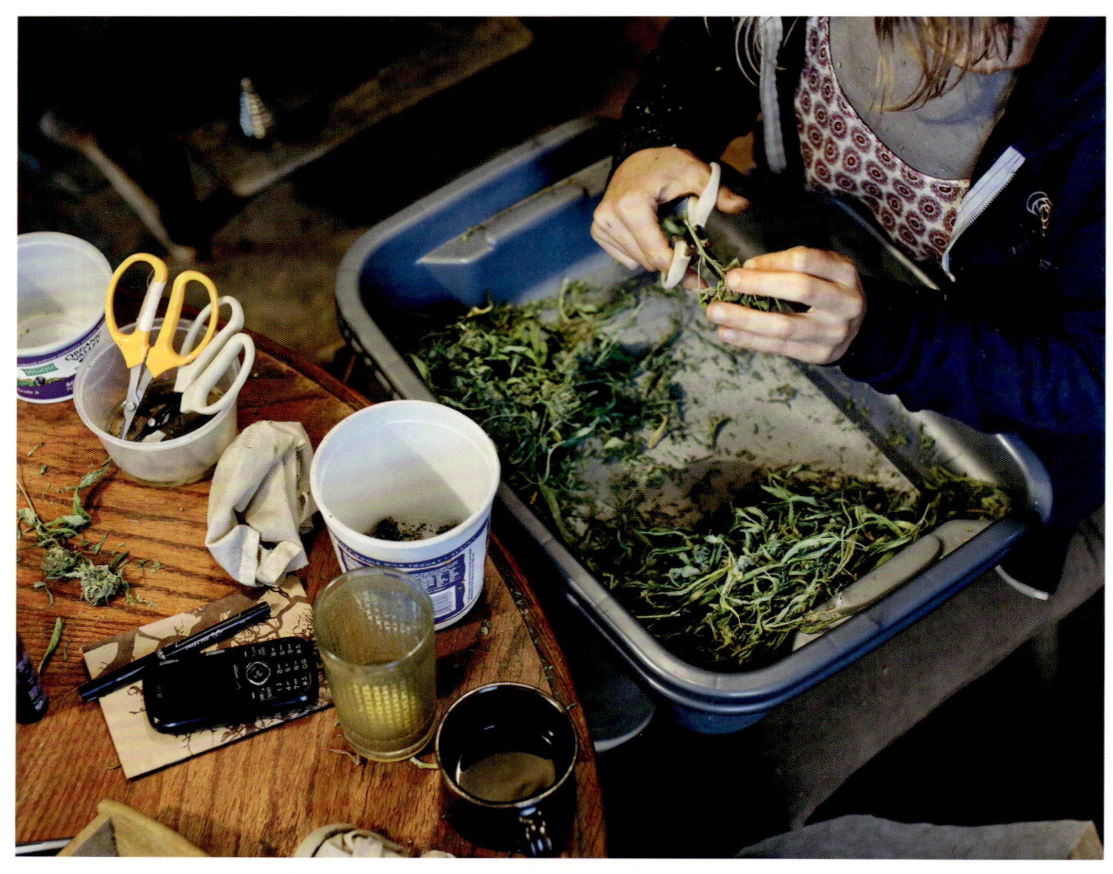

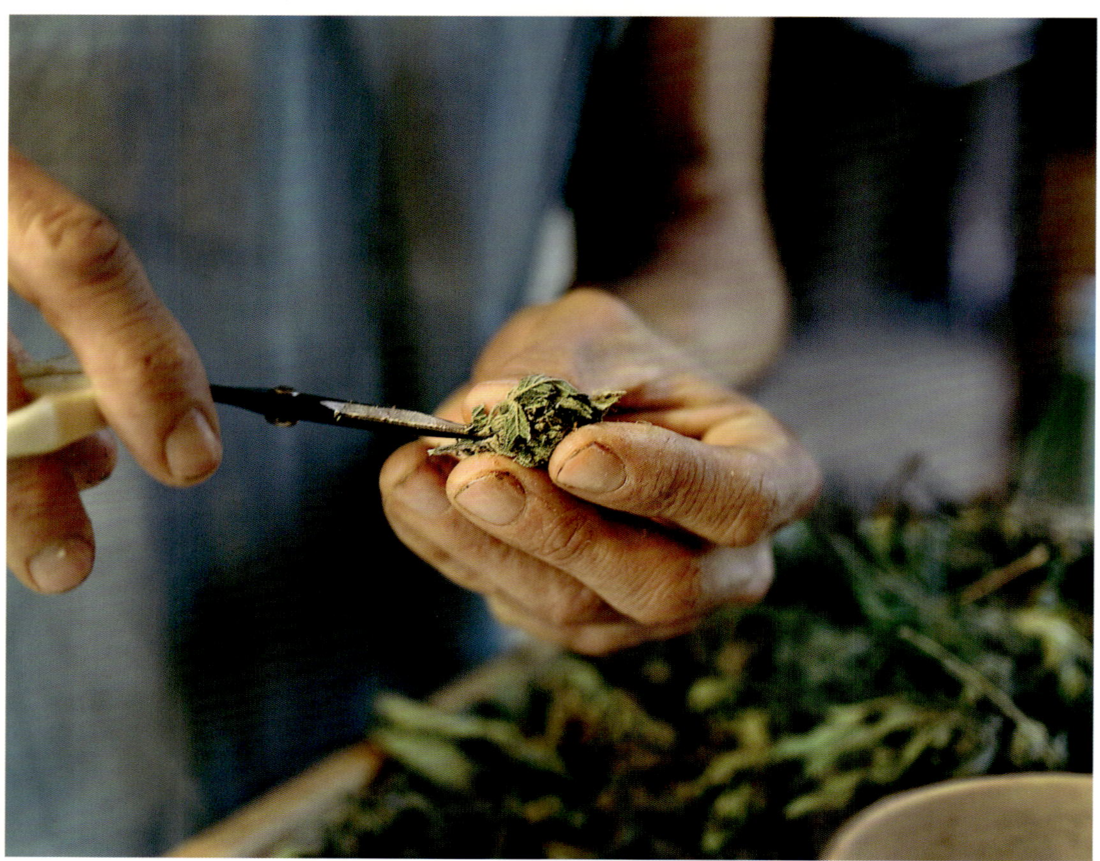

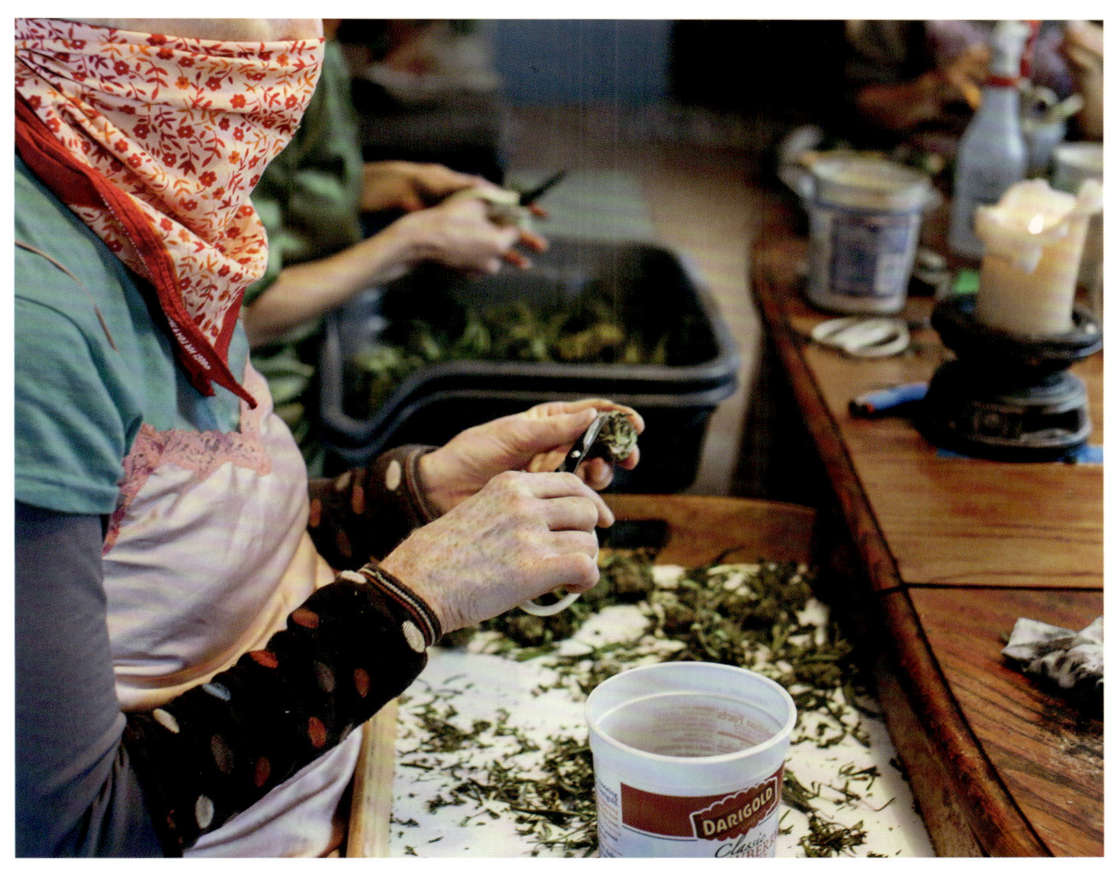

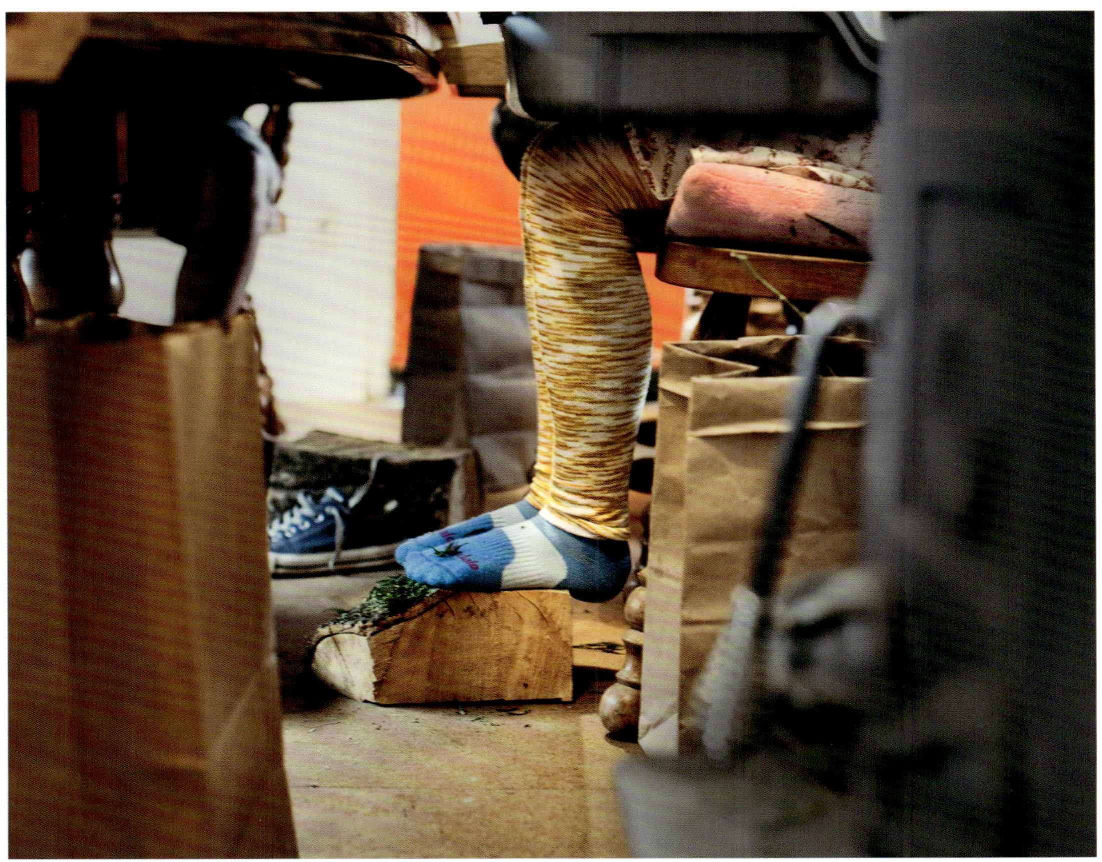

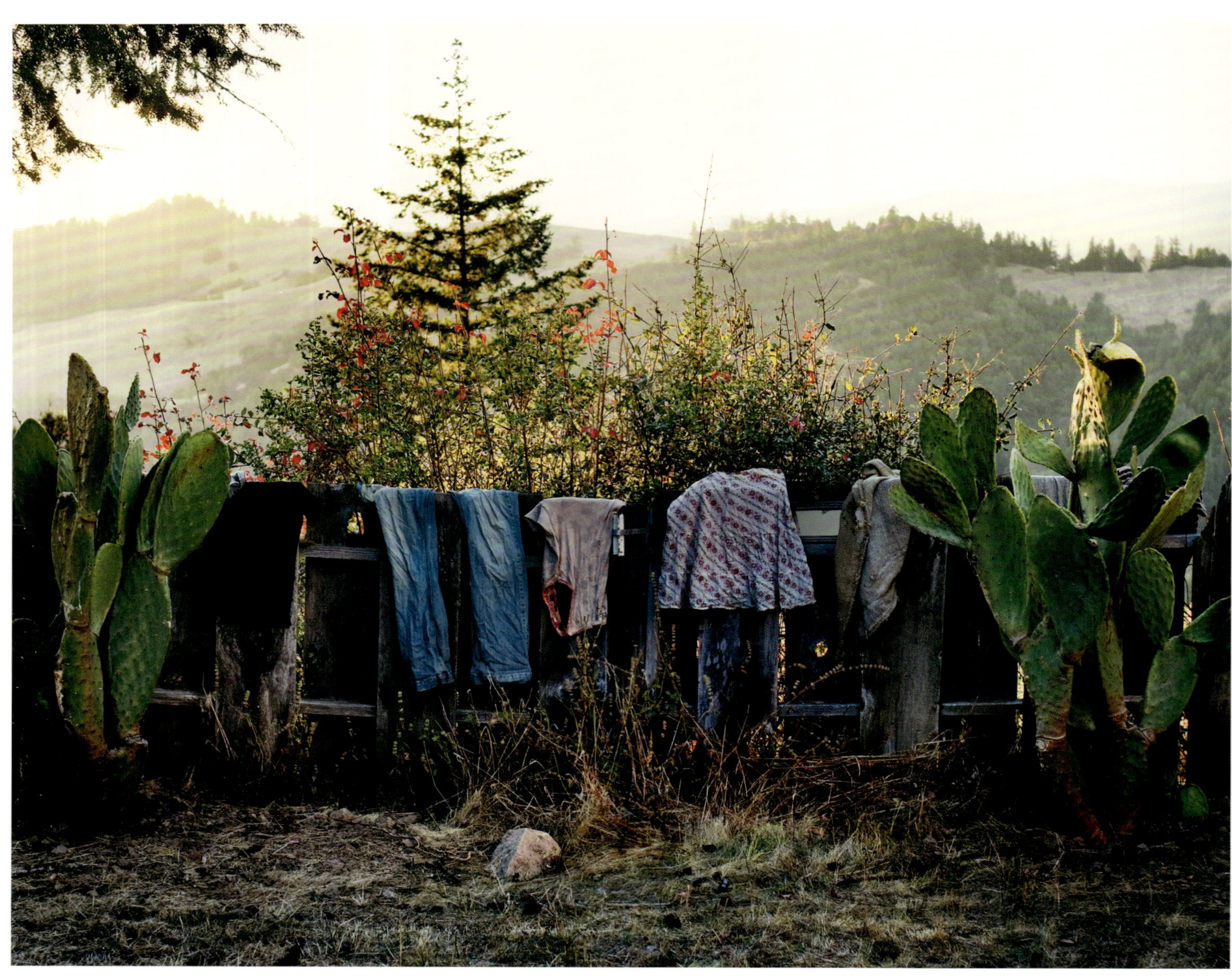

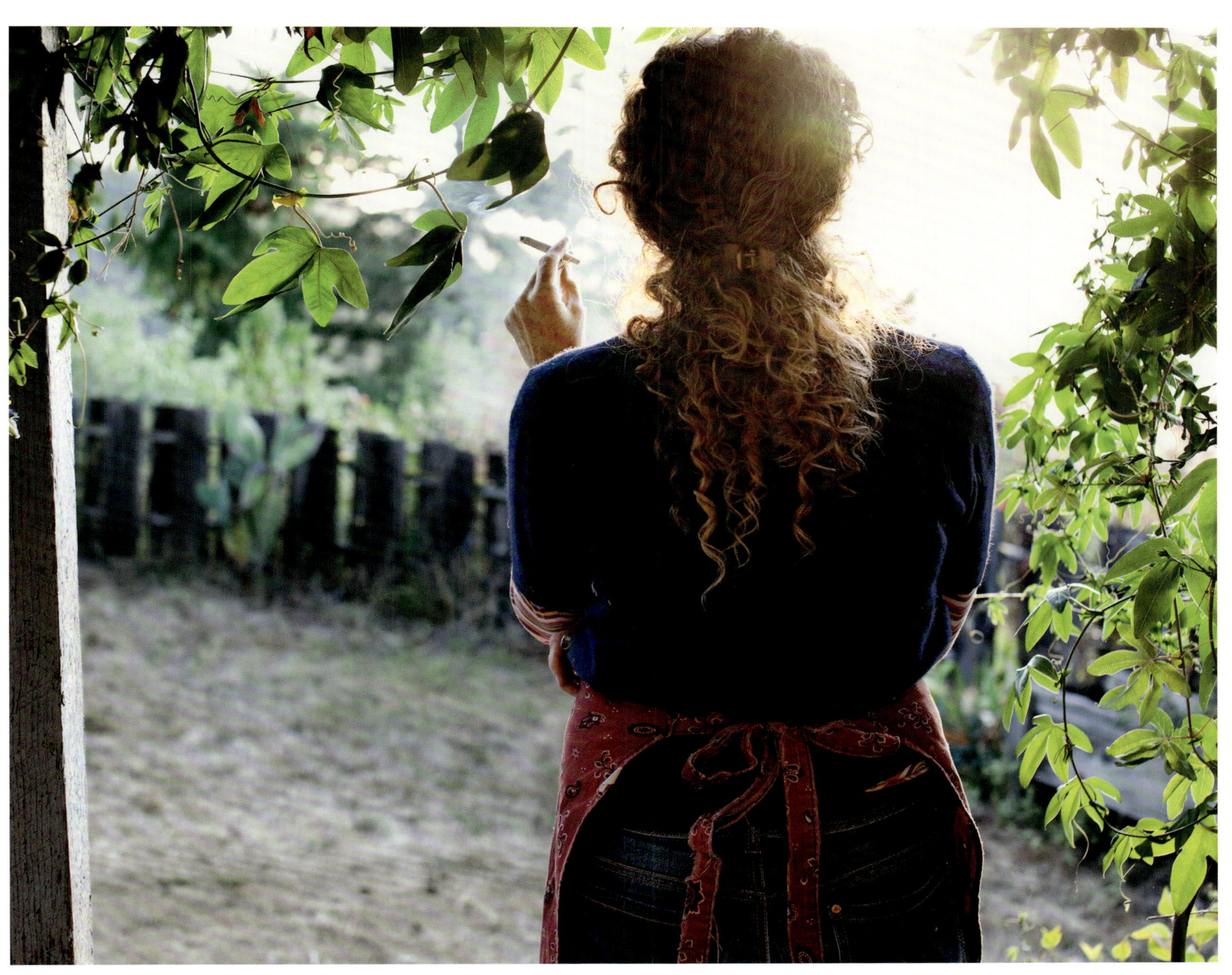

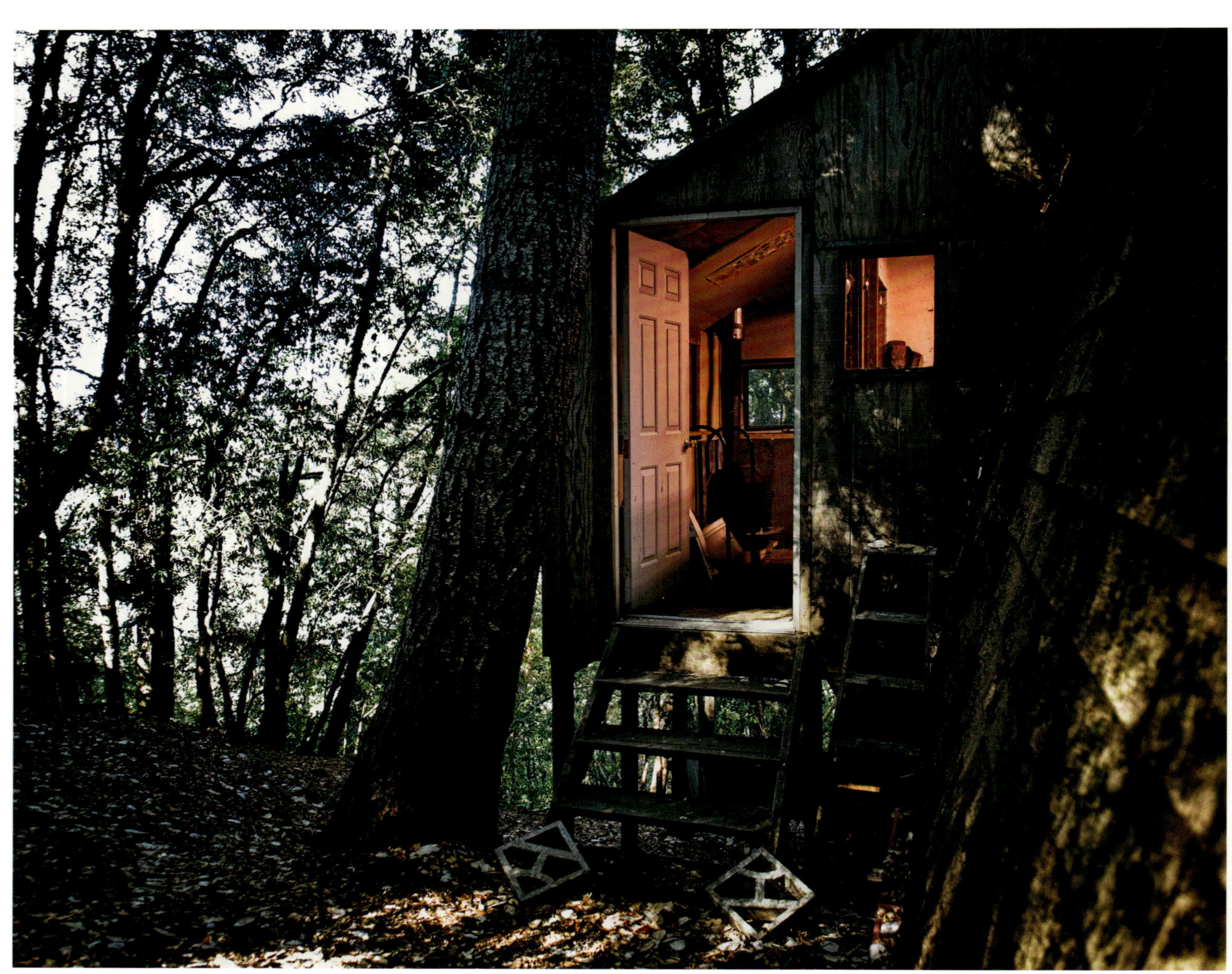

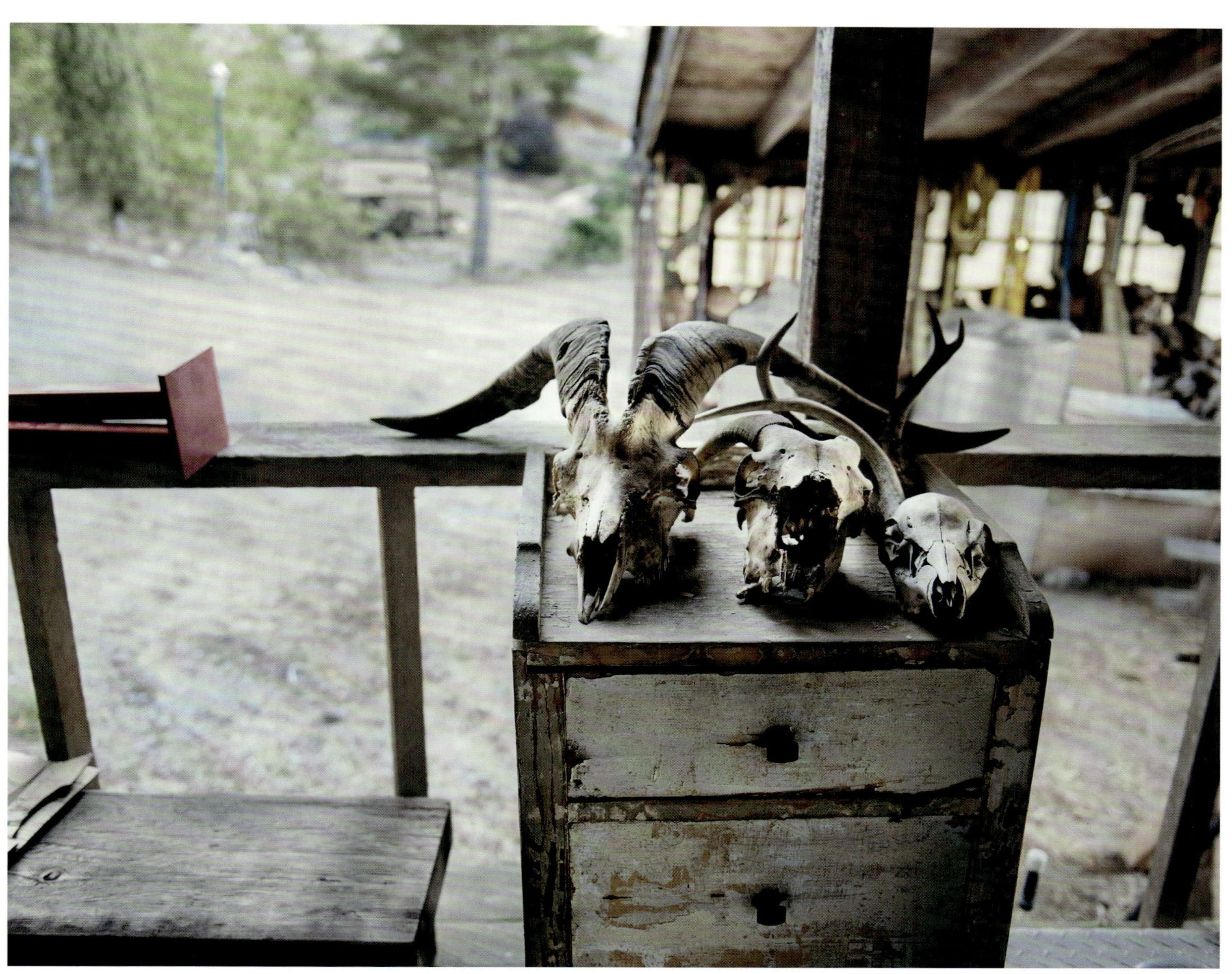

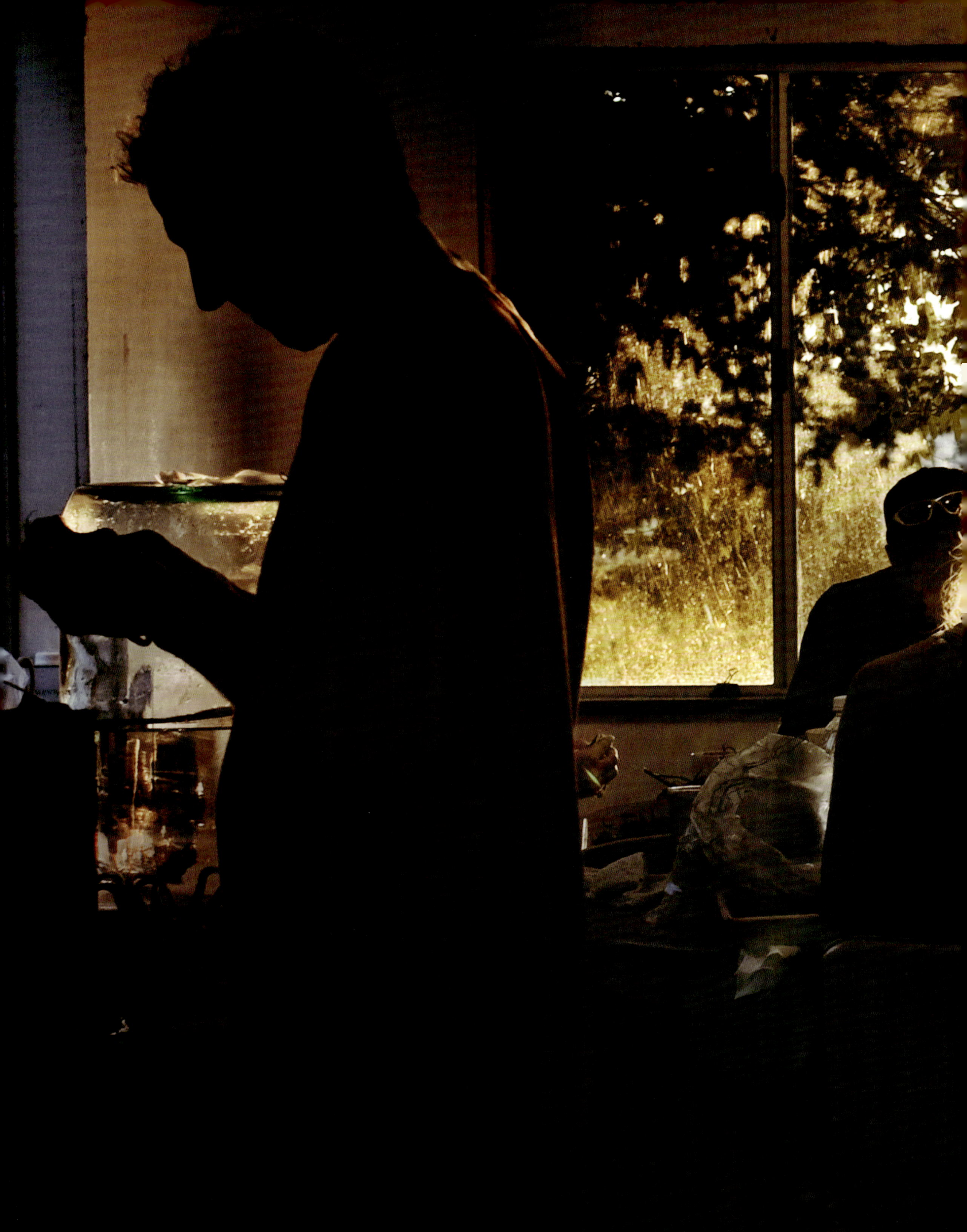

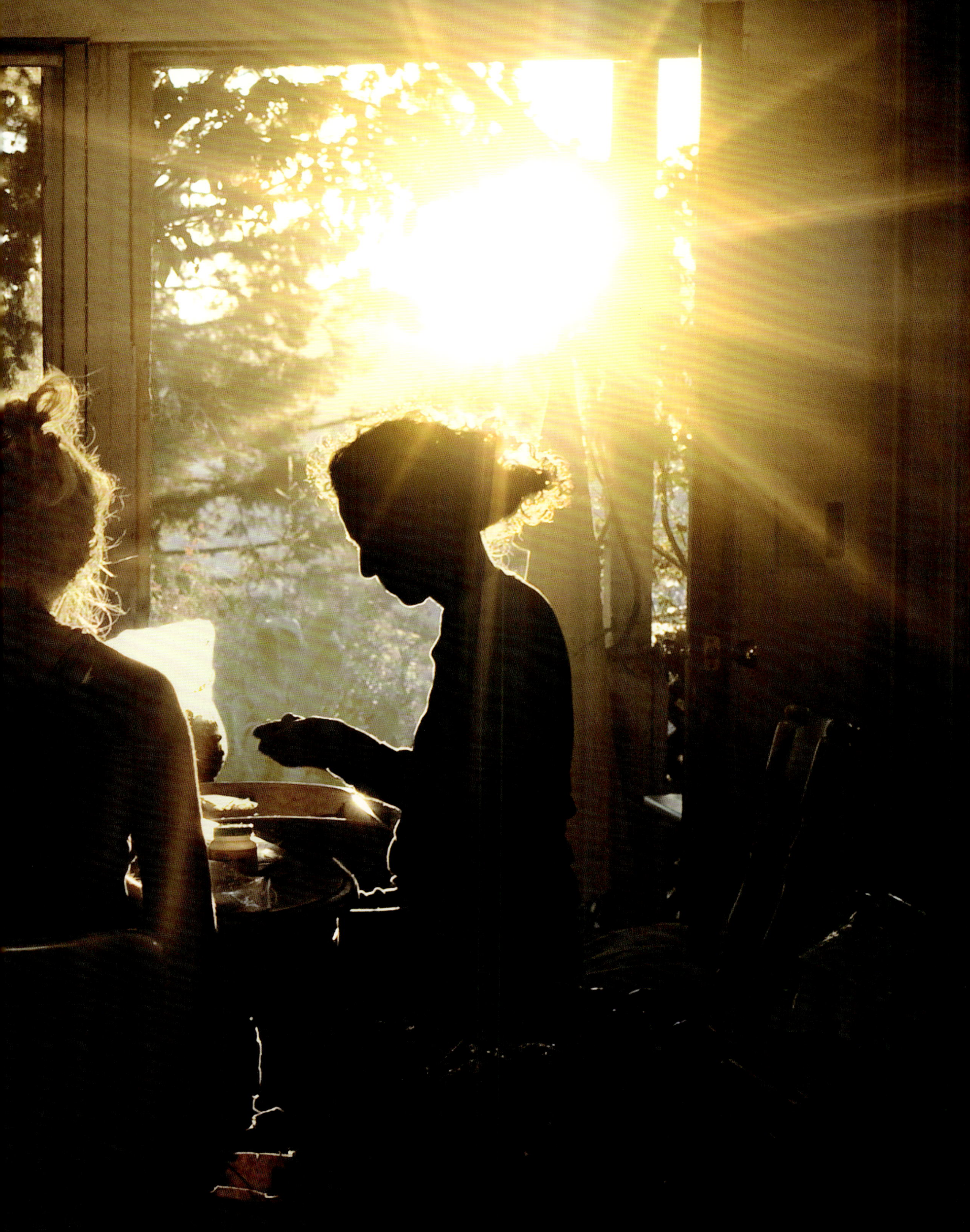

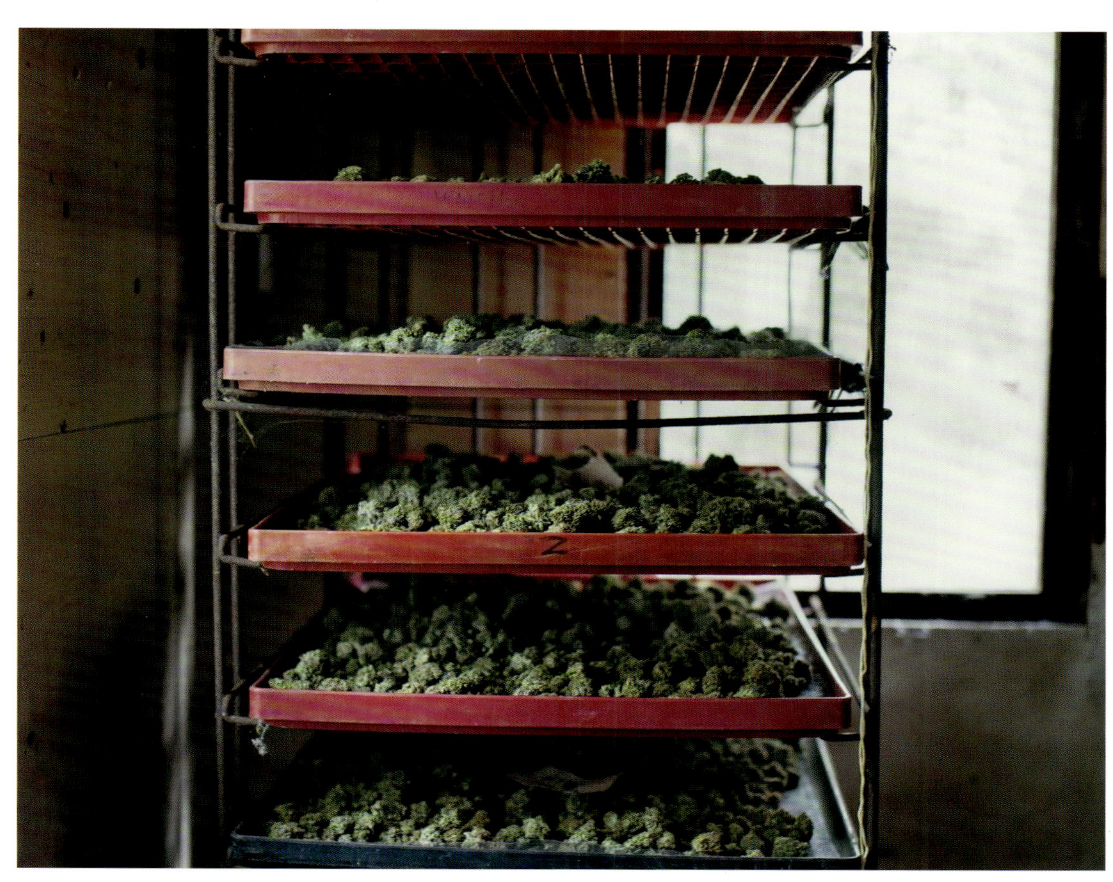

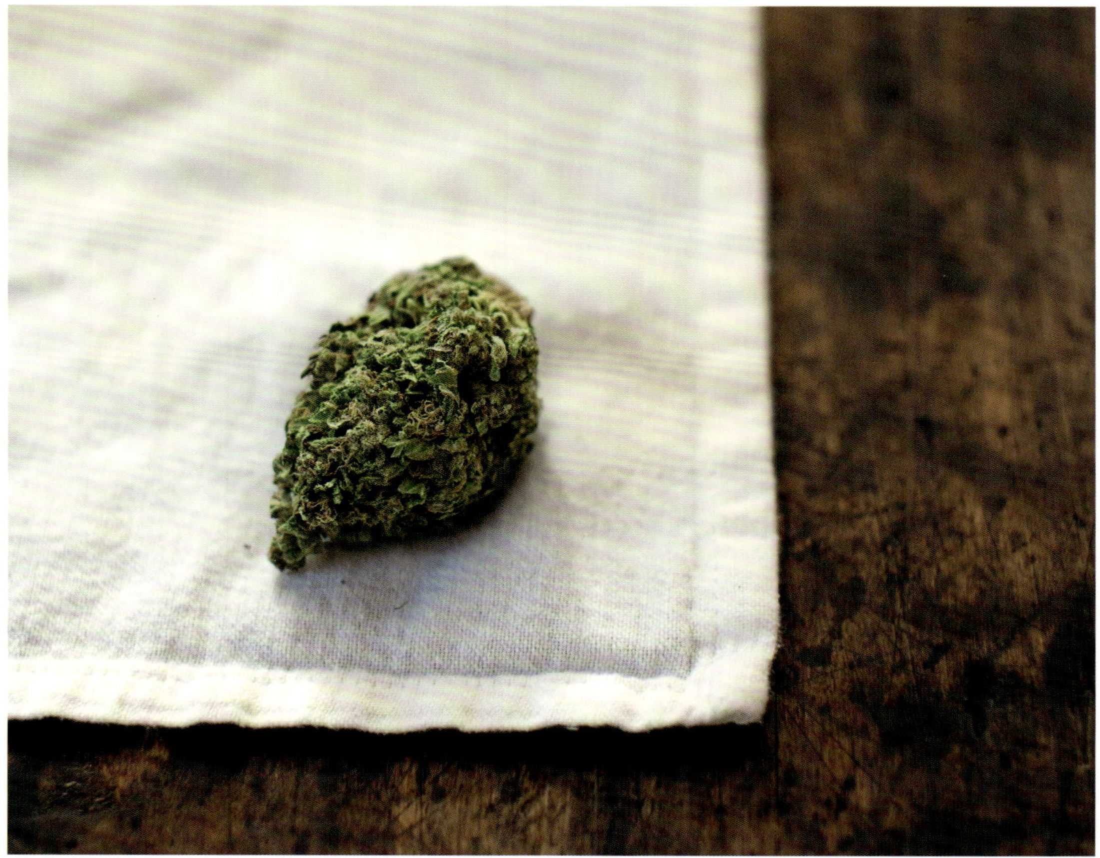

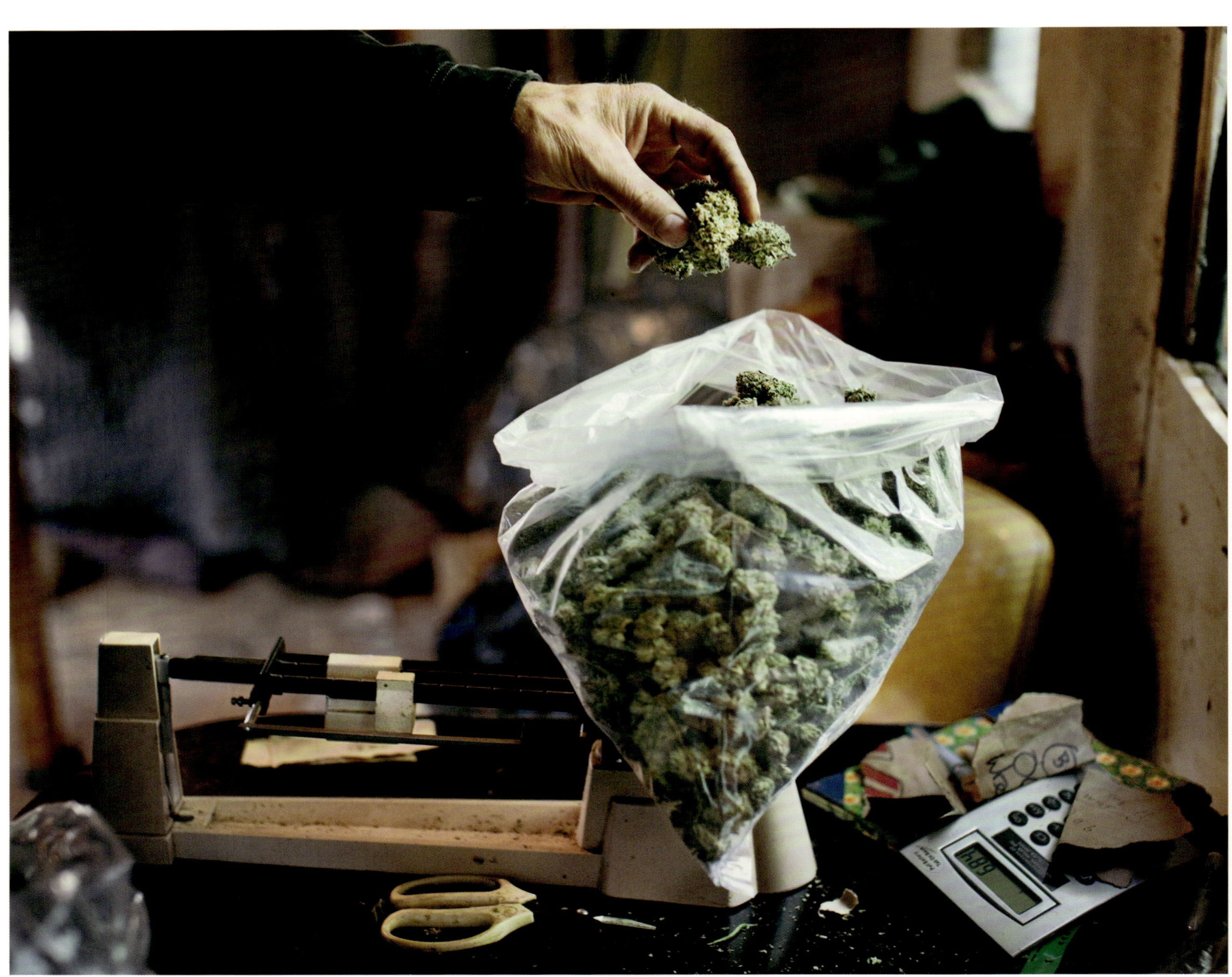

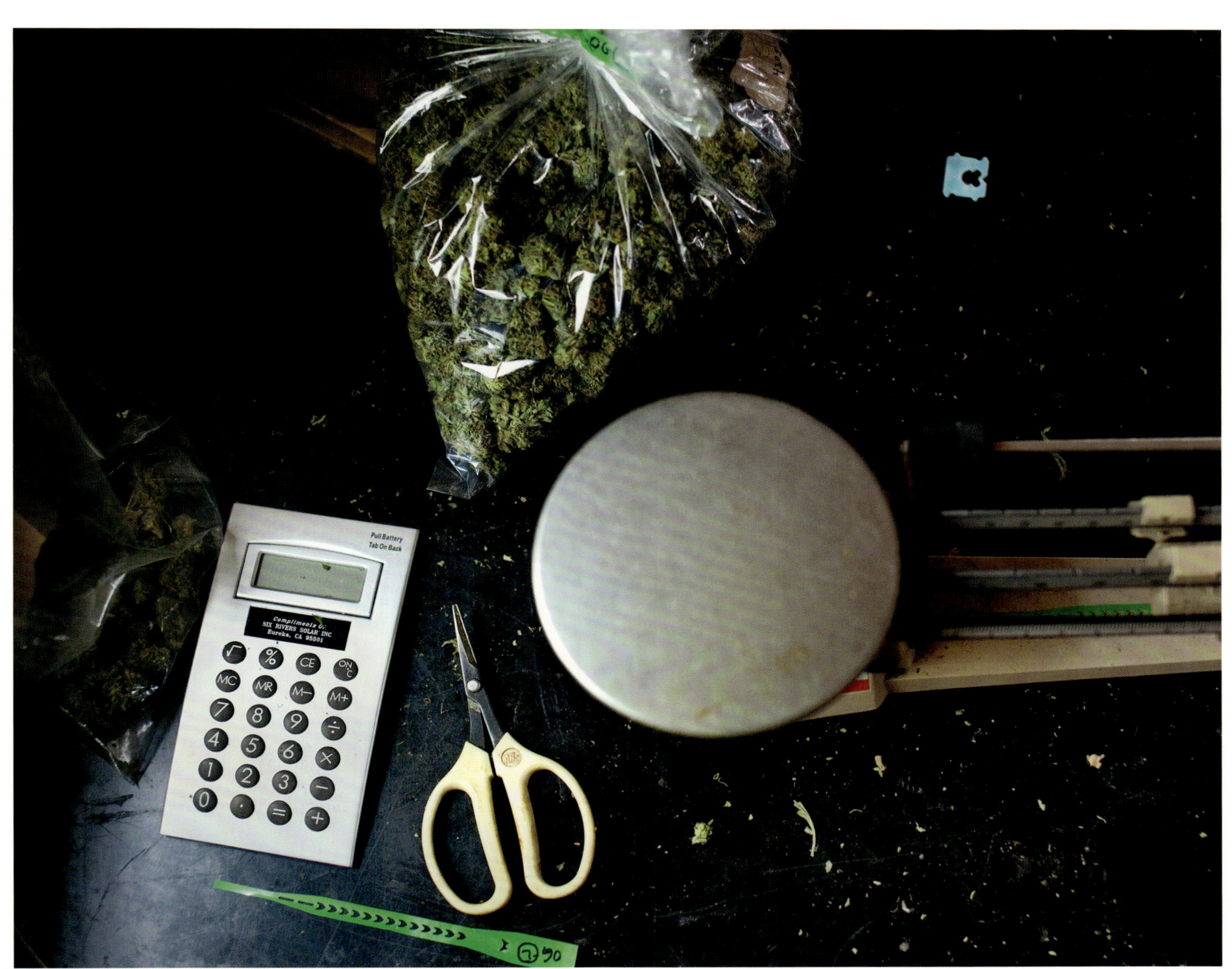

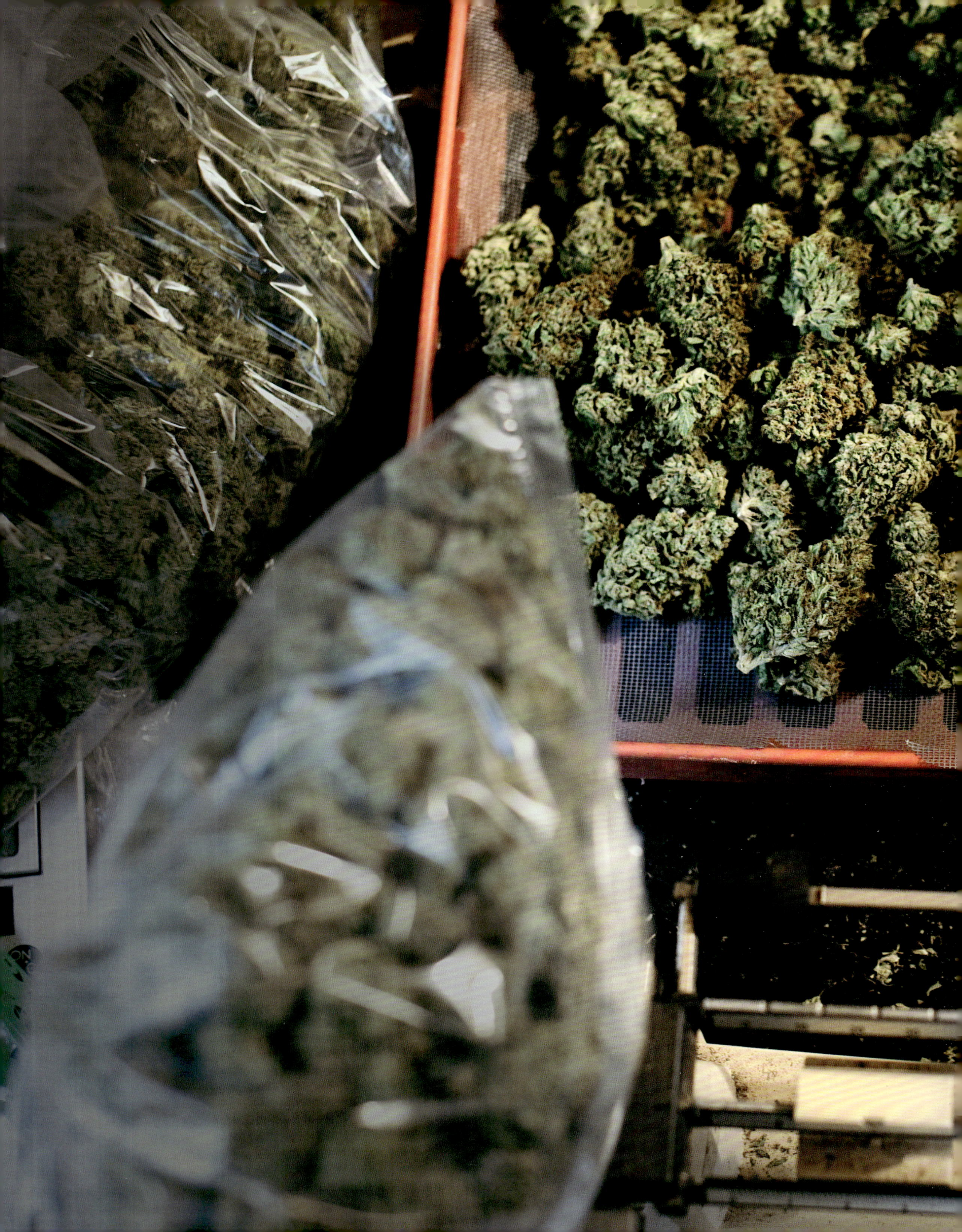

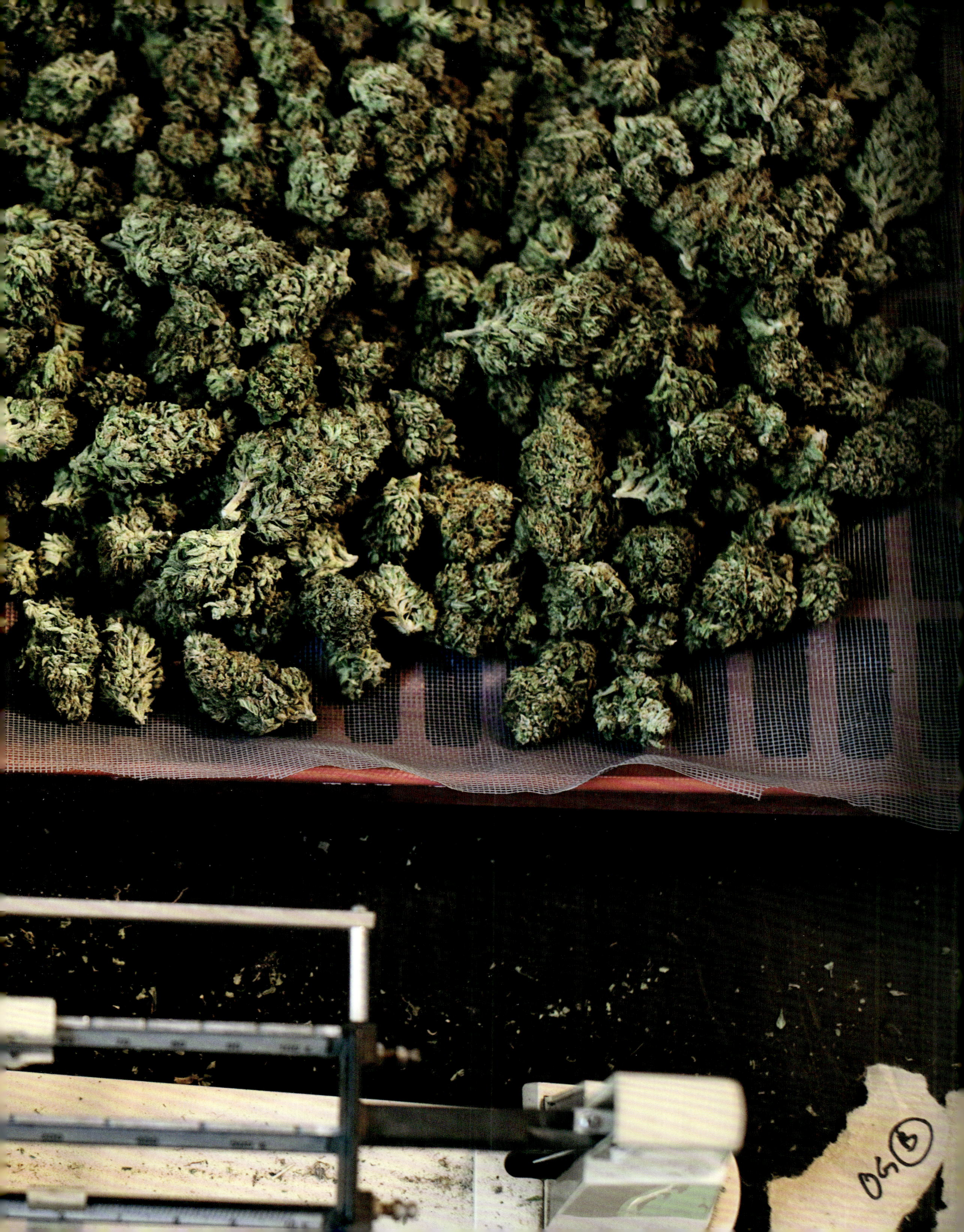

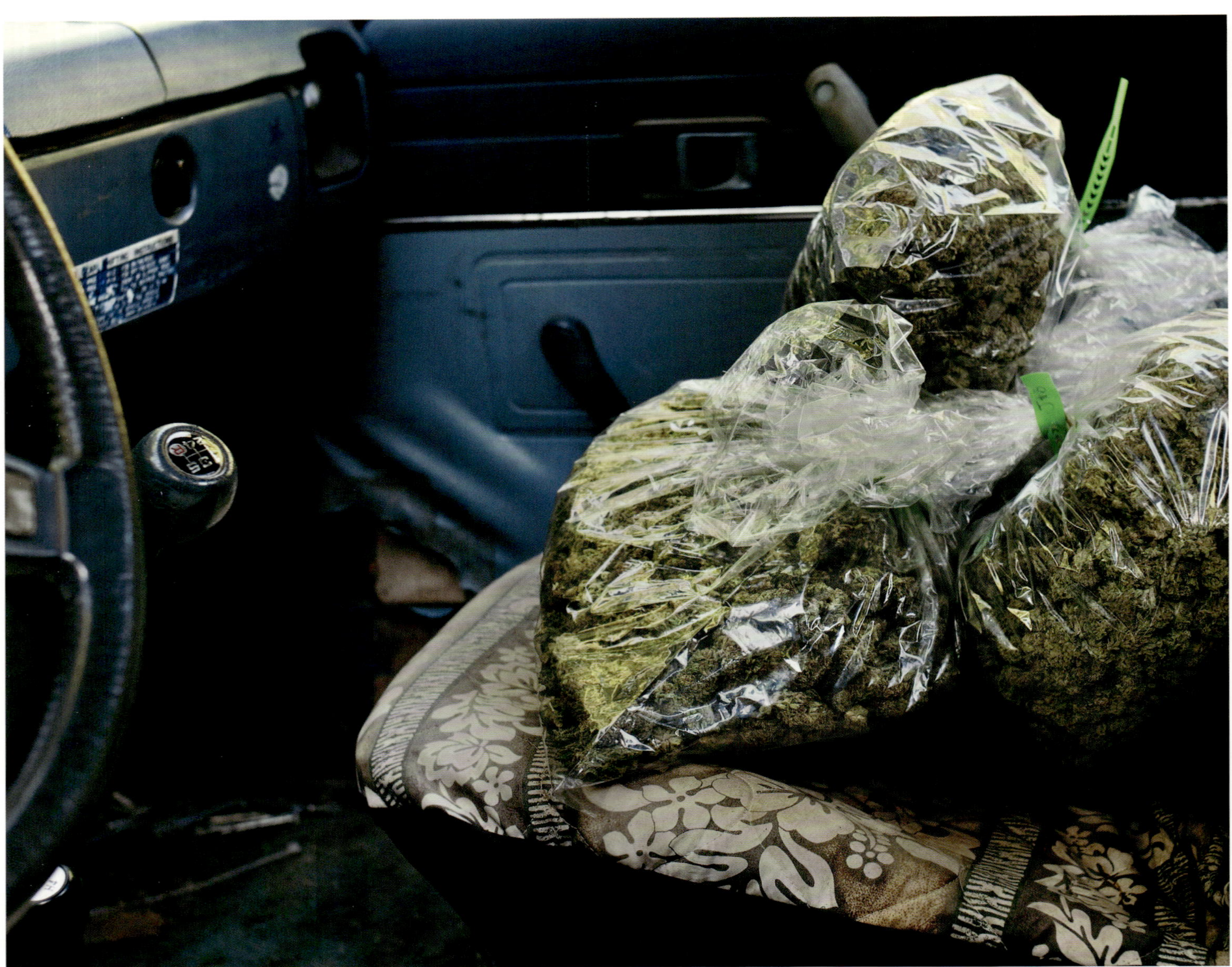

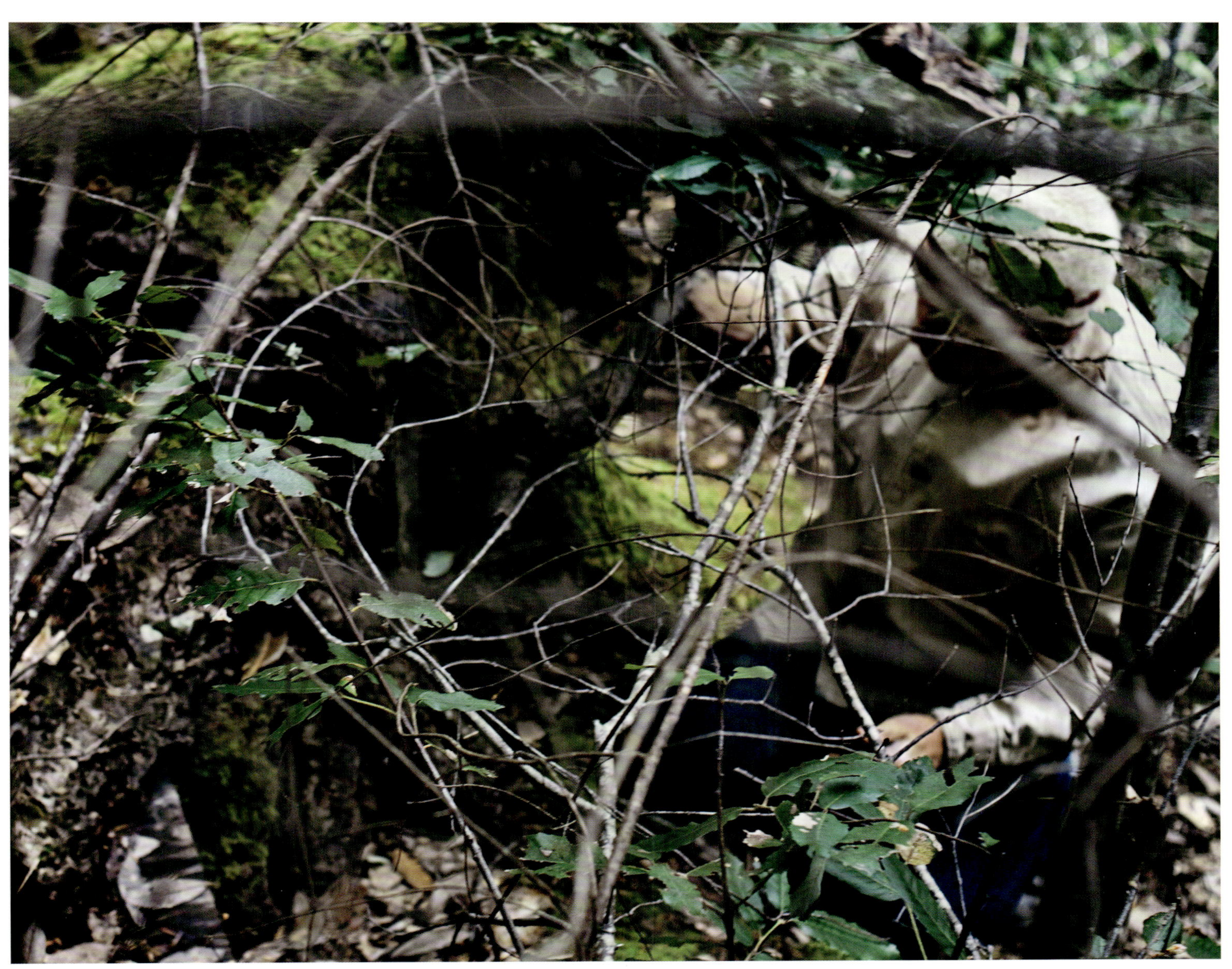

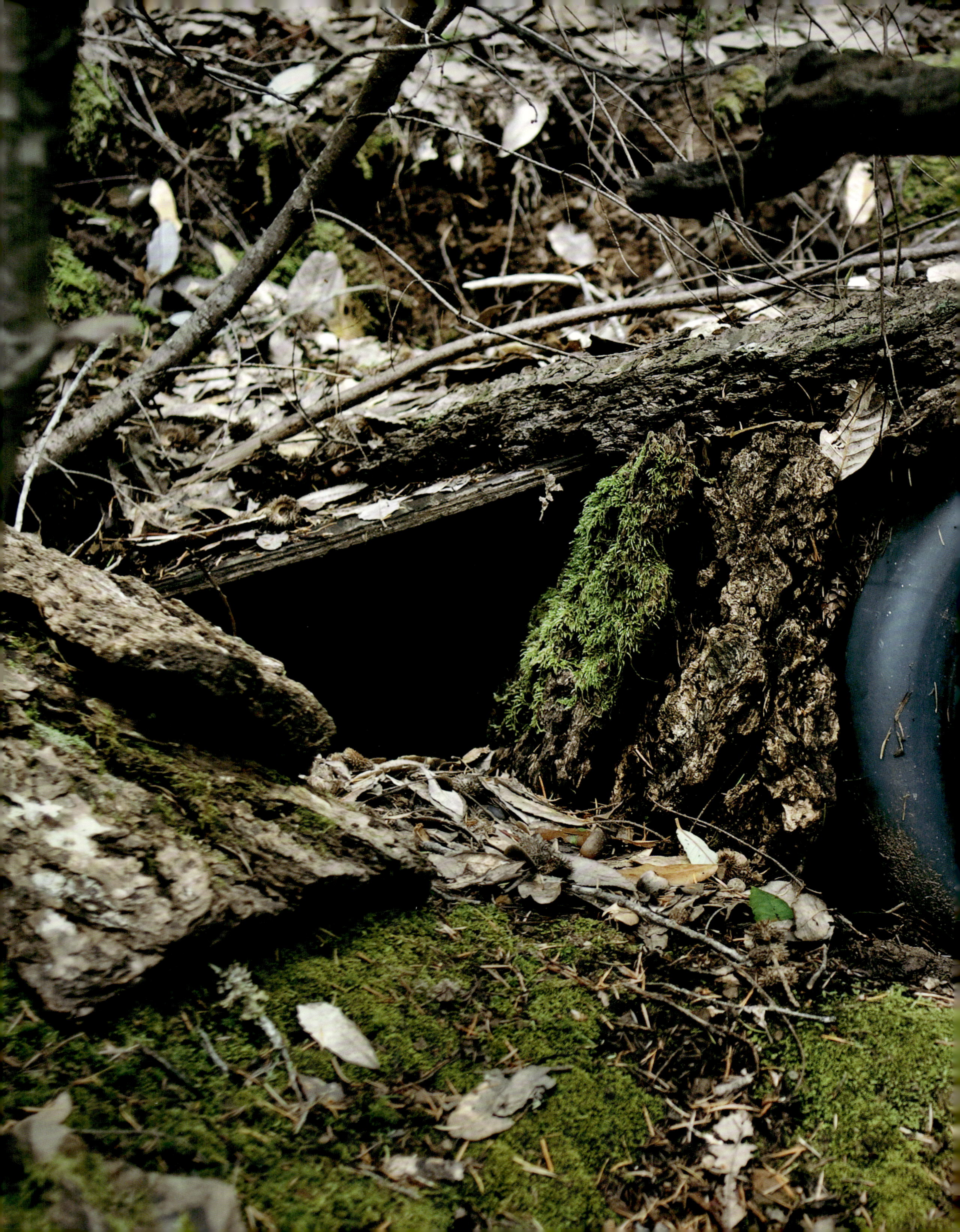

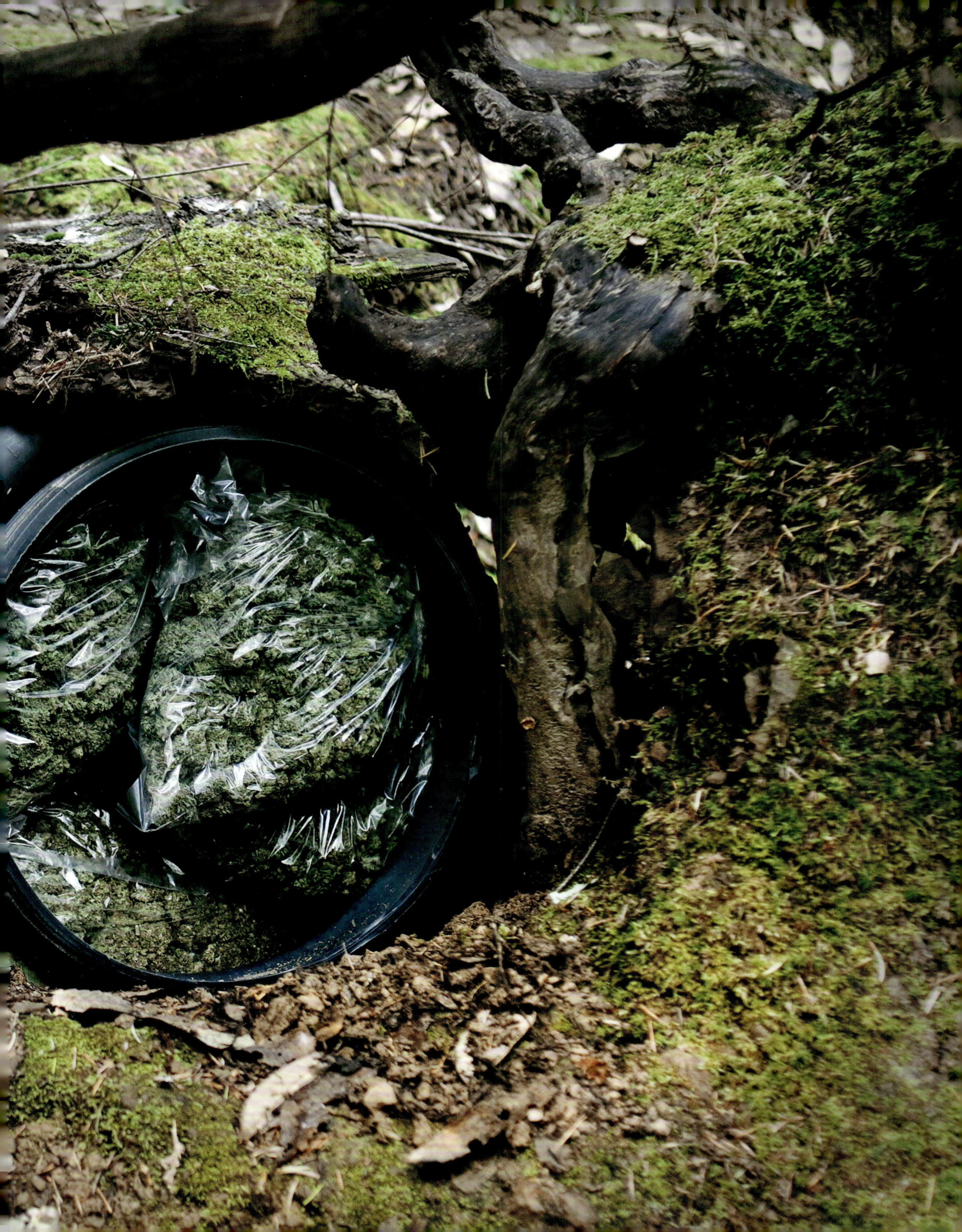

Once, decades ago, I was the editor of *High Times* magazine. It was then and it remains—I believe—the leading periodical on the subject of marijuana, and I certainly learned a lot while I was there. I sampled quite a variety of product. I met users, sellers, growers, smugglers, and all sorts of enthusiasts, theorists, and even detractors. But I wasn't really interested in the business side—legal, illegal, or quasi-legal. I left that to the reporters. I was amused by certain products, such as the electronic bong that looked like a CB radio and shot smoke into your mouth, and I was amazed by the adventurous tales of daring smugglers. But, personally, I was more interested in the culture around the plant. I had once worked for *Playboy*, and there was a certain similarity between the magazines—both were philosophical advocates of controversial positions, and *High Times* also had a famous centerfold. Although its subject was from the plant kingdom, it did inspire a certain lust among the readers.

Often, when it came to the real world of marijuana, I simply didn't want to know. My life was complicated enough. I liked to smoke, and I liked the culture around it—the art, the music, and the lore. I never saw a grow light or visited an American grower, indoor or outdoor. I did have opinions about the agricultural side—I was a big seed advocate. But I was more focused on the user experience and cultural impact of ganja.

I have been a champagne enthusiast for decades, but I never actually visited the Champagne region of France until two years ago. The place was so charming that I immediately regretted having waited so long to get there. Maybe I'll get to Humboldt one of these days too, but until now the closest I've come is eating the fabulous Humboldt Fog cheese—the goat cheese with a little layer of ash in it. I'm not sure what that ash is, but it's fun to imagine its presence was inspired by a cheesemaker dropping his spliff. Anyway, I was delighted to see the photographs in this book, which show me what I've missed by not visiting the area: a rich culture of outlaw artisans and rebel botanists. Humboldt was called by *The New Yorker* "the heartland of high-grade marijuana growing in California." Now that things are changing faster and faster, maybe I'll visit one day soon, if it's doctor's orders.

As someone with a long history with marijuana and as a supporter of its legalization and availability, I thought I'd share some reflections on the culture of this extraordinary plant.

✳

Marijuana?

The first things I remember hearing about marijuana were the names of the famous people who got arrested for it. Gene Krupa, Robert Mitchum, Louis Armstrong, Lester Young. They were "hopped up on pot." I believe I was supposed to watch Krupa's drum solo on "Sing, Sing, Sing" and be horrified. Instead I wanted to take off my clothes and dance. Whatever Krupa was doing looked like fun. Maybe it was worth getting arrested.

My parents never really defined "hopped up," but I thought, "If that's hopped up, I probably wanna get hopped up too." Krupa, Mitchum, Pops, and Prez seemed like pretty good testimonials for whatever marijuana did. And how could you not be interested in something called "boo" or "muggles" or "gage"?

But it seemed like it was going to get you in trouble. Lester Young, *Down Beat*'s best tenor saxophone in 1944, was drafted the same year and put in the brig after telling the doctor he had smoked every day since 1933. Being a hipster head seemed like a hard row to hoe.

When I transferred to an urban high school in tenth grade, my mother told me not to walk around the neighborhood of my school because someone might try to sell me pot, and so I began walking in ever larger circles around the school. But nobody ever stepped forward with a sales proposition. I wasn't sure what grass would do, but I was intrigued. The propaganda campaign against marijuana was based on so many lies and fantasies that it was hard to know the truth without firsthand knowledge. In *The Basketball Diaries*, Jim Carroll wrote that in high school he could never remember whether it was heroin or marijuana that was supposed to be addictive. Although Bob Dylan says that "Rainy Day Women #12 & #35" wasn't a drug song and that he was talking about stoning in the biblical sense, everybody said it was about reefer, which we had never experienced. Whatever it was about, it sure seemed like there were many suitable occasions for stoning and that there was a certain amount of fun involved.

Finally, in my first year of college, I managed to acquire some cannabis and was immediately charmed by its effects. I didn't really know what to expect, but it wasn't dramatic. I remember thinking, "I don't feel anything." Then I noticed that I had been standing in a corridor, looking at a photograph of the surface of the moon for maybe ten minutes. It's hard to put the effect into a few words, but I would say that marijuana put things in perspective. What does it do? It shifts perspective. I'd have to say that it makes you more like yourself. It summons a kind of bemused reserve, thoughtfulness, a certain clarity, calmness, body consciousness. And, of course, stonedness. Where did I put that joint?

It seems normal for people first trying marijuana to say they don't feel anything and then start laughing. The head reveals itself at its own pace. What starts casually works up to revelation.

You can do things on it, like drive or play sport. But I never thought it was much good for golf. You don't want to see the swing differently each time, but exactly the same. We still smoked, but we said, "Take a toke, add a stroke."

What was then widely known as grass certainly improved my attitude. Since it was associated with what was then widely known as hippies, one picked up certain habits or clichés surrounding it. If you took acid you were an acid head, but if you smoked reefer you were a head. If you were a head, chances are you had long hair, and if you saw other longhairs on the road you gave them the V peace sign.

The marijuana I smoked as a college student was far different from what goes around today. It was virtually all *Cannabis sativa*, and some of it was probably intended to make rope. It was usually artisanally smuggled, probably by some poor dude wading across the Rio Grande. Then it became professionally smuggled "commercial Columbian," which was not the stuff of magicians.

At the age of 29, I joined *High Times* magazine as articles editor. I was thrilled. The job enabled me to leave Chicago, where I worked for *Playboy*, and return to New York, which I still considered my home. During my one-year employ at *Playboy* I never had a haircut and, for at least the last six months, I didn't shave. I think my appearance was meant not just to distinguish me from my fellow employees but somehow also to make up for the fact that I could never really find a good smoke in Chicago.

New York was a different matter. Working at ground zero, I had the best in the world. We had this and we had that. It turned out that marijuana growers were strangely amenable to a certain discreet publicity, and there was never any shortage of exotic product for centerfold shoots or reviewing purposes. Sinsemilla was coming in, with growers aiming for maximum THC and minimal CBDs, but there were also exotics, including Thai sticks and the weed of the future, skunk, with its oriental roots. It was very nice. It went well with jazz, rhythm and blues, and reggae, all of which had been made in that spirit. And the new, improved grower marijuana went well with dub, an abstract variety of reggae, which explored a new spatial dimension of sound.

I was, in fact, a sinsemilla dissenter and had endless arguments with my friends over what made the best smoke. I said it had to have some seeds, but it was really about lineage. Thai sticks had some seeds, and, as far as I can recall, the best stuff was sent to me in the mail from Thailand, by a guy in the U.S. Air Force. And then, of course, there was charas, the black hash from Nepal or Afghanistan.

The improvement in the professionalism of the marijuana trade had some unfortunate consequences. See Oliver Stone's *Savages*. The distribution end of the system had plenty of similarities with the distributors of alcohol during Prohibition. If one wasn't a thug, one was in a world where thugs were encountered. Alas. But somehow a righteous spirit seems to evolve where good weed is smoked, and the times have changed more than I ever thought possible back in the hippie days. Marijuana has regained its place in American culture, the place it held until race-motivated legislation made it illegal in 1937. I knew that was possible. I had seen it in Jamaica, where herb is smoked with religious devotion.

The first time I went to Jamaica, I think it was 1973—it was the same year that *Catch a Fire* and *Burnin'* by the Wailers came out in the U.S., the year after *The Harder They Come*. I stayed in Port Antonio, which is near where the Blue Mountains meet the sea. I figured that it might just be possible to do some smoking in this beautiful place, so I decided to get into my little rental car and drive up into the mountains until I saw someone smoking a spliff. I actually thought this would work, and it did. As things were getting pretty rural, I saw three young guys sitting on a fence smoking. I stopped and asked if they knew where I could get some of that. They got in the car and said they would take me to a guy.

The guy was a farmer up in the hills, in a very beautiful place. He looked kind of like Al Green with dreads, wearing sandals and jeans. He asked me what I wanted, and I said I wanted some smoke. He said, "How much?" I said, "An ounce?" He just laughed. He asked if I had a plane or a boat. "Would you like a ton?" he asked. I would have loved it, but it wasn't going to fit into my luggage.

He put a handful of buds on a butcher block and whacked at it with a machete, chopping it up nicely. "Roll a spliff," he said. He gave me paper from a bread bag. I rolled a New York-sized joint, and they all laughed.

"That's no spliff, mon," he said.

He took a much larger piece of paper and rolled up a joint the size of the one Bob is smoking on *Catch a Fire*. He handed it to me. "Smoke."

I lit it up, took a few drags, and tried to pass it. Again, they laughed. Jah Al Greene said, "No, that's for you, mon."

I smoked it.

This seemed to prove something. After a little more lighthearted chatter about me buying a ton, the farmer wrapped a nice "lid"-size package for me. My friends, none of whom had ever heard of Bob Marley, flattened it out and put it under the floor mat of the car, and I drove down the mountain, dropping them where we'd met. What nice fellows, I thought. I wondered what my mom would have thought of me up there in the mountains with dope-smoking black strangers and a guy swinging a machete.

I always wished I'd had a boat.

Within a year I met Bob Marley and Peter Tosh. I could never be a Rasta, but I believed what they believed. In my own way. I believed in the Wailers' "Get Up, Stand Up": "Most people think, Great God will come from the sky, take away everything and make everybody feel high, but if you know what life is worth, you will look for yours on earth. And now you see the light, you'd better stand up for your rights. Jah!"

Rastafarianism is a religion I can live with because "we know and we understand, almighty God is a living man." It's all about understanding. Or, as Peter Tosh would say, "overstanding." Today we hear a lot about how marijuana is no worse than alcohol, but we've been lied to about it ever since it was made illegal in 1937, primarily because it was used by blacks and other non-whites, and probably because someone on it might be motivated to stand up for their rights. Rasta is not knowledge or belief that is disseminated from on high; it is knowledge that is perceived directly by the individual. It's herb-facilitated gnosis. If there is a god, Rasta is God's democracy.

"When you dance you just are Jah," said Bob.

In the same Wailers song, Peter Tosh sings, "You can fool some people sometimes, but you can't fool all the people all the time. So now we see the light, we're gonna stand up for our rights."

I might not believe in the same god or gods as you, but I say, if marijuana is your line of work, then you're doing God's work.

A lot of people I know either never liked marijuana or stopped using it because it made them "paranoid." I had housemates in college who thought the cops parked in front of our house were watching us. I thought they were drinking coffee and eating doughnuts. Some people get high and freak out: "It didn't make me feel good."

I think that's good paranoia. Keep going and it'll get better. Whatever fear comes with pot is merely the realization of how you really feel. It puts you in touch with your body. This is why so many heads are into health foods and various healing disciplines. I think when you encounter that fear, you have to give in to it. Indulge it. Pot doesn't tolerate "Ignore it and it will go away." It is gently confrontational. It reveals yourself to yourself.

Judging from Colorado and Washington and the states that have accepted marijuana as medicine, a lot of the people haven't been fooled for quite some time. Marijuana is its own best witness. It conveys knowledge of what it is directly, no explanation needed.

Governor Cuomo of New York, seeing what all the other liberal states are doing, seems to have taken some time out from pushing legal gambling to suggest that maybe it's time for medical marijuana in New York, but very controlled, of course. You'd have to go to a hospital to get it. Ironically, marijuana, unlike many other drugs, tends to keep people out of the hospital.

The handwriting is on the wall. The truth cannot be contained. The war is over. Herb won. You don't want to stand in the way, not when you can see the future from here and now. Bob Marley said, "Herb is the healing of the nation." Shall we proceed?

Excuse me while I light my spliff.

—Glenn O'Brien, New York

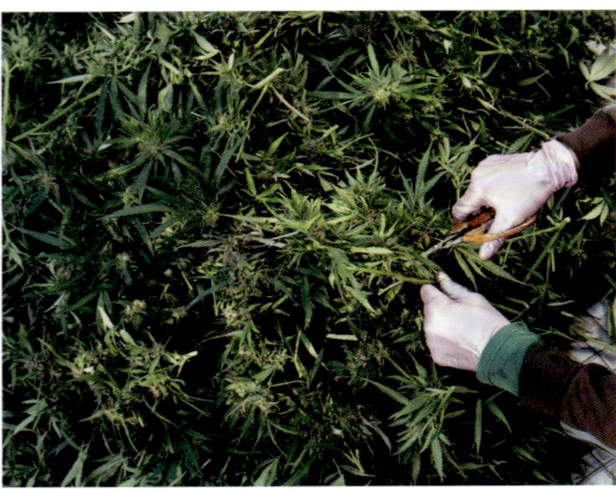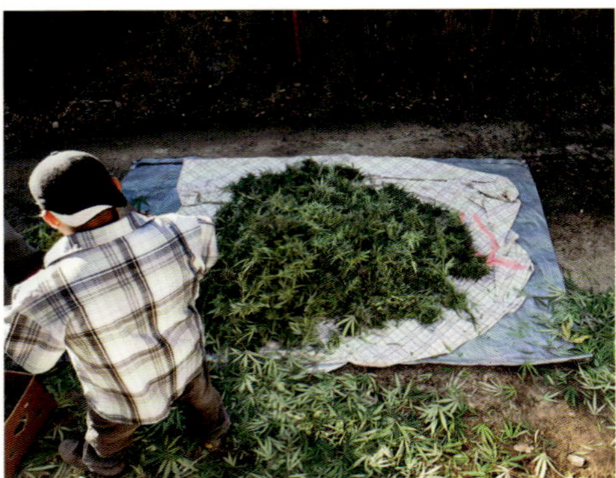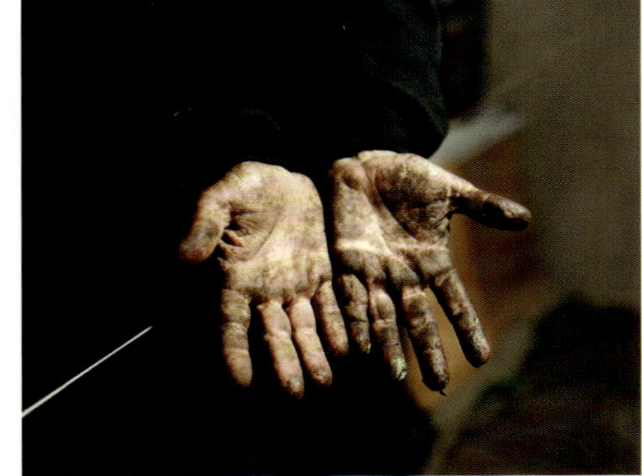

Left to right: Latex gloves protect hands from plant resin while fan leaves are removed from just-harvested buds / First day of harvest, 2013 / Resin on hands, after a day of harvesting. If collected, resin can be used to make hashish

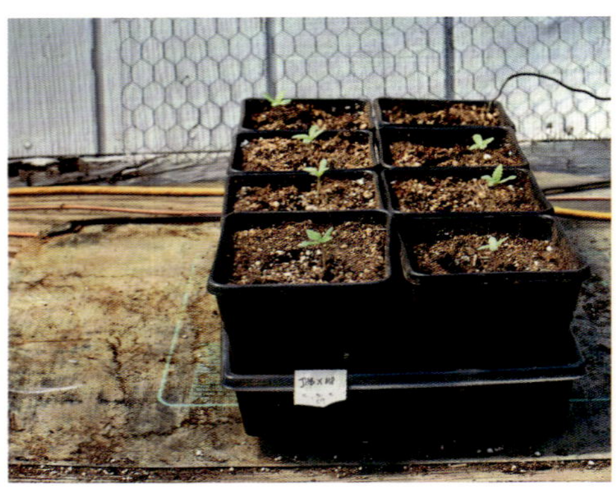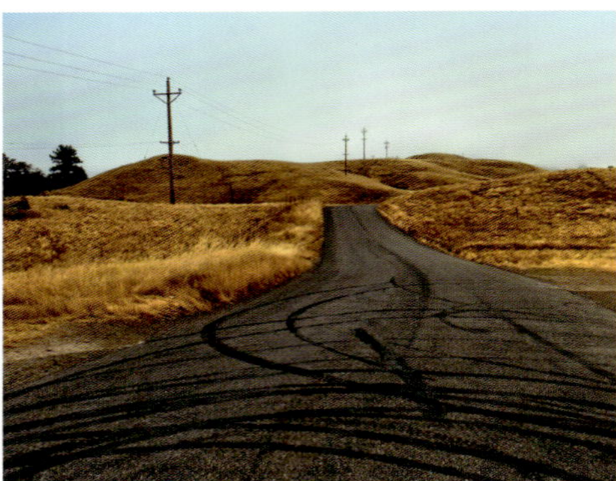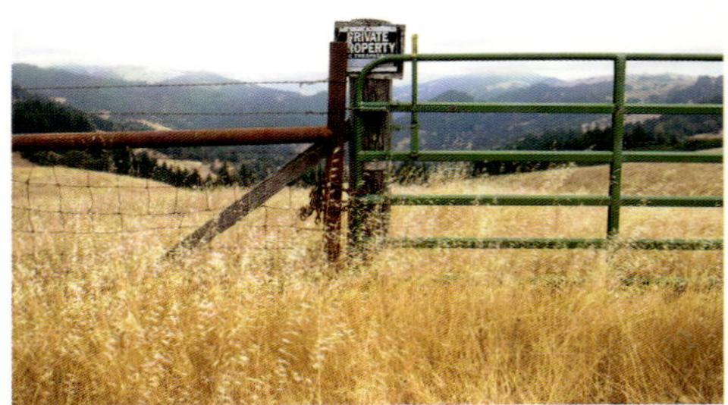

Left to right: Growing from seed: JHB stands for this grower's strain, Jack Harer Banana / Temperatures can rise to 100 degrees during Humboldt's extreme dry summers / Common signs in the Emerald Triangle: no trespassing, private property, and padlocked gates

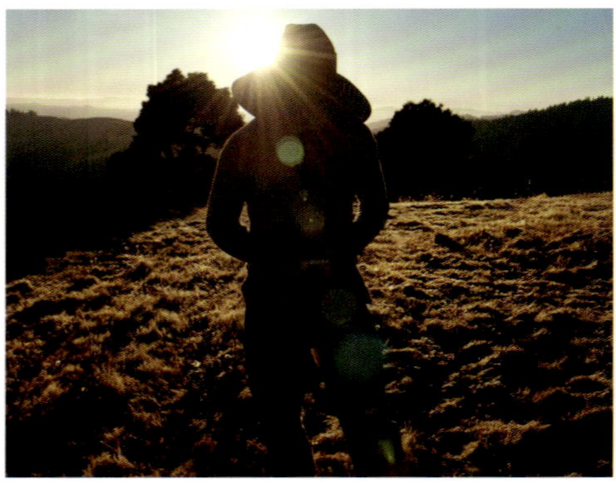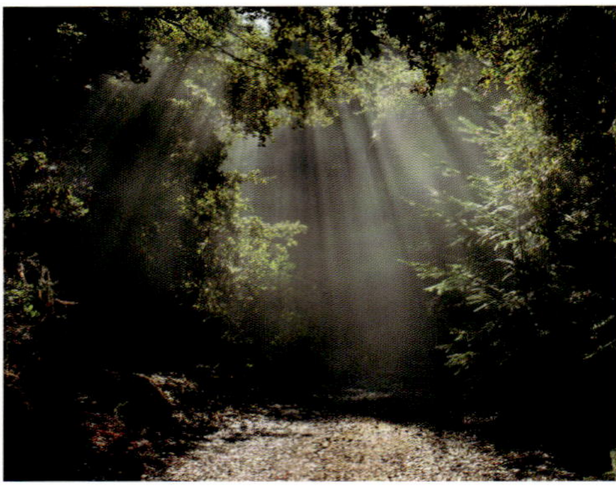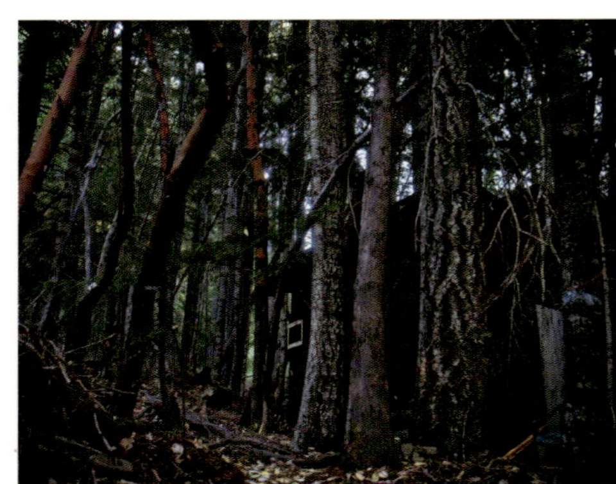

Left to right: Repairing a timer for an automated irrigation system / On the way to a marijuana patch deep in the woods / A deserted structure is converted into a well-camouflaged drying shed

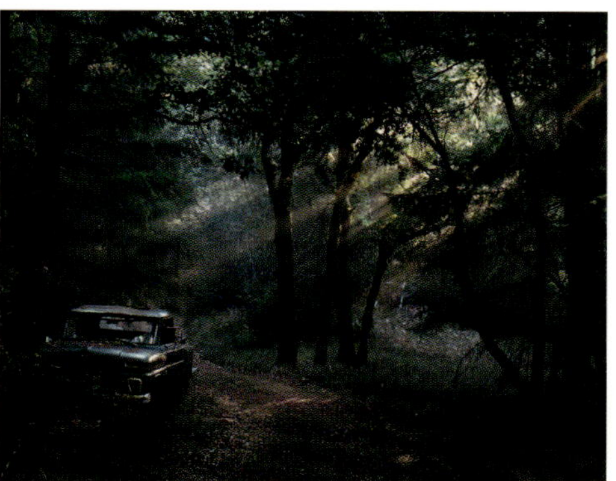 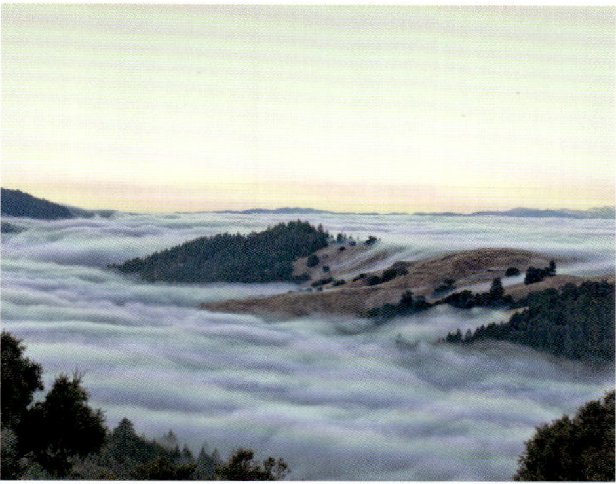 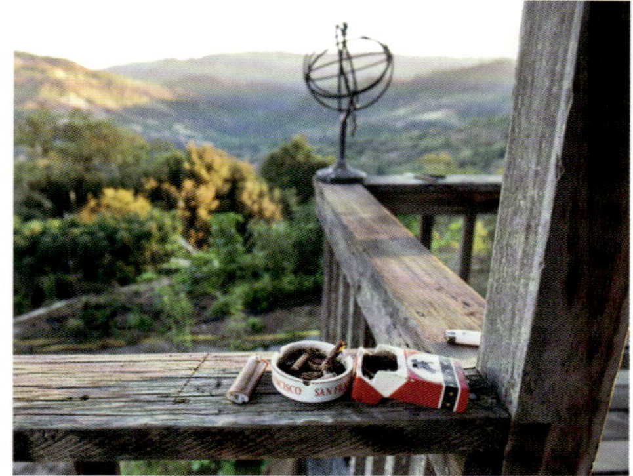

Left to right: Abandoned vehicles scattered around properties are a common sight / Coastal fog creeps across the hills on cool fall mornings, creating an ideal environment for ripening buds / Terraces of pot plants grow just below this house

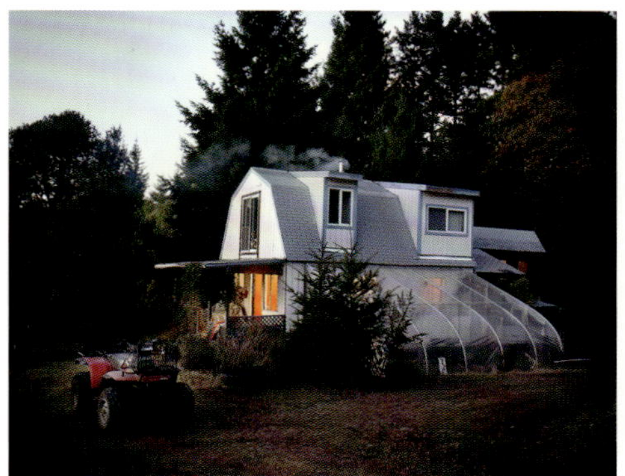 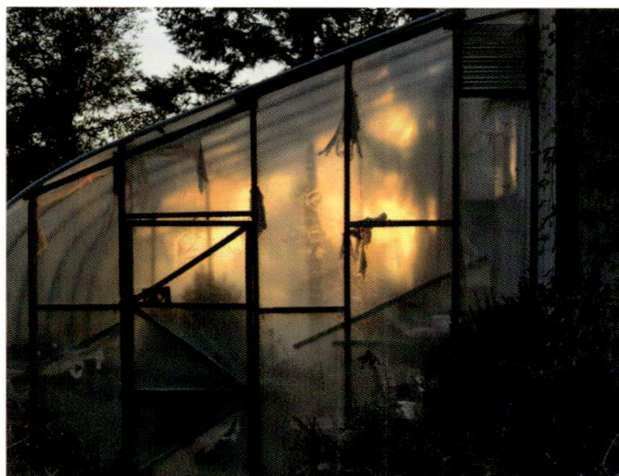 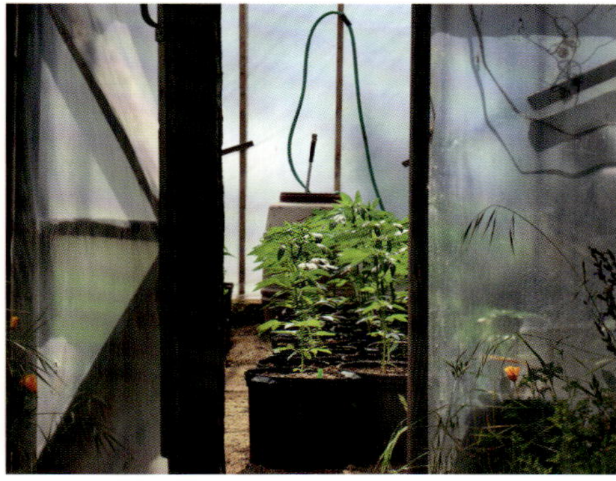

Left to right: Growers make their rounds easily on ATVs / This greenhouse is used for both starting seeds at the beginning of the season and drying weed at the end / Waiting for the plants to sex: the females will be transplanted and the males discarded

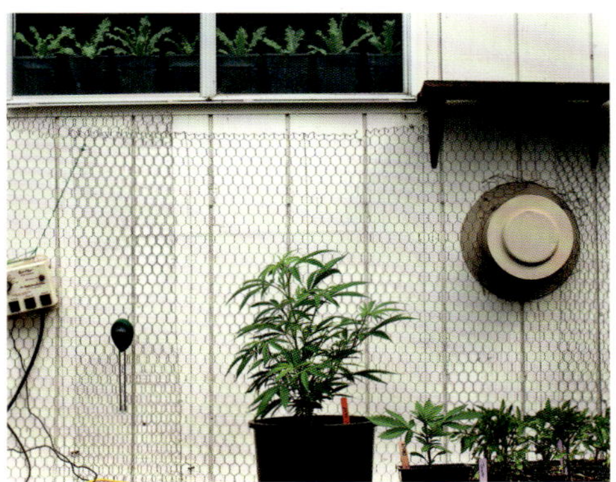 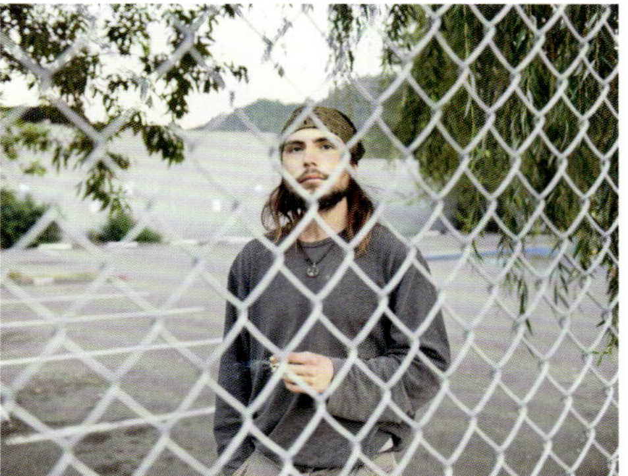 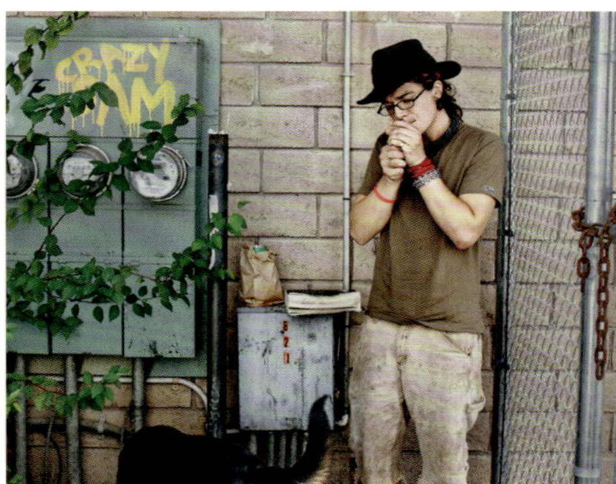

Left to right: A few select males are kept in isolated areas to cross-pollinate with the best females to create new seeds for the next season / For many, it is an hour's drive to food and garden suppliers and to the dump, making trips to nearby small towns an all-day adventure / Seasonal workers and travelers pass through, taking a break in town or looking for work

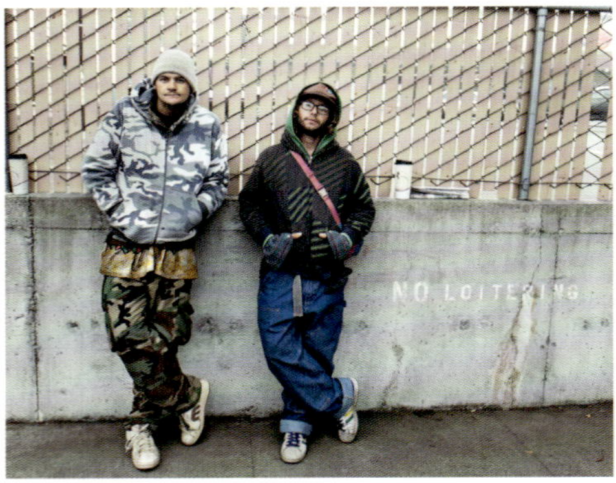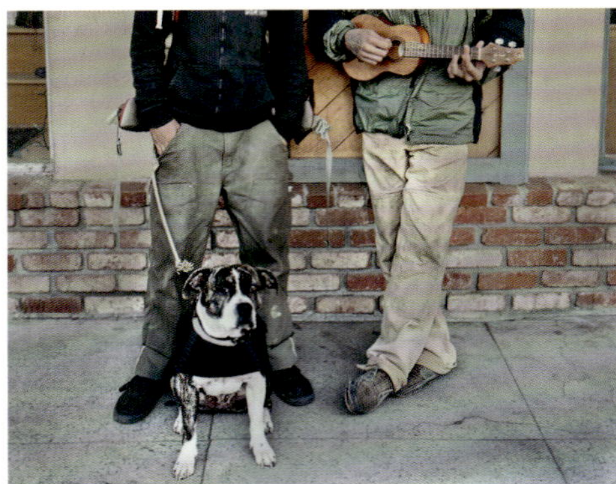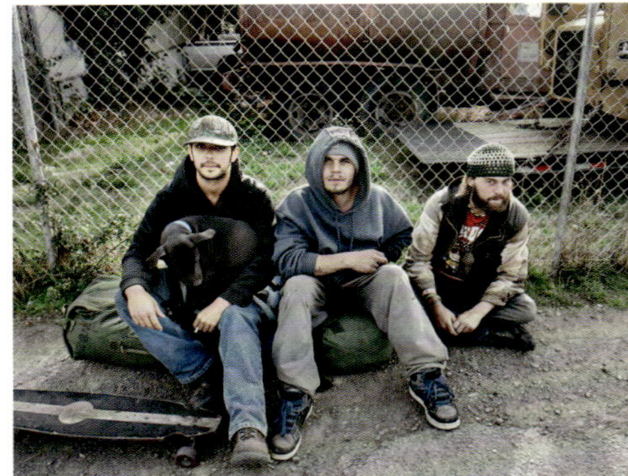

Left to right: Seasonal workers and travelers pass through, taking a break in town or looking for work

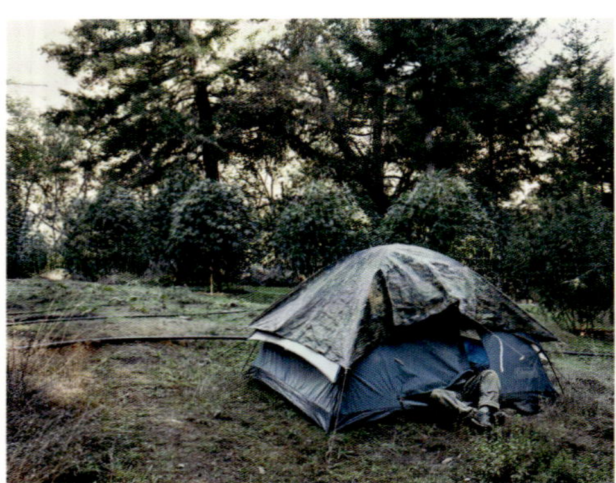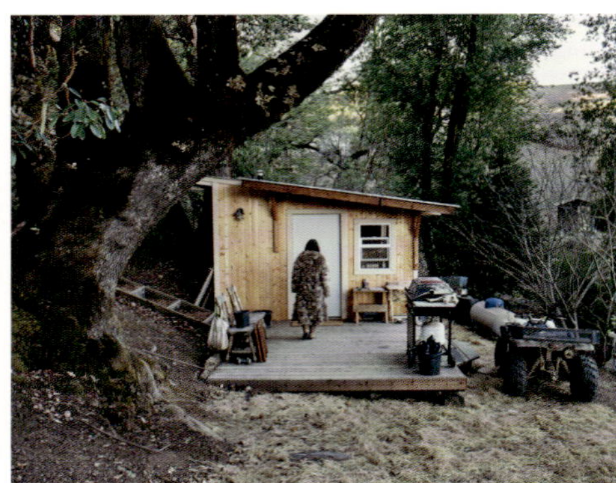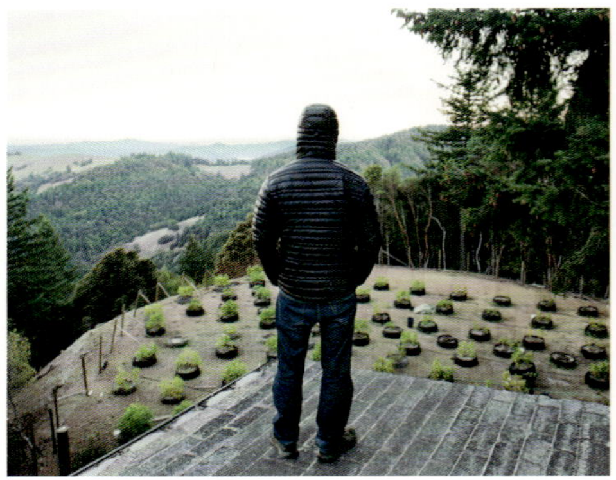

Left to right: Helpers throughout the season might live in trailers, vans, or tents for weeks or months / Structures, both new and old, sit on many properties / A grower surveys his just-harvested crop planted in Smart Pots; he doubled his production in the last two years

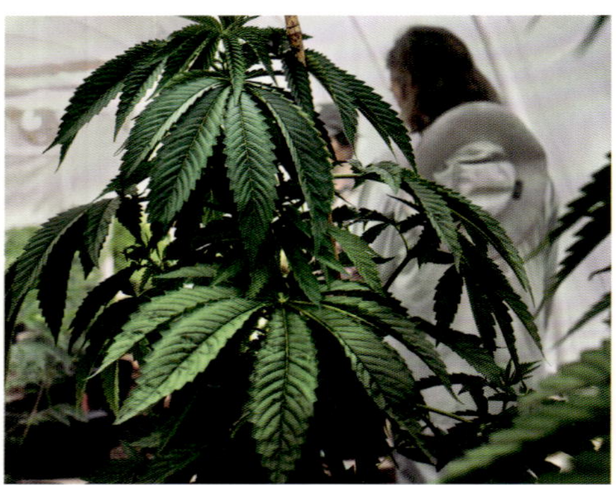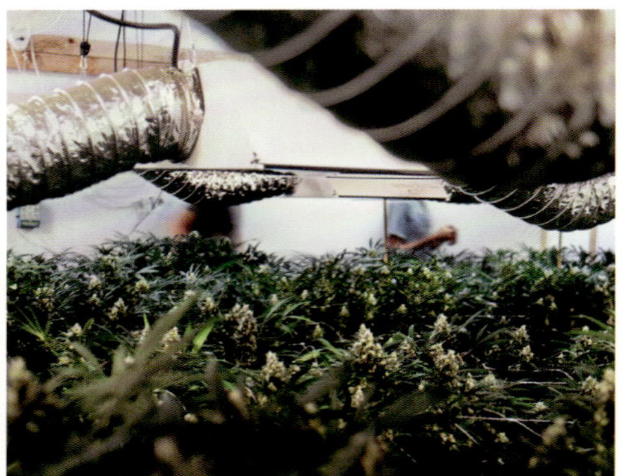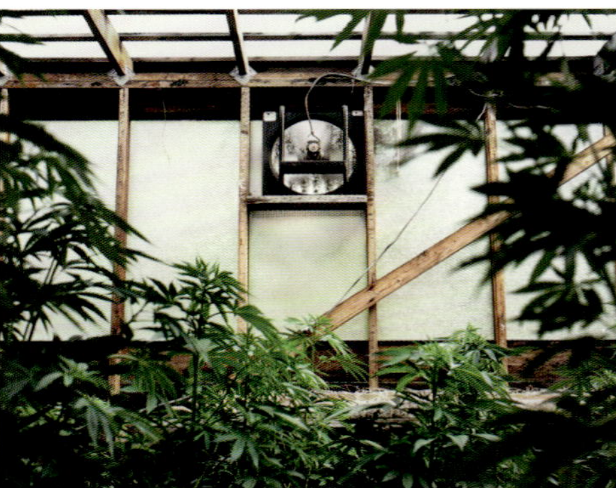

Left to right: Checking for spider mites and powdery mildew / Between seasons, some growers take their operations indoors to grow more during the cold weather / Good ventilation is a requirement

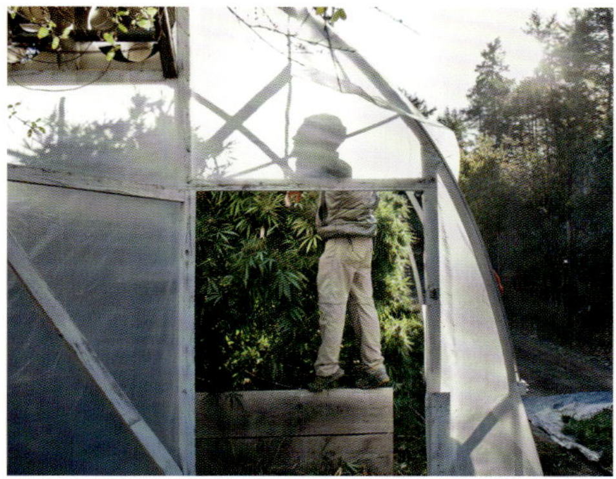 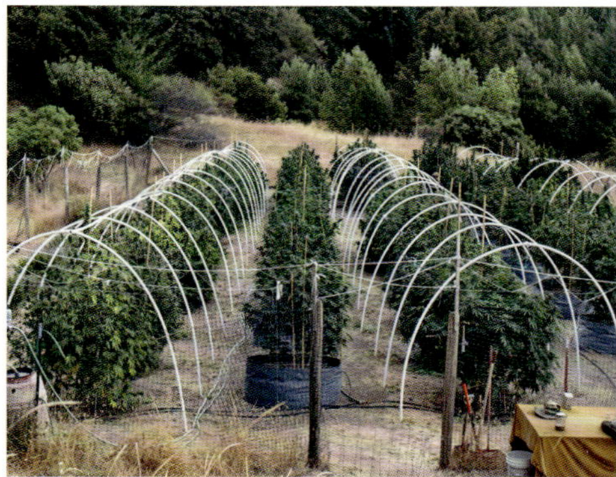 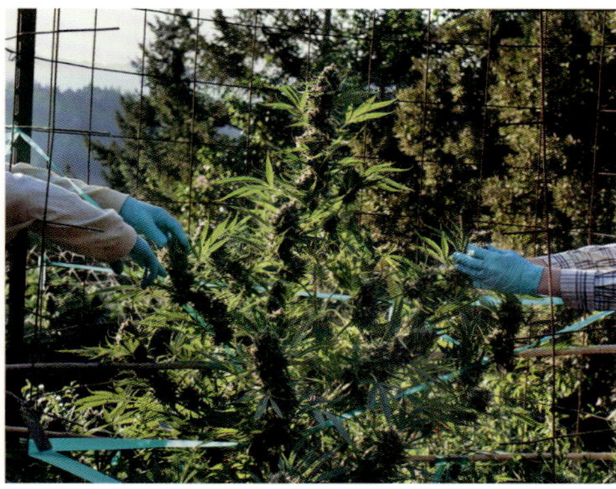

Left to right: Some plants will stay inside a greenhouse for an entire 6–8-month season; others will be transplanted in full sun / Branches are affixed to PVC hoops in this garden, where big plants grow uncovered, visible only to a helicopter / As buds get weightier, it is crucial to tie them to a trellis system to prevent breakage

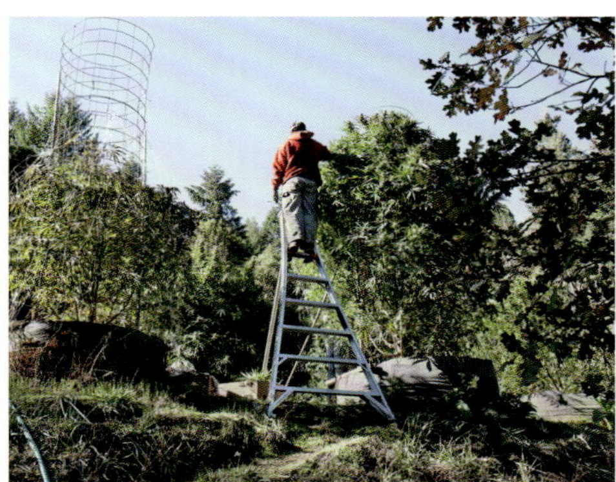 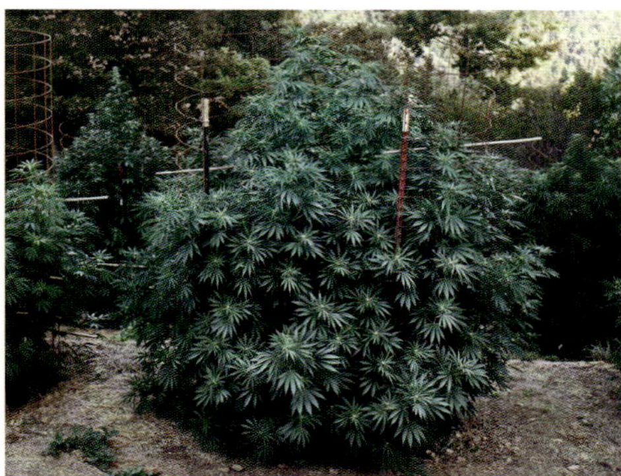 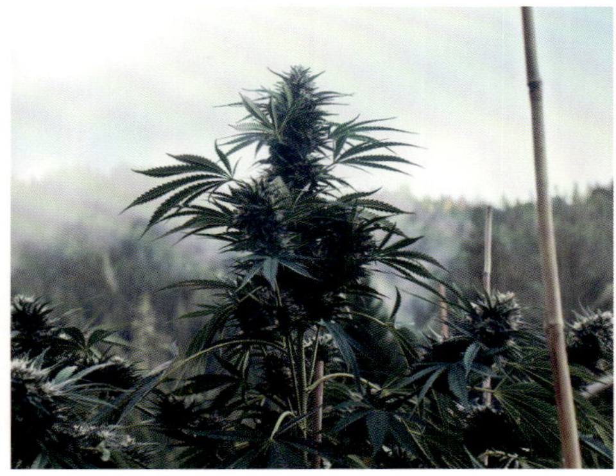

Left to right: Harvesting a plant, which will yield roughly 8–10 pounds / A bud's maturation depends on the strain; earlier is ideal to avoid the change in fall climate, and rain and mold / Firm clusters, strong fragrance, change of color in tiny hairs, and opal-hued trichomes mean the plant is ready to harvest

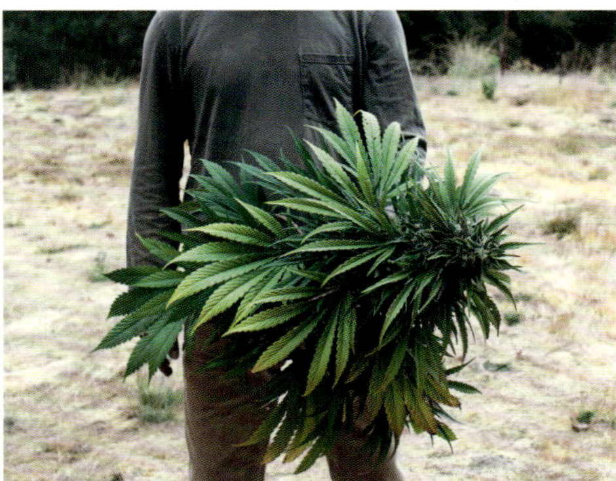 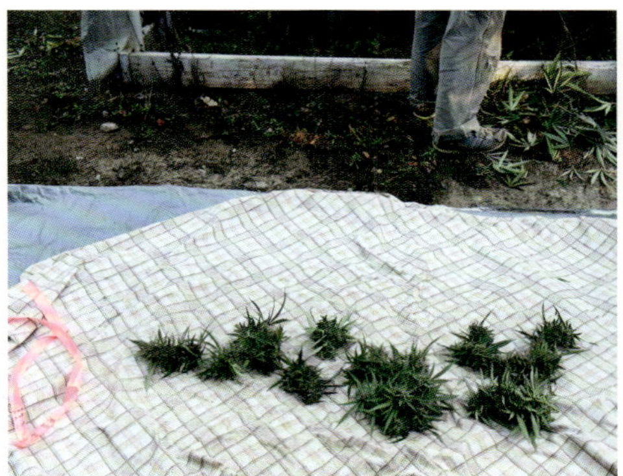 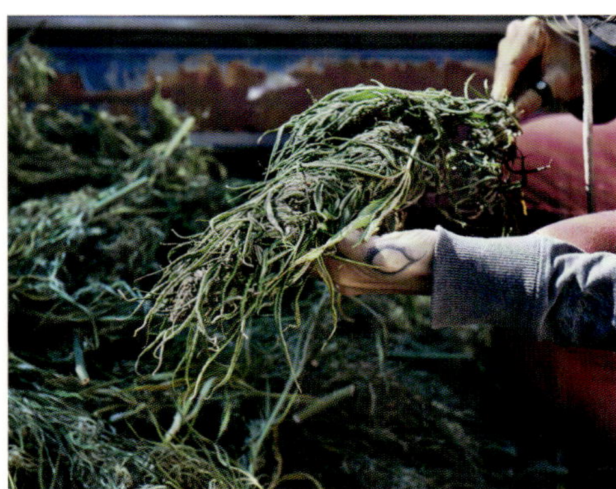

Left to right: A just-cut healthy cola / Harvested weed, readying for a drying scene / The top of a pot plant damaged by mold

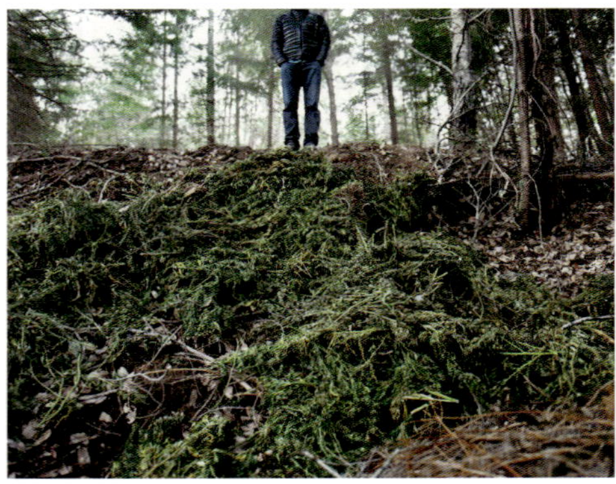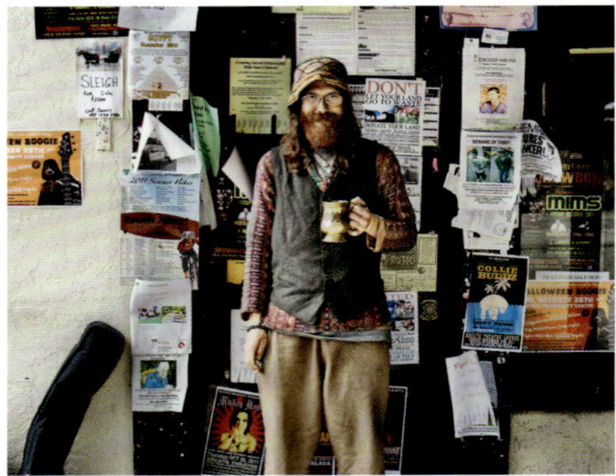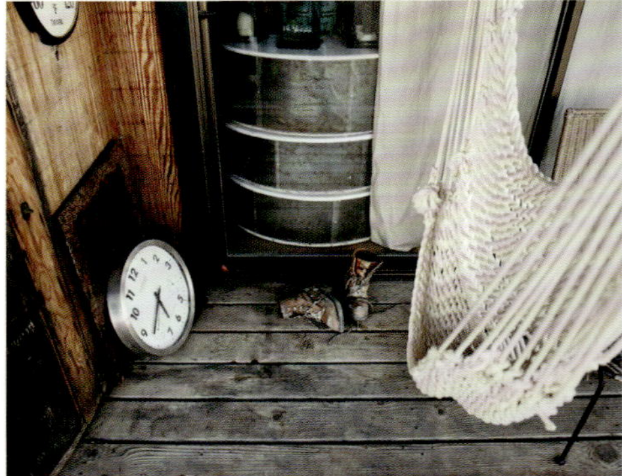

Left to right: Mold ripped through an entire drying room of one grower's weed, all of which had to be tossed down a hillside / Humboldt boasts a colorful cast of characters / Long summer days mean heavy watering and keeping an eye out for pests like moles and spider mites

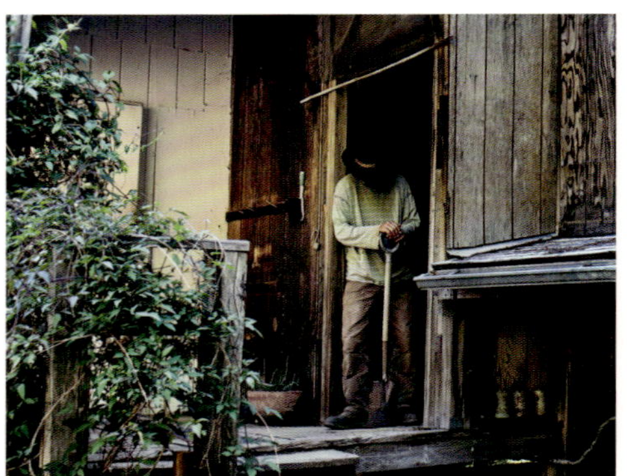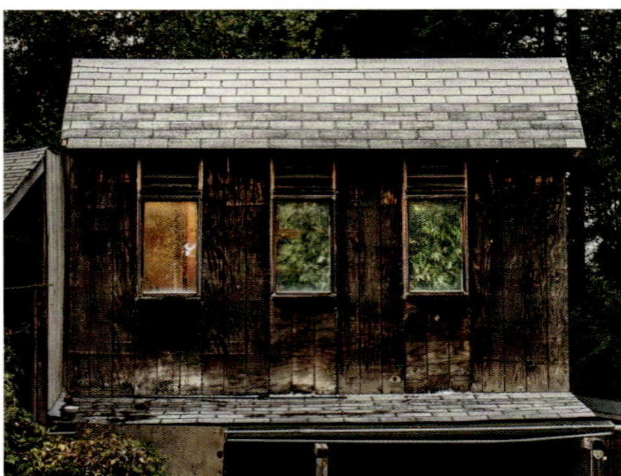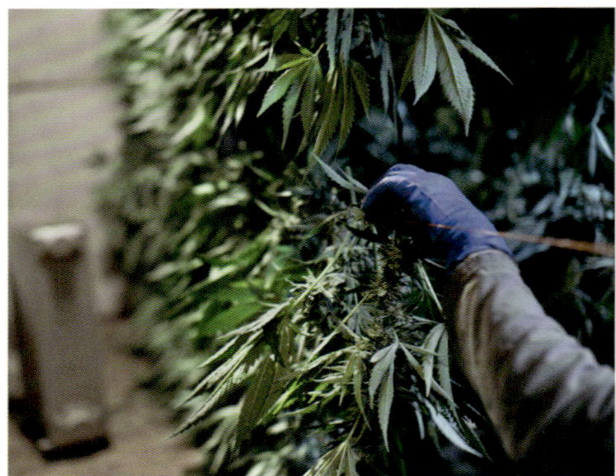

Left to right: On a break from digging holes / A last-minute drying room is constructed in this shed, where the careful curing process will take place / Electric heaters help keep the drying room at an ideal 68 degrees

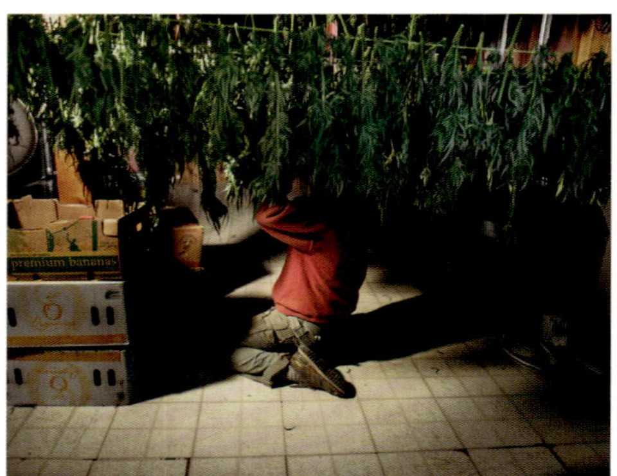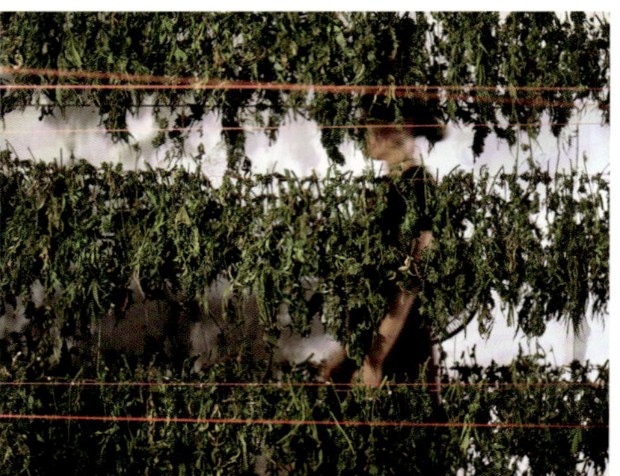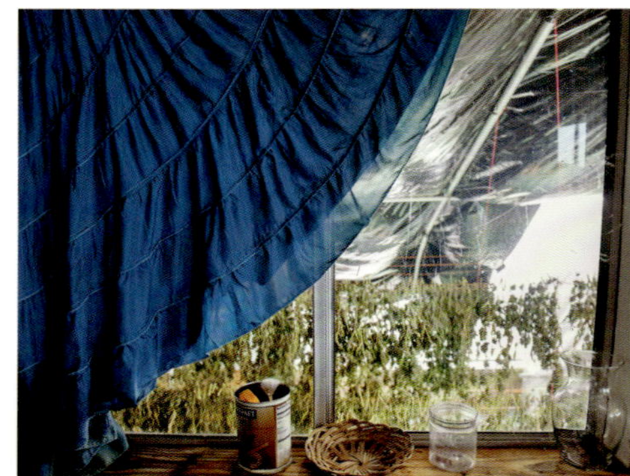

Left to right: Some say that the drying process is the key to producing quality herb / Cut plants are hung by their branches on twine or wire until they are dry to the touch / A greenhouse used for baby plants at the season's start is transformed into an extra drying room

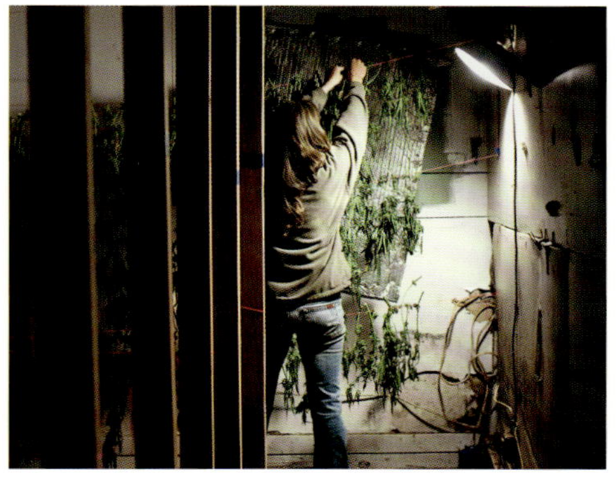 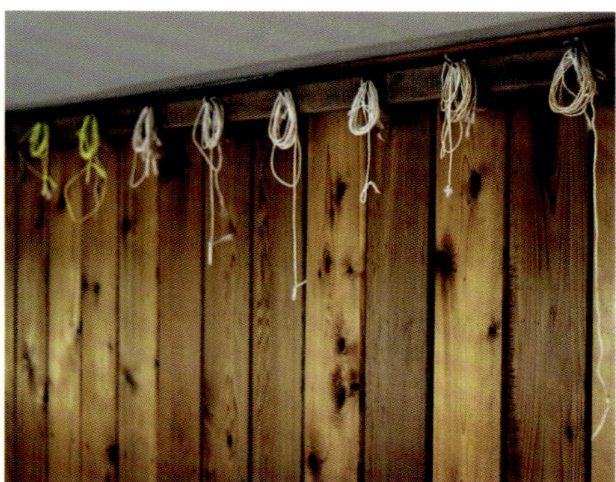 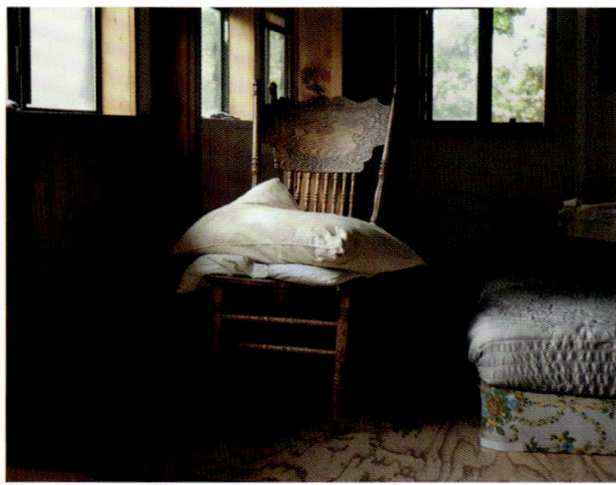

Left to right: At the peak of harvest, growers desperate for space will use anything dry, from vans to old trailers and living rooms / String, ready to be tied into drying lines / An extra bed for a temporary worker

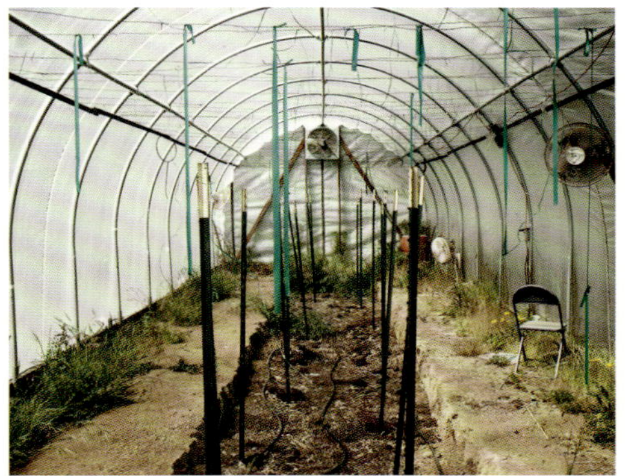 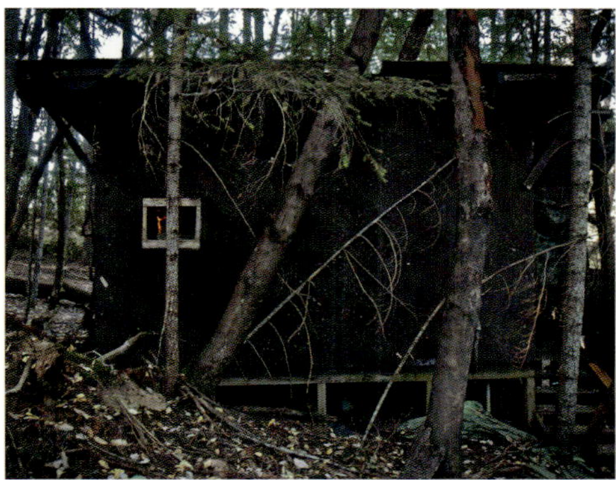 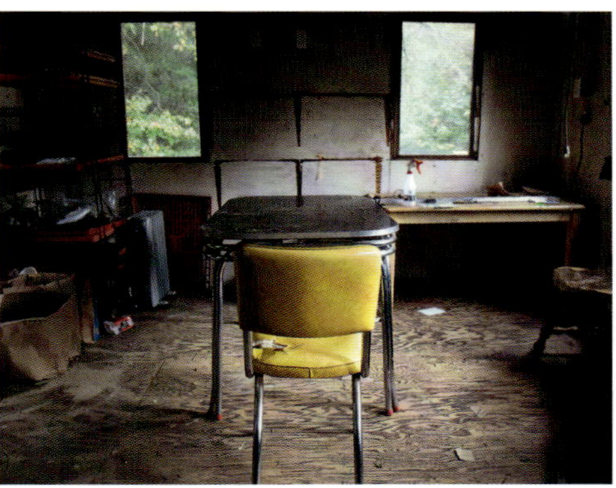

Left to right: After it is fully harvested, the finished pot plant is pulled by its roots and tossed or burned / A shed used for drying, trimming, or storage, hidden deep in the woods, unseen from land or air / Prepping for a trim scene

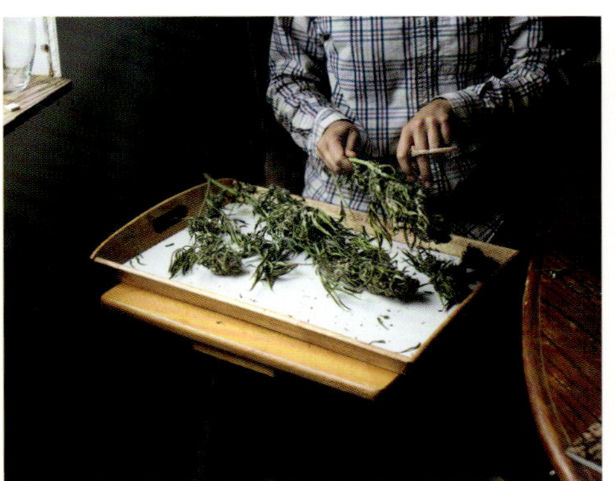 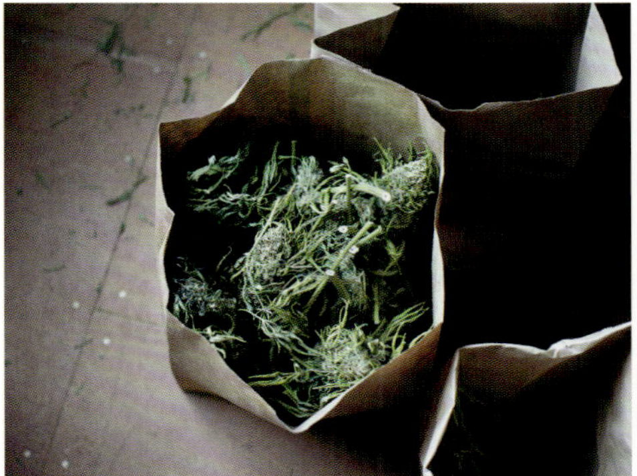 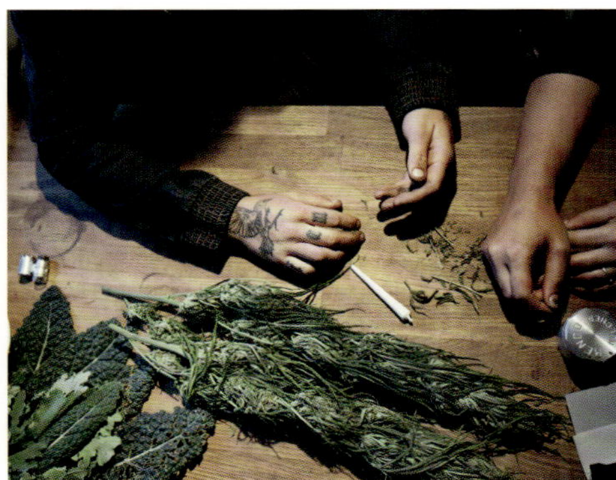

Left to right: The leaves and branches of the pot are discarded and buds are sculpted into neat nuggets / Dried branches are dispersed to trimmers in paper bags, which helps to further the curing process / Trim scenes look something akin to a knitting circle: people sitting around a table for hours, swapping stories, listening to music, and clipping and smoking weed

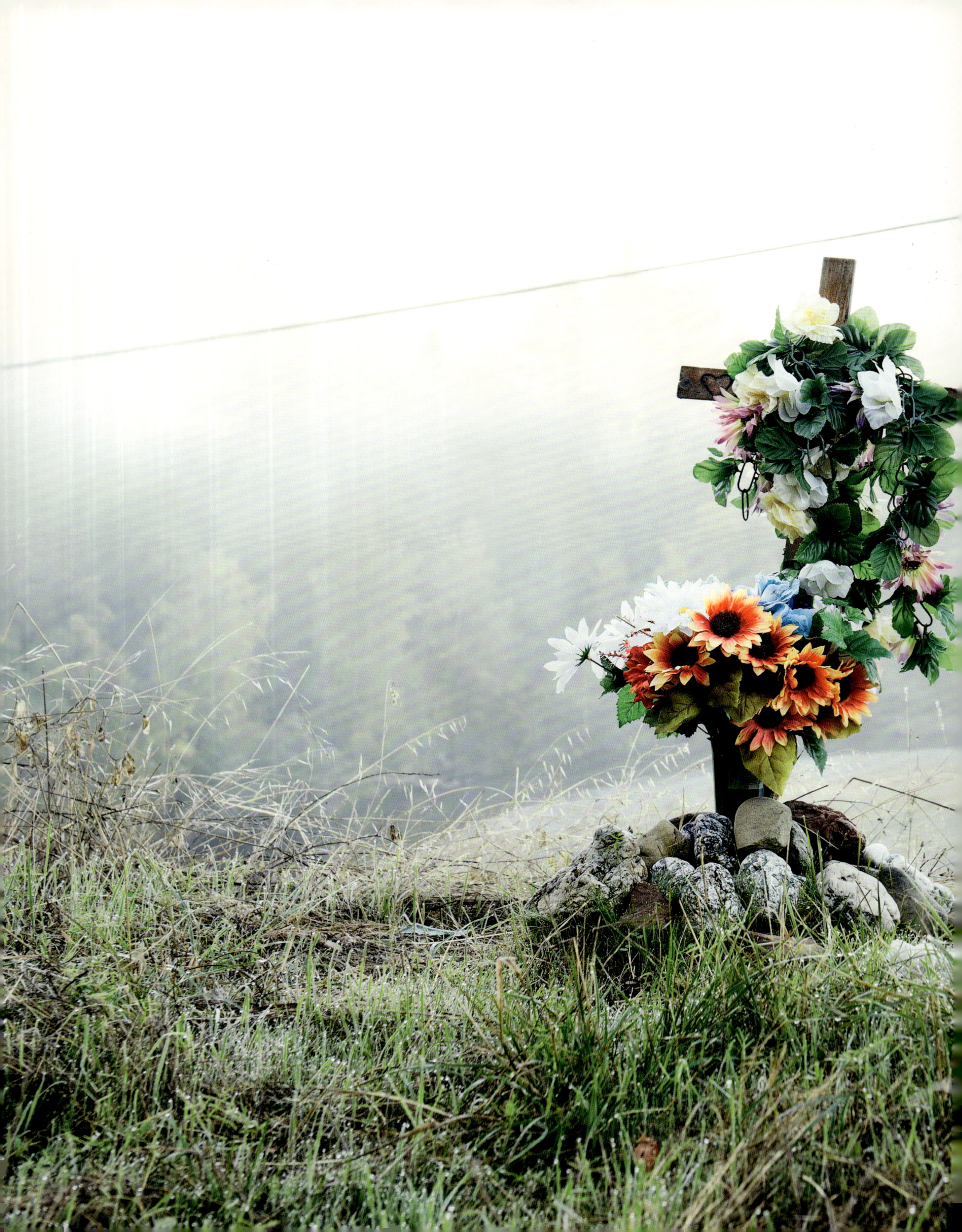

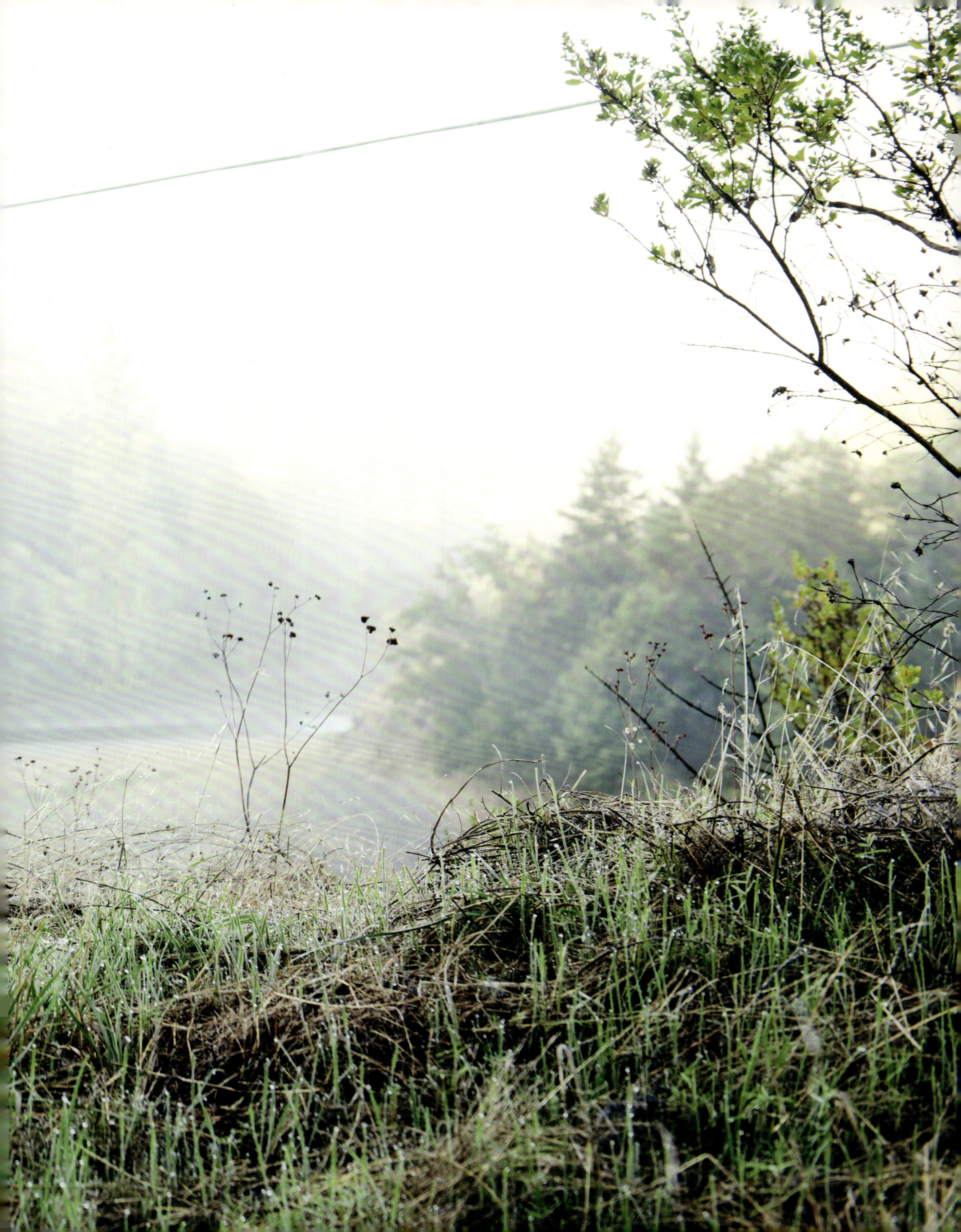

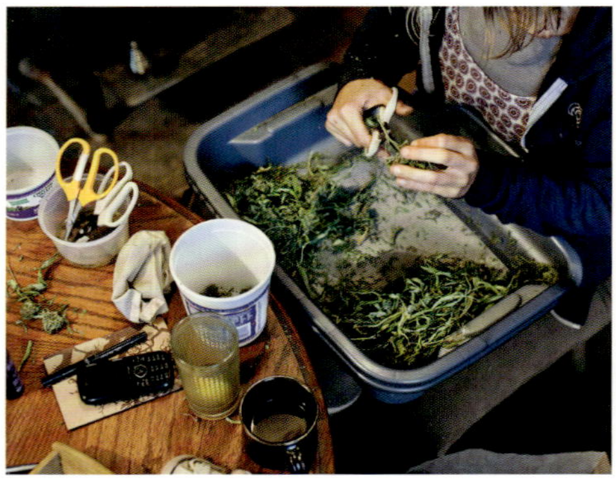 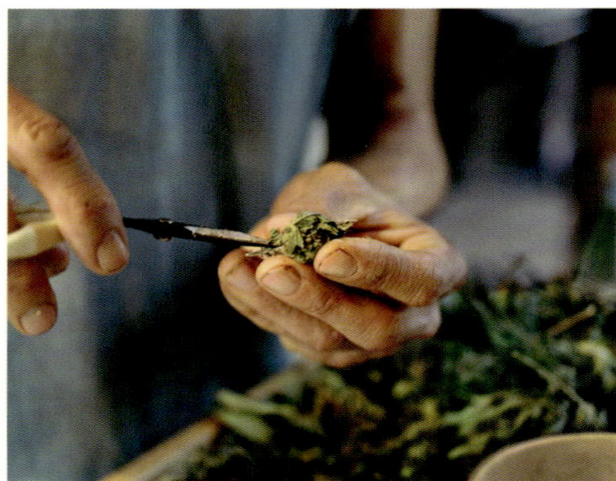 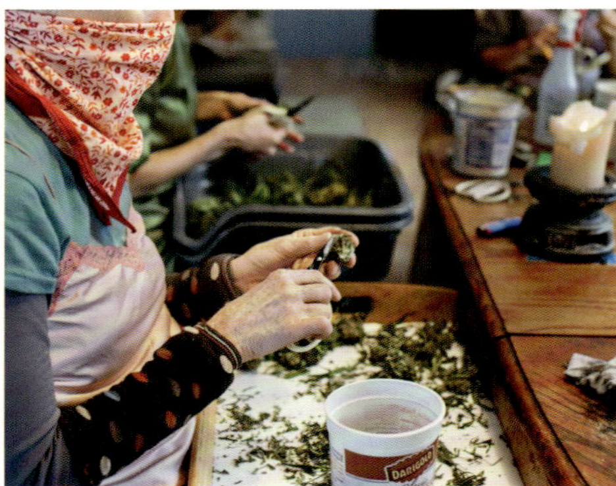

Left to right: Tools of the trade: Fiskars scissors, yogurt containers, and a lot of coffee / Meticulous clipping, while watching for unwanted seeds and signs of mold / Paid per pound, a fast trimmer can work for 12 plus hours a day and pocket a good amount of cash

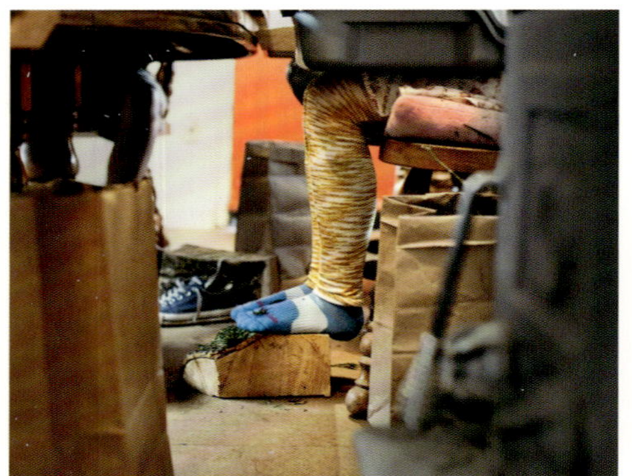 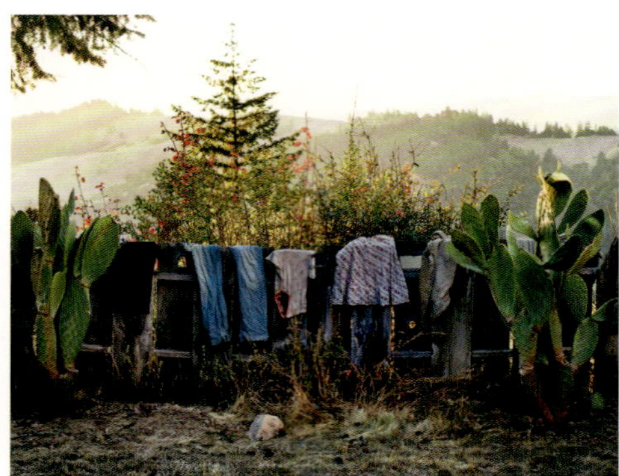 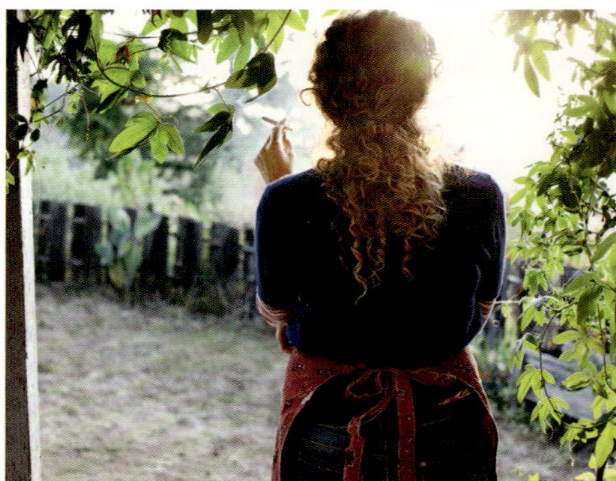

Left to right: An arduous task, trimming requires patience, agility, and commitment / After weeks of trimming, clothes and hair are suffused with shake and an overpowering smell of weed / Catching the sunset on a smoke break

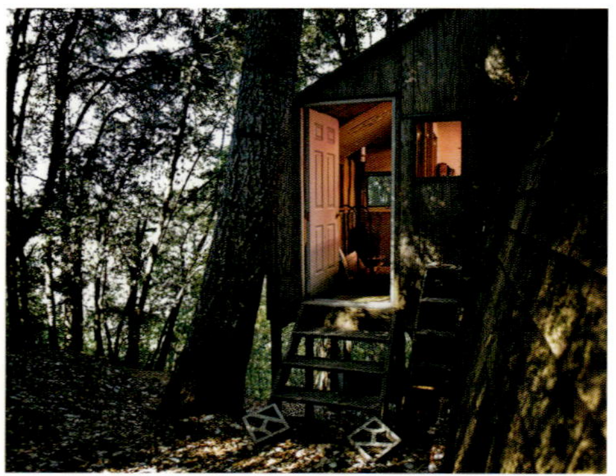 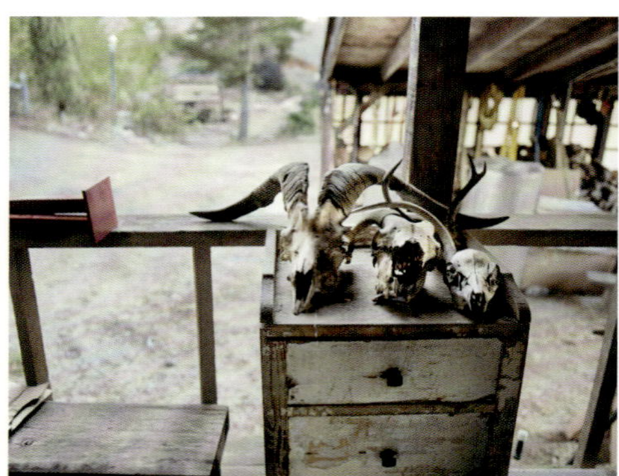 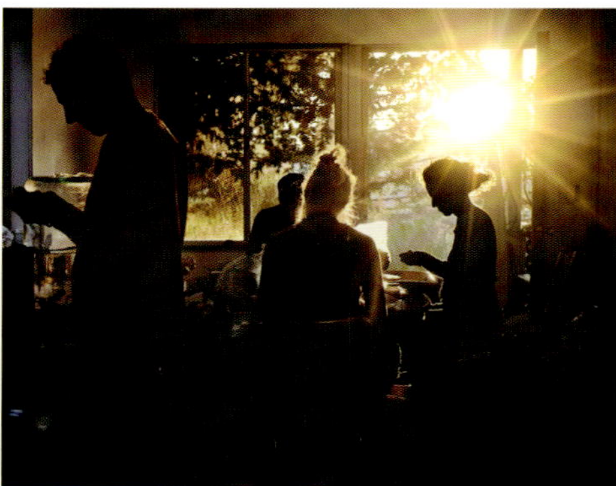

Left to right: Meeting wildlife is a natural part of a grower's world and that of workers who inhabit the forests, even temporarily / Deer, wild boar, and bear are all threats to the crop; many growers own a gun, protection from unwanted intruders of any kind / Though trimming is demanding work, the sense of community on the north coast peaks during this time

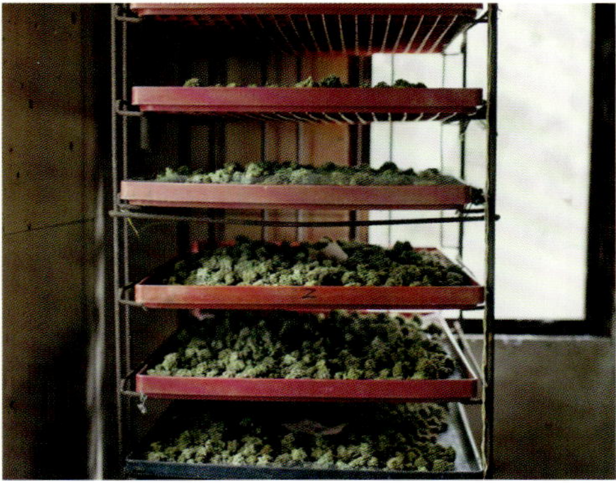 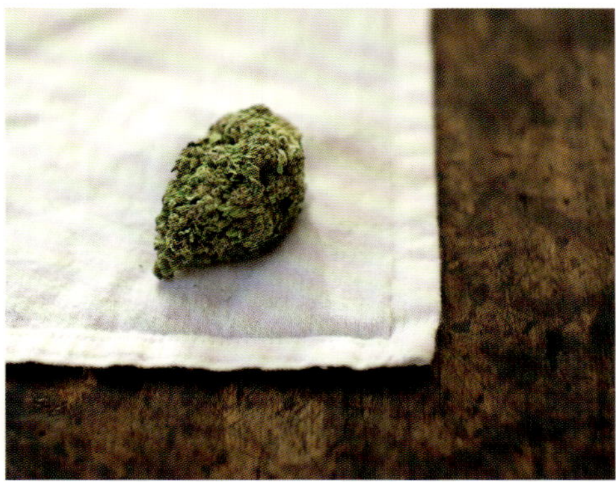 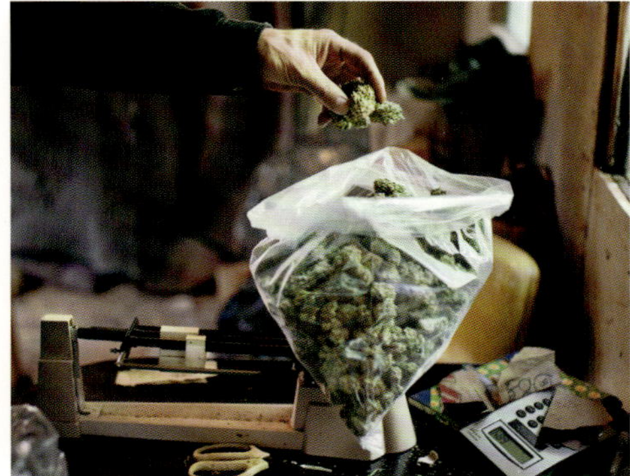

Left to right: Drying racks are used for the final cure / A tighter trim can fetch a higher price in a flooded market / Tallying up a day's work and batching it by the pound

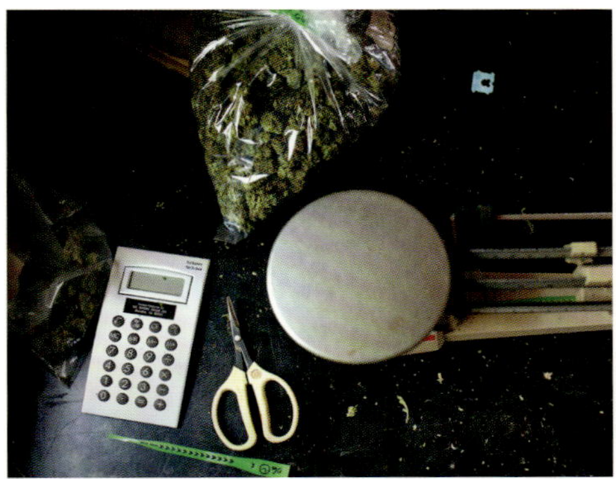 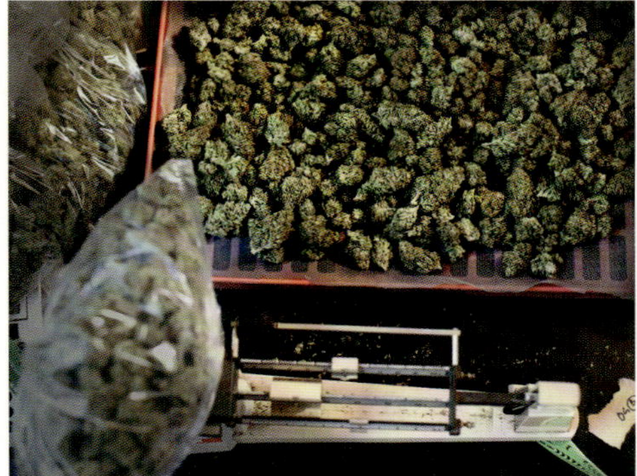 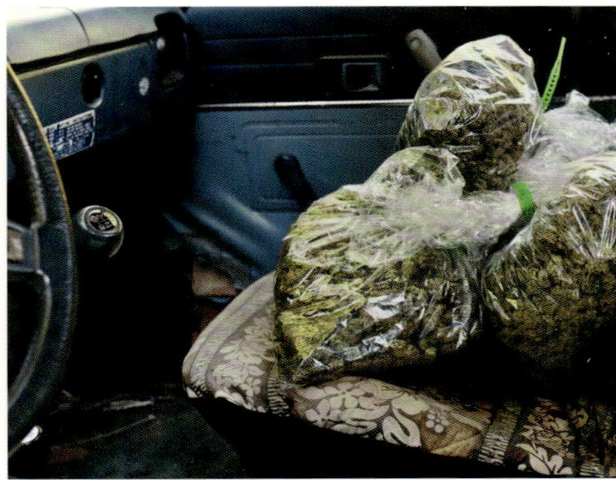

Left to right: Ordinary turkey bags hold a pound perfectly and conceal the smell of pot / A trimmer's finished nuggets, weighing nearly two pounds / Bagged and marked by strain, pounds are transported to storage

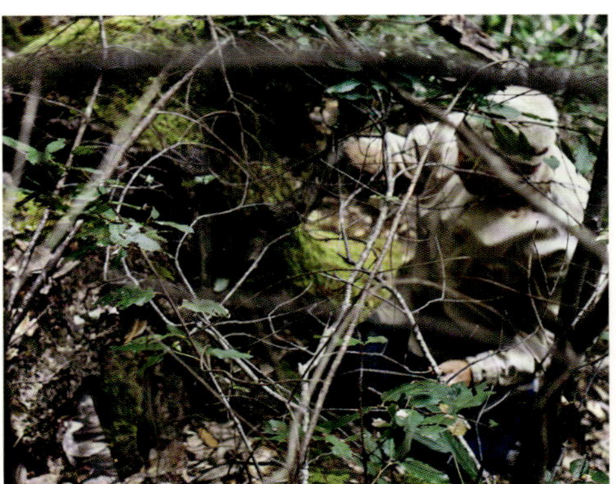 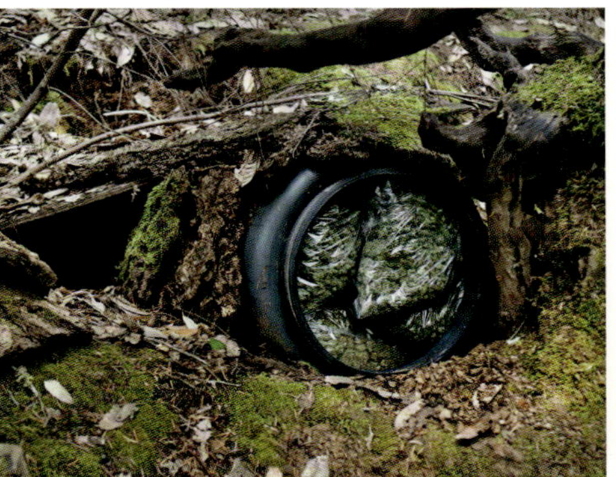 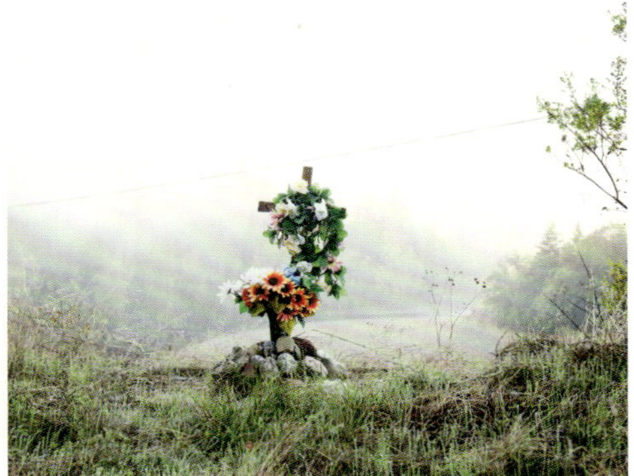

Left to right: The woods are a common hiding place for weed as well as for sequestering cash / Buried pickle barrels keep plastic bags of marijuana dry and out of sight; this one holds nearly 30 pounds / A lawless community can translate to reckless living; car accidents are common

Acknowledgments

For John.

To the Kehrer Verlag crew, notably Alexa Becker and Klaus Kehrer, thank you for believing in *Grassland* and this anonymous photographer, and for making the "making of" so extraordinarily smooth. Much gratitude goes to the talented hands and eyes that helped to piece together the pages so beautifully—Pascale, Gregor, and Sonny. To Emily and Glenn for giving *Grassland* a voice; thank you for contributing. And finally—and most importantly—endless appreciation goes to the growers, trimmers, good friends, and strangers who allowed me into their clandestine worlds. This book is only possible because of you.

New York-based photographer H. Lee (a pseudonym) spent a year documenting the culture of cannabis in Humboldt County, capturing intimate moments as she lived among the growers.

Emily Brady is the author of *Humboldt: Life on America's Marijuana Frontier*. She was born and raised in Northern California. A graduate of Columbia University's School of Journalism, she has written for *The New York Times*, *Time*, and the *Village Voice* and reported from Latin America, Europe, Asia, and New York City.

Glenn O'Brien is the author of *Soapbox*, *Human Nature (Dub Version)*, and *How To Be a Man*. A former editor at *Interview*, *Rolling Stone*, *Spin*, and *High Times*, he writes frequently on contemporary art, supplied the lead catalog essay for the 1996 exhibition *Beat Culture and the New America: 1950–65* at the Whitney Museum of American Art, New York, and is a contributing editor at *Ten*, *L'Officiel Homme*, and *GQ*, where he writes the "Style Guy" column.

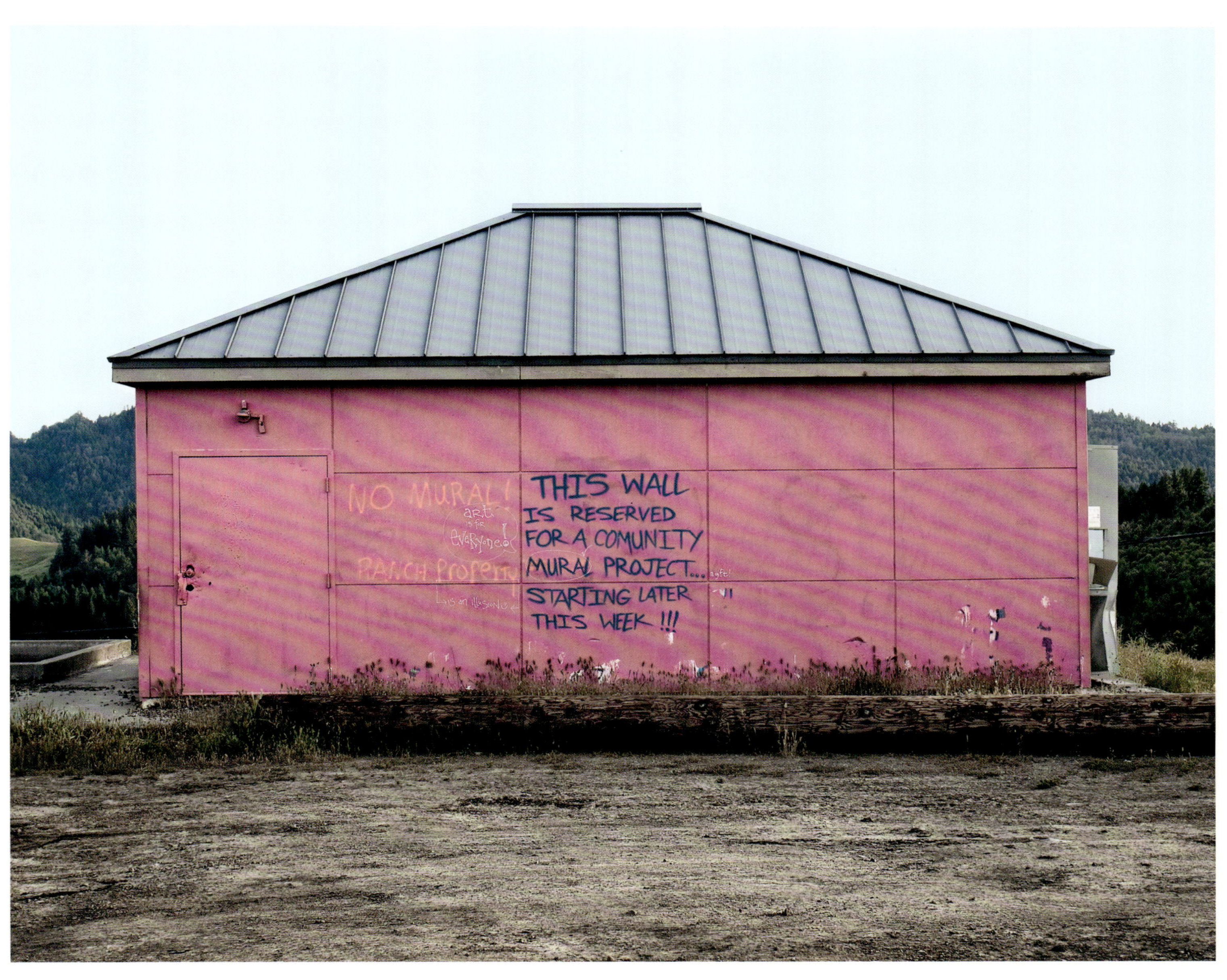
NO MURAL!
art is for
everyone!
RANCH property
→ is an illusion
THIS WALL
IS RESERVED
FOR A COMUNITY
MURAL PROJECT...
STARTING LATER
THIS WEEK !!!

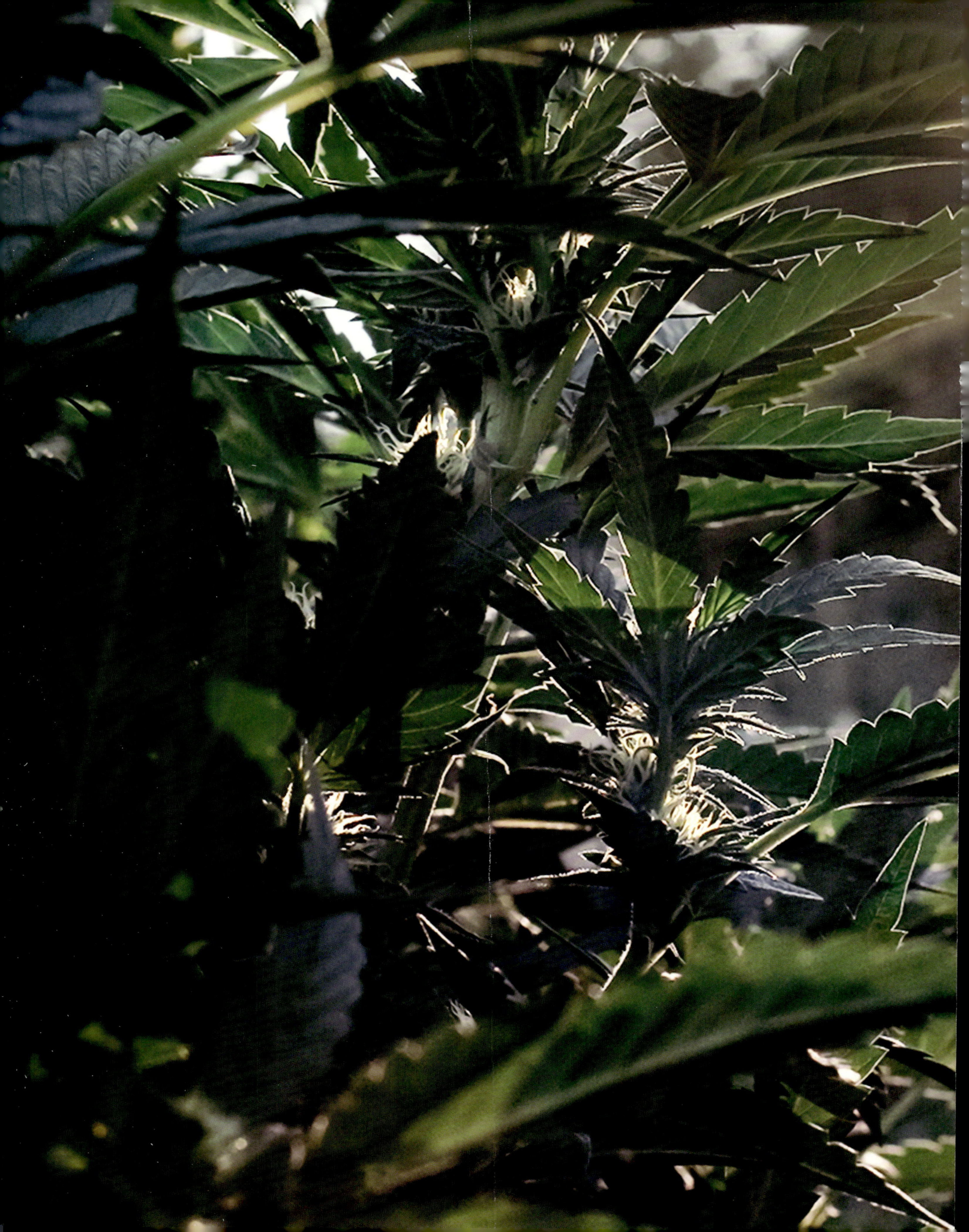

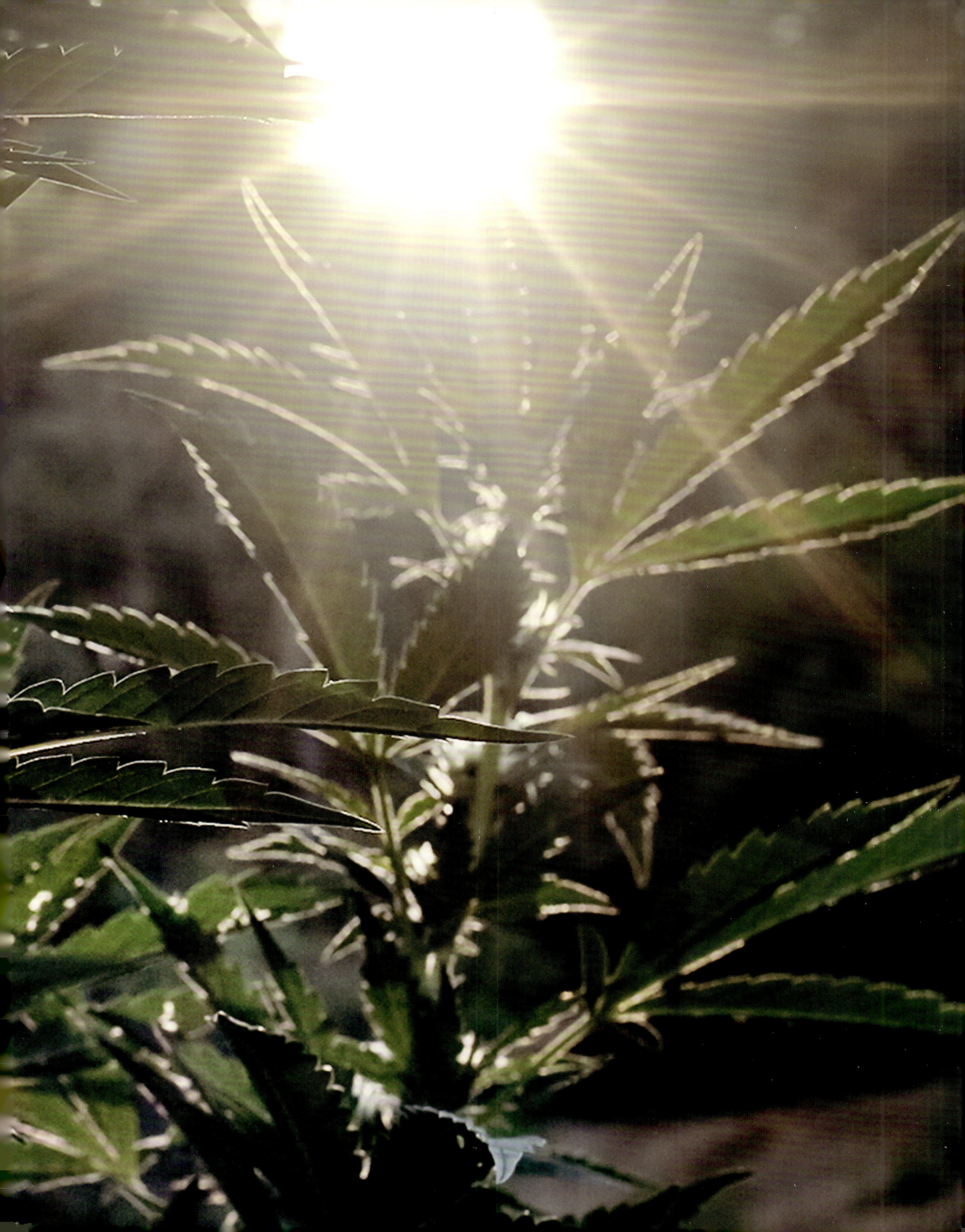

Concept & photography by H. Lee
Edited by Gregor Ehrlich
Designed by Pascale Willi
Image processing by Salvatore M. Fabbri and Kehrer Design Heidelberg (René Henoch)
Proofread by Rebecca Roberts and Wendy Brouwer
Production by Kehrer Design Heidelberg (Andreas Schubert)

Bibliographic information published by the Deutsche Nationalbibliothek.
The Deutsche Nationalbibliothek lists this publication in the Deutsche Nationalbibliografie;
detailed bibliographic data is available on the Internet at http://dnb.d-nb.de.

Printed and bound in Germany

ISBN 978-3-86828-481-2

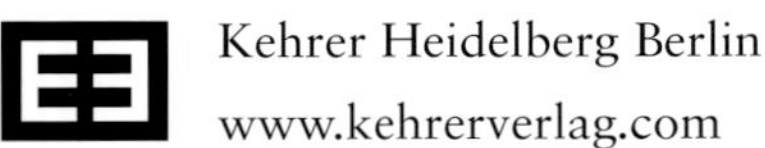

Kehrer Heidelberg Berlin
www.kehrerverlag.com